CIN15

W9-DJP-392

gull

"wilson"

European Business
Four Centuries of Foreign Expansion

European Business
Four Centuries of Foreign Expansion

Advisory Editor
Mira Wilkins

Editorial Board
Rondo Cameron
Charles Wilson

THE
SUEZ CANAL

ARNOLD T. WILSON

ARNO PRESS

A New York Times Company

New York / 1977

Editorial Supervision: ANDREA HICKS

———◆———

Reprint Edition 1977 by Arno Press Inc.

This reprint has been authorized by the
    Oxford University Press
Copyright Oxford University Press 1933

Reprinted from a copy in
    The University of Illinois Library

EUROPEAN BUSINESS:
Four Centuries of Foreign Expansion
ISBN for complete set: 0-405-09715-8
See last pages of this volume for titles.

Manufactured in the United States of America

———◆———

Library of Congress Cataloging in Publication Data

Wilson, Arnold Talbot, Sir, 1884-1940.
    The Suez Canal.

    (European business)
    Reprint of the ed. published by Oxford University
Press, London.
    Includes bibliographies.
    1. Suez Canal.   I. Title.   II.   Series.
HE543.W52 1977   386'.43   76-29990
ISBN 0-405-09722-0

THE SUEZ CANAL

Its Past, Present, and Future

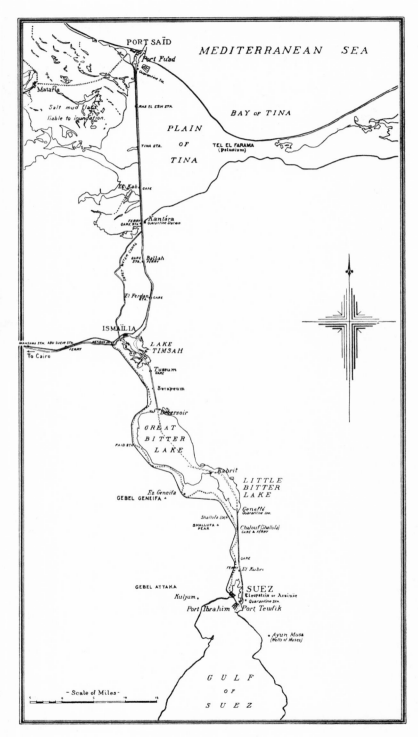

THE SUEZ CANAL

THE
SUEZ CANAL

Its Past, Present, and Future

BY

LT.-COL. SIR ARNOLD T. WILSON

K.C.I.E., C.S.I., C.M.G., D.S.O., M.P.

'The question of the Suez Canal Company's concession is a very complicated matter, which requires to be elucidated.'

SIR E. GREY
in House of Commons, *July* 1910.

'The prosperity of the East is now dependent upon the interests of civilization at large, and the best means of contributing to its welfare, as well as to that of humanity, is to break down the barriers which still divide men, races, and nations.'

DE LESSEPS, *July* 1855.

'He that taketh away weights doth as much advantage motion as he that addeth wings.'

LORD CHANCELLOR BACON.

OXFORD UNIVERSITY PRESS
LONDON : HUMPHREY MILFORD
1933

OXFORD UNIVERSITY PRESS
AMEN HOUSE, E.C. 4
LONDON EDINBURGH GLASGOW
LEIPZIG NEW YORK TORONTO
MELBOURNE CAPETOWN BOMBAY
CALCUTTA MADRAS SHANGHAI
HUMPHREY MILFORD
PUBLISHER TO THE
UNIVERSITY

PRINTED IN GREAT BRITAIN AT THE UNIVERSITY PRESS, OXFORD
BY JOHN JOHNSON, PRINTER TO THE UNIVERSITY

'Much can be done by temperate and courteous discussion. It is impossible that two great nations like France and England should not have clashing and conflicting interests, for they have possessions and protectorates in every quarter of the globe, and they touch each other in almost every part of the world. If they had not competing interests and rival ambitions they would not be the great nations they are. Rivalry in every direction is the very essence of their greatness, and neither can complain of the other because it is ambitious and far-reaching. Neither could forgo its ambitions without descending in the scale of nations.'

Monsieur WADDINGTON
French Ambassador, at the Mansion House
6 March 1893

PREFACE

OF all the great engineering works of the nineteenth century none has proved of more enduring value, none more permanently profitable to its owners, than the Suez Canal. It is a monument to the technical skill of French engineers, to the patient labour of the Egyptian peasantry, and to the laudable ambitions of the rulers of Egypt. Above them all towers the mighty figure of de Lesseps, whose extraordinary pertinacity, combined with rare diplomatic genius, enabled him almost single handed to overcome political difficulties compared with which the hidden rocks and shifting sands of the desert were trifling obstacles.

For nearly forty years, from 1840 onwards, the question of the Suez Canal was, in one form or another, an important though never a ruling factor in diplomatic discussions between the Great Powers. Not until it was actually completed could de Lesseps convince the world that it was practicable, and the English Government that it was desirable. It took him another seven years to prove it financially successful. The problems of international law created by its construction remained in doubt until 1904 and are not yet completely solved.

The question of the Suez Canal to-day is two-fold—firstly, is the control of a great international highway by a commercial company, bent on paying as large dividends as possible, consistent with modern ideas and modern needs? Upon the answer to this question depends the reply that must eventually be returned to the second—should the concession, which terminates in 1968, be renewed; if so, in what form and on what terms?

The literature on the subject is of very unequal value. The references to a maritime canal in ancient and medieval histories are incidental to the general narrative and often contradictory. The developments of the eighteenth century are fully treated by Ch. Roux's two works, which are based mainly on original material, both English and French, but his treatment of the question from 1855 onwards is less satisfactory. He drew his information almost exclusively from de Lesseps' published works; he made little use of British documentary sources, and adopted an attitude uniformly hostile to the British Government, showing little understanding of public opinion in England or of its effect upon Government policy. Public archives were not accessible when he wrote and, perhaps for this reason, current history becomes in his hands a fortuitous concatenation of events.

Another French writer, Monsieur Voisin, deals mainly with the engineering problems of the canal, though his first volume, based on de Lesseps' writings, is devoted to political history. Subsequent writers, British and American, German and French, were until recently content to draw upon these works and upon ephemeral journalistic studies and technical writings.

An Egyptian student of London University, Muhammad Kassim, wi te in April 1924 a thesis on *The History of the Suez Canal Question 1854–66* in which, for the first time, the Archives of the Public Record Offices in London, Paris, Amsterdam, and Vienna were laid under tribute. His thesis, which earned him a Doctorate of Philosophy, is a lucid and admirably documented history which merits publication, whether in English or French. In 1928 appeared *British Routes to India*, a work of great merit, by Dr. Halford Lancaster Hoskins of Tufts College, Massachusetts, U.S.A., in which, for the first time, the Suez Canal question was dealt with as part of a wider problem. In 1930 was published *The Suez Canal*, by Dr. Charles W. Hallberg of Syracuse University. He, too, has drawn extensively on original sources and within his self-imposed limits is accurate and reliable. To both these authors I make grateful acknowledgement.

No Englishman appears to have made a comprehensive study of the Suez Canal since Fitzgerald, who wrote his two volumes in 1876. Recent literature published in England consists almost exclusively of topical, rather than critical, articles in monthly and quarterly reviews, *The Times*[1] and the latest issue of *The Encyclopaedia Britannica*, all alike from the pen of Sir Ian Malcolm, the Senior British Government Director, who has been at pains in every case to avoid any reference to the financial aspect of the operations of the Company.

In an article in *The Quarterly Review* of January 1930 he observed that

'No foreigner who visits the canal annually can fail to note the extraordinary happy family feeling which exists between all classes of the Company's servants: there is general satisfaction with the existing condition of things . . . there is a great desire in every grade to get sons and nephews taken into the service. One need not disguise one's own pleasure in sharing in so admirable a state of affairs, for which friendship, enlightened generosity, gratitude and glad co-operation are about equally responsible. Long may it continue for the advantage of all concerned.'

This frank admission was followed by the statement that

'Sooner, rather than later, the question of the future of the Canal will come up again, although not until all parties are agreed that the question is ripe for dis-

[1] Special articles and illustrations celebrating the Jubilee of the Suez Canal, and 'The Diamond Wedding' of the two oceans, appeared in *The Times* of 15 November 1929.

cussion. The parties primarily concerned are Egypt, the Suez Canal Company, and the British Empire.'

This announcement, made at a moment when the profits of the Company had reached the highest level in history, and when British shipping, and indeed that of the world at large, was finding it difficult to pay any dividends at all, suggested to my mind a series of investigations which have led to the publication of the present work.

I take this opportunity of acknowledging with gratitude the invaluable assistance which I have received from Mr. H. W. Macrosty, O.B.E., formerly Chief Statistical Officer to the Board of Trade and now Honorary Secretary of the Royal Statistical Society. The statistical and comparative tables prepared by him for inclusion in Chapters VIII and X are for the most part quite new and, though based wholly on official data, have not, for the most part, been published elsewhere, nor are the requisite data easily accessible.

The extension or renewal of the Suez Canal Company's concession, contemplated in 1883, and pressed upon the Egyptian Government in 1910, was again brought forward in Anglo-Egyptian negotiations in 1921. On the 17th August and again on 13th October of that year, the Foreign Office desired to provide in the Treaty of Alliance for the prolongation of the Suez Canal Concession for a further forty years, on the lines advocated in 1910 by Sir E. Gorst. No agreement was reached and the question is still governed by the Declaration of 28th Feb. 1922, which read as follows:

'Whereas H.M.'s Government, in accordance with their declared intentions, desire forthwith to recognize Egypt as an independent sovereign State, and whereas the relations between H.M.'s Government and Egypt are of vital interest to the British Empire;

The following principles are hereby declared:

1. The British Protectorate over Egypt is terminated and Egypt is declared to be an independent sovereign state. . . .

3. The following matters are absolutely reserved to the discretion of His Majesty's Government until such time as it may be possible by free discussion and friendly accommodation on both sides to conclude agreements in regard thereto between H.M. Government and the Government of Egypt.

(*a*) The security of the communications of the British Empire in Egypt.
(*b*) The defence of Egypt against all foreign aggression or interference, direct or indirect.
(*c*) The protection of foreign interests in Egypt and the protection of minorities.
(*d*) The Sudan.

Pending conclusion of such agreement the status quo in all these matters shall remain intact.'

At first sight it would appear that this document must preclude

b

ad hoc negotiations for the renewal of the Company's concession. But it was stated in 1910 that the consent of the Egyptian National Assembly to such renewal was not necessary: still less requisite is the prior approval of the British House of Commons, and subsequent constitutional developments since that date have tended to weaken rather than to strengthen the control exercised by parliaments over governments. Apart from this, however, though it is generally believed in Egypt that the renewal of the Concession is still a cardinal point in the policy of the British Government, much study has brought me to the conclusion that to renew the Concession in its present form would be injurious not only to the interests of His Majesty's Dominions and Dependencies east of Suez and to those of Great Britain, but to the commerce of Europe and Asia.

De Lesseps at every stage in his career regarded the construction of the canal not primarily as a money-making enterprise, but as a service to be rendered to the commerce of the world—an enterprise of public utility to be conducted on an international basis by a Company in the management of which no one nation would predominate. It was not to the cupidity of French investors, but to their patriotism and to their imagination that he appealed: it was not the *bourgeoisie*, but the Bourse that brought pressure to bear on him to pay large dividends, and until his death in 1894 he was well content to regard 25 per cent. as a reasonable maximum dividend. The management is no longer international: the Statute which requires direction to be drawn from 'the nationalities principally interested' is ignored. The only nation now represented, other than Great Britain or France, is Holland, and commercial interests other than shipping are almost unrepresented.

The fortunes of the Canal Company are to a large extent unaffected by the vicissitudes of prices, markets, or fashion. Its monopoly is indeed threatened, in some directions, by the Panama Canal; in others by the construction of pipe lines across the Arabian desert, by the growth of air transport, and by increasing enthusiasm in every country for policies of national self-sufficiency. But its monopolistic position is not as yet seriously threatened. In the words of Mr. Baldwin (House of Commons 1929).

'The Public is best served by an efficient industry operating freely. But special considerations arise where a single undertaking dominates . . . (its duty is, in such circumstances) . . . to supply on reasonable terms: and the public have a right to be satisfied that those terms are reasonable.'

It is time to apply this principle to the Suez Canal, and the sooner the task is taken in hand the more favourable the prospect of a just solution. *Augescunt aliae gentes, aliae minuuntur.* The proportion of

British shipping using the canal is falling slowly but steadily, that of French shipping is not increasing. The question can only be solved in connexion with, or as a result of a settlement of Anglo-Egyptian relations, but it does not concern only the Governments of Great Britain and Egypt and the Suez Canal Company. The Governments of India, Australia, New Zealand and S. Africa, of Germany, Italy, the Netherlands and France, of China, Japan, and Siam, of British possessions and protectorates in Africa and Asia are also entitled to be heard.

In this connexion the protests of the Australian Government, made as long ago as 1906 and reproduced as an Appendix to this volume, are of particular interest.

The problem is thorny, and discussions must of necessity reveal many divergent claims and interests, but that is no reason why it should be shelved or avoided at the cost of perpetuating the present unsatisfactory state of affairs.

'The government of the world', said Disraeli in the House of Commons on 9th February 1876, with reference to complaints then being made against the Canal Company,

'is not a mere alternation between abstract right and overwhelming force. . . . The world is governed by conciliation, compromise, influence, varied interests, the recognition of the rights of others, coupled with the assertion of one's own; and, in addition, a general conviction, resulting from explanation and good understanding, that it is for the interest of all parties that matters should be conducted in a satisfactory and peaceful manner.'

To secure such a settlement by agreement is the fittest tribute that we of this generation can pay to the work of the illustrious Frenchman who has deserved so well of his country and of all civilized nations.

A. T. WILSON

CONTENTS

CHAPTER IX. THE SUEZ CANAL DURING THE GREAT WAR
Position on outbreak of war. Enemy merchant ships. Declaration of War by Turkey. Canal defended. Activity of spies. Sir John Maxwell takes command. Defensive system. Attacks by the Turks. Mines placed in canal. Advanced line of defence organized. Effect of abandonment of Gallipoli. Sir A. Murray succeeds Sir John Maxwell. Ocean wharves constructed at Qantara: railway developments. Lt.-Col. Elgood's comments.

CHAPTER X. THE PANAMA CANAL: A RIVAL ROUTE
The Panama and Suez Canals compared. Tolls. Transits. Tonnage. Receipts. Expenses. Deficits. Nationality of Shipping. Effect on Trade of U.S.A. Relative distances via Suez and Panama.

CHAPTER XI. COMMENTS, CRITICISMS, AND REPLIES, 1931–3
Post-War decline in Shipping. Protests of Liverpool Steamship Owners' Association. Reply of Suez Canal Company. Protest of British Shipping and Commerical Interests. Reply of Lord Inchcape. Rejoinder of Liverpool Steamship Owners' Association. Questions and Answers in Parliament. The question reopened in March 1933. Views expressed to Royal Central Asian Society. Reply of Marquis de Vorgüé. Further Addresses. Article in *The Nineteenth Century and After*.

1. ACT OF CONCESSION OF THE VICEROY OF EGYPT FOR THE CONSTRUCTION AND WORKING OF THE SUEZ MARITIME CANAL AND ITS DEPENDENCIES FROM THE MEDITERRANEAN TO THE RED SEA. Cairo, 30 November 1854.
2. ACT OF CONCESSION OF THE VICEROY OF EGYPT AND 'CAHIER DES CHARGES' FOR THE CONSTRUCTION AND WORKING OF THE SUEZ MARITIME CANAL AND ITS DEPENDENCIES. Alexandria, 5 January 1856.
3. STATUTES OF THE UNIVERSAL COMPANY OF THE SUEZ MARITIME CANAL. Alexandria, 5 January 1856.
4. CONVENTION BETWEEN THE VICEROY OF EGYPT AND THE SUEZ MARITIME CANAL COMPANY. Signed at Cairo, 22 February 1866. (Extract.)
5. SUEZ CANAL. RULES OF NAVIGATION, Jan. 1933.
6. CORRESPONDENCE RELATING TO SUEZ CANAL DUES. Presented to Parliament in March 1907. Cd. 3345.
7. NOTE ON EFFECT OF SUEZ CANAL ON MIGRATION OF MARINE FAUNA.

CHAPTER I

FIRST BEGINNINGS

Geological aspects of Isthmus. Trans-Isthmian canals in Herodotus, Strabo, Diodorus, and Pliny. Changes in Geography of Nile. Early canals between Nile and Red Sea. Great canals in Mesopotamia. Ptolemy. The Khalifs. The Venetians. Napoleon Bonaparte. The first surveys. Chesney's report. Muhammad Ali's scheme for a Suez–Cairo Canal. Proposed Alexandria–Cairo Railway. Monsieur Enfantin. Arthur Anderson. Lord Palmerston. Robert Stephenson. Thomas Waghorn. Abbas Pasha. Saïd Pasha. Ferdinand de Lesseps. Bibliography.

WE first trace the area now occupied by Egypt and Sinai as a land surface of granite on which were deposited the Nubian sandstones. After this land had sunk beneath the sea, Cretaceous and Eocene limestones were laid down. At the end of the Eocene period the whole area was folded and raised again above sea-level. In this process the trench of the Gulf of Suez and the Red Sea came into being.

In Miocene times this trench was invaded by the waters of the Mediterranean; there was, however, as yet no water connexion with the Indian Ocean. The fauna was purely Mediterranean until Middle Pliocene times, when the waters of the Southern Seas entered the trench and the marine creatures of the two seas began to mingle.

When and how the Gulf of Suez was cut off from the Mediterranean we do not know; we do know, however, that in the past three millennia the land between the Bitter Lakes and Suez has risen by three metres: the process may have started in Late Pliocene times and may still persist. It is certain that in Pleistocene times a fresh-water lake, fed presumably from the Nile, existed on the Isthmus.[1]

The boundaries of this lake are not known, but we know that in early historical times the Bitter Lakes were connected with, and were in fact an extension of, the Gulf of Suez. Either Sesostris (2000 B.C.) or Necho (600 B.C.) or both these Pharaohs in turn dug a canal joining the most easterly or Pelusiac branch of the Nile to this northern extremity of the Erythrean Sea.

Herodotus is the first writer who tells us anything on the subject, in his *Euterpe*, c. 158:

'Psammitichus had a son whose name was Necho, by whom he was succeeded in his authority. This Prince first commenced that canal leading to the Red Sea which Darius, King of Persia, afterwards continued. The length of this canal is equal to a four days' voyage, and is wide enough to admit two triremes abreast. The

---

[1] Hume, quoted in *Trans. Zool. Soc.*, 1926.

B

water enters it from the Nile, a little above the city of Bubastis. It terminated in the Red Sea, not far from Patumos, an Arabian town. They began to dig this canal in that part of Egypt which is nearest to Arabia. Contiguous to it is a mountain which stretches towards Memphis, and contains quarries of stone. Commencing at the foot of this, it extends, from west to east, through a considerable tract of country and, where a mountain opens to the south, is discharged into the Arabian Gulf. In the prosecution of this work under Necho no less than 100,000 Egyptians perished. He at length desisted from his undertaking, being admonished by an oracle that all his labour would turn to the advantage of a barbarian.'

Strabo gives the following account:

'There is another canal terminating in the Arabian Gulf at the city of Arsinöe, sometimes called Cleopatris (Suez).[1] It passes through the Bitter Lakes, whose waters were, indeed, formerly bitter but which, sweetened since the cutting of this canal by an admixture with those of the Nile, now abound with delicate fish, and are crowded with waterfowl. This canal was first made by Sesostris before the war of Troy. Some say that the son of Psammitichus (Necho) first began the work and then died. The first Darius carried on the undertaking, but desisted from finishing it on a false opinion that as the Red Sea is higher than Egypt, the cutting of the isthmus between them would necessarily lay that under water. The Ptolemies disproved this error, and by means of weirs or locks rendered the canal navigable to the sea without obstruction or inconvenience. Near to Arsinöe stand the cities of Heroum and Cleopatris, the latter of which is on that recess of the Arabian Gulf which penetrates into Egypt. Here are harbours and dwellings and several canals with lakes adjacent to them. The canal leading to the Red Sea begins at Phaccusa, to which the village of Philon is immediately contiguous.'

Diodorus has the following version:

'From Pelusium[2] to the Arabian Sea a canal was made. Necho, son of Psammitichus, first began the work; after him Darius the Persian carried it on, but left it unfinished, being told that if he cut through the isthmus, Egypt would be laid

---

[1] Suez al Hajar (Suez the Stony) occupies the site of several former cities. Ancient Egyptian remains have been found, and on an adjacent eminence (Kūm al Kulzum) are the ruins of the Ptolemaic fortress of Clysma Praesidium, the Kulzum of Arab geographers. Nearby are the earlier ruins of Arsinöe built by Ptolemy Philadelphus (c. 230 B.C.) and later named Cleopatris. It was a naval station in the time of Selim I (1517), water being brought by aqueduct from a well on the Cairo road a league and a quarter distant, as well as from the Wells of Moses eight miles away.

Yaqut mentions the presence here of magnetic rock (maghnāṭīs). Encyclopaedia of Islam.

[2] Pelusium (pelos=mud) was anciently a strong city with a circumference, according to Strabo, of 2⅓ miles. It occupied a site near the present Arab village Tineh (mud)—the Sin of Exod. xvi. 1. Ezekiel (xxx. 15) refers to the place as the strength of Egypt and it was still so regarded in Roman times. Here the army of Sennacherib lost 185,000 men in one night by the angel of death; here it was that Cambyses defeated the Egyptians, and here Pompey was assassinated. The ruins are still extensive and include a fort of Roman construction placed upon an eminence (Nourse).

under water, as the Red Sea was higher than Egypt. The last attempt was made by Ptolemy the Second, who succeeded by means of a new canal with sluices which were opened and shut as convenience required. The canal opened by Ptolemy was called after his name, and fell into the sea at Arsinöe.'

Pliny says:

'Sesostris, King of Egypt, was the first that planned the scheme for uniting the Red Sea with the Nile by a navigable canal of 62 thousand paces, which is the space that intervenes between them. In this he was followed by Darius, King of Persia, and also by Ptolemy of Egypt, the second of that name, who made a canal of 100 feet wide by 30 feet in depth, continuing it $37\frac{1}{2}$ thousand paces, to the Bitter Fountains. At this point the work was interrupted, for it was found that the Red Sea lay higher than the land of Egypt by 3 cubits, and a general inundation was feared. But some will have it that the true cause was, that if the sea was let into the Nile, the water of it, of which alone the inhabitants drink, would be spoiled.'

It will be observed that whilst Herodotus and Diodorus both give Necho credit for the original design and commencement of the work, Strabo and Pliny ascribe it to Sesostris. All, however, agree that Darius Hystaspes continued and, according to Herodotus, completed it, whereas Diodorus and Strabo agree that Ptolemy the Second was the person who actually completed it. Pliny, however, does not admit that it was ever finished.

To explain the situation of these ancient canals, it is necessary first of all to remember the changes which have taken place in the geography of the Nile during the last two thousand years. A little distance below Babylon (now modern Cairo, very nearly) the river divided itself, in ancient times, into three great branches. Two of these are still extant, viz. the western one, discharging into the Mediterranean at the Rosetta Mouth, the middle one, or Damietta River; whilst the third, or eastern branch, called the Pelusiac, has disappeared. It is with this one, however, we have to deal. Leaving the main stream below Babylon or Cairo, it flowed north-easterly, and discharged into the Mediterranean near modern Tineh, anciently Pelusium. About midway on its length there was a large fresh-water lake adjoining the ancient city of Bubastis; and it was from this lake, and not from the Mediterranean Sea, that the canal of Necho was carried towards Arsinöe or Suez,[1] but terminating in the Bitter Lakes, which lie some distance north-west of the head of the Red Sea. From these Bitter Lakes the canal of Ptolemy extended to the Red Sea itself; at Suez passing on its way through the city of Heroöpolis, which was, it is

---

[1] To the west of Suez lie the steep cliffs of Attakah, on whose heights ages ago Phoenician sailors bound for Ophir lighted fires and offered sacrifices to Baal Zephon, god of the north wind.

supposed, situated some 5 or 6 miles to the south-east of them, and about 15 miles north-west of Suez. And many writers agree that the Red Sea in ancient times extended much farther north: indeed, if not as far as the Bitter Lakes themselves, certainly to Heroöpolis. The indications of the retreat of the sea southwards are so manifest in various places as to make it clear that the waters of the Mediterranean and the Red Sea were at one time commingled.

It has been observed that the head of the canal of Necho at Bubastis was about the same distance from the Mediterranean as from the Red Sea; and this was probably done with a view of securing a current all the way from the Nile into the Red Sea, and so as to prevent the return of the salt water inland. That this actually took place there is little doubt, now that the levels are actually known: indeed, Herodotus confirms the fact, for he says that 'it entered the canal from the Nile, and discharged itself into the Arabian Gulf'.

With respect to the dimensions of these canals, according to Herodotus that of Necho and Darius was wide enough to admit *two triremes abreast*; and Strabo says that the canal of Ptolemy was 100 cubits broad, and had a depth sufficient for the largest merchant ships. Pliny, however, only allows 100 feet for the breadth, and 30 feet for the depth, which must clearly be erroneous. A work of such proportions would not stand.

There is no reason to regard these statements with suspicion, for the construction of great canals, for purposes of irrigation, was brought, both in Egypt and in Mesopotamia, to a high degree of perfection in the second millennium before Christ. The great Nahrwan Canal on the Tigris above Baghdad, with its three heads, which still exists almost intact, is 400 feet wide and 17 feet deep. Nimrod is credited with having constructed the dam and turned the river. This work existed for over 3,000 years, and was only swept away in the time of the last feeble Khalifs. The ancient Babylonians controlled the Euphrates by means of powerful escapes into two depressions capable of holding six milliards of tons of water, of which about a quarter was utilized for feeding the rivers, in time of low supply, at the rate, during sixty days, of over 40,000 cubic feet a second. They made of the Euphrates delta a country so rich that Alexander the Great would, but for his untimely death, have made Babylon the capital of the world. Long after its glory had departed, the son of Harun er Rashid is reported to have exclaimed, on ascending the Mokattam Hill, which overlooks Cairo: 'Cursed be Pharaoh who said in his pride, "Am I not Pharaoh, King of Egypt". Had he seen Babylonia, he would have said it with humility.'

With such traditions, and with such examples before their eyes, it is not surprising that the question of a canal across the Isthmus of Suez

was a matter of practical interest to successive rulers of Egypt.[1] The
object to be thus obtained varied, however, with the requirements of
each period. For many centuries the primary purpose was a passage
for sailing ships between the Red Sea and the Nile, in order to facilitate
commerce between Egypt and Arabia, which from the remotest ages
was of high importance. When the natural channel between the Bitter
Lakes and the present Gulf of Suez silted up Darius and Xerxes
(5th century B.C.) built a ship canal to facilitate navigation between the
Bitter Lakes and the Gulf. Under Ptolemy II (3rd century B.C.) this
work was completed and direct water connexion from the Gulf to the
Nile restored. So long as the largest vessels in use at that time could
pass up the Nile, no other solution of the problem was required. Again
and again, as empires rose and fell, such waterways fell into decay and
ruin, and were restored, or not, according to the political or strategical
conceptions of the rulers of Egypt. Under Roman rule, the needs of
commerce differed little from those of the past, but the Pelusiac branch
was at this time silting up. This circumstance, and the increased
draught of vessels, having rendered the navigable channel between
Bubastis (the modern Zagazig) and the Red Sea precarious, in the
second century A.D. the canal was deepened by Trajan, and a new
head constructed, taking off from the main stream above the Delta,
near the spot where Cairo now stands. Thence it ran eastwards till it
met the canal of Necho, near the modern Belbeis at a point half-way
between the Bubastis and the Bitter Lakes.

The new canal does not seem to have long remained navigable:
Ptolemy the geographer does not refer to it, though he lived within
fifty years of the time of Trajan. Centuries later, at the time of the
Arab invasion in A.D. 639, Amru ibn el Aas, the lieutenant of the
Khalif Omar, joined the two seas by a direct canal from Suez to
the Nile at Cairo, following the line of Trajan's canal, to facilitate
the transport of foodstuffs to Arabian ports. Omar, however, moved
by the fear of laying open to Christian vessels a path to Arabia,
closed Egypt herself to the trade of Europe,[2] but his successor the
Khalif Abu Jafar Abdullah el Mansur filled it up in A.D. 767 at the
junction of Necho's canal and the Bitter Lakes in order to reduce to
starvation the insurgents of Medina, then, as now, wholly dependent
upon imported foodstuffs. The winds and the sands did the rest, and

---

[1] A comprehensive survey of ancient canal works in Egypt is given in Roux, *L'Isthme et
le Canal de Suez*, 2 vols., vol. i, ch. i, Paris, 1901. See also Grover, Hamley and Warmington.

[2] Amr is also said to have contemplated the construction of a branch canal from Lake
Timsah northwards to the Mediterranean, and to have been forbidden by Omar to proceed with the project. Vide Butler, p. 345 note.

produced the ridge of Serapeum, which probably covers the site of Heroöpolis.

The Venetians, in the fifteenth century, urged the need for a marine canal to counteract the diversion of their trade into Portuguese hands. They could not, however, finance the venture themselves, and the Mameluke Sultans saw no profit in it.

From the sixteenth century until the middle of the nineteenth, Egypt played an unimportant part in the Oriental trade, but the project of a marine canal was never wholly forgotten, especially in France. It was recommended to Louis XIV by Leibniz. Colbert played with the idea, as did the Ministers of Louis XV and Louis XVI.

Not, however, until almost the beginning of the nineteenth century were facilities for navigation between the Mediterranean Sea and the Indian Ocean needed, or such provision likely to be commercially profitable or politically desirable.

The conquest of Egypt by the French revived the long dormant project of a canal which would take the largest ocean vessels. It appealed strongly to Napoleon Bonaparte as a means whereby the English might be circumvented and French commercial interests advanced. Among the scientists who accompanied him to Egypt in 1798 were several surveyors, charged with the duty of running lines of levels from sea to sea.

In December 1798 Bonaparte, accompanied by Berthier and Caffarelli and several scientists, spent ten days in Suez. He condemned it as a squalid and filthy place. Everywhere was neglect and decay, the harbour choked with sand, the shipyards deserted, the transit trade ruined by three centuries of Turkish and Mameluke misrule. Could he pierce the Isthmus he might destroy England's commercial supremacy. It would be a stupendous achievement, if it were practicable. The aims of Bonaparte's Egyptian expedition, as officially defined by a secret decree on 12th April, included the capture of Egypt and the exclusion of the English from 'all their possessions in the East to which the general can come'. He was also to have the Isthmus of Suez cut through and to assure 'the *free and exclusive possession* of the Red Sea to the French Republic'.[1] (Here, perhaps, we have the key to the determined opposition offered by Great Britain, for more than half a century to the schemes of de Lesseps.) Riding into the desert he discovered traces of Amru's canal, and decided to re-excavate this ancient waterway, deferring the greater scheme to a more favourable juncture.[2]

Fate decided otherwise, and he gave his name to neither. He was not well served by his engineers, under Monsieur Lepère, and the

[1] Rose, i. 181.   [2] Elgood (pp. 184–5), whom I have here and elsewhere followed closely.

survey of the Isthmus was bungled. It began in January 1799; interrupted in February, it was resumed in September and completed in December. The surveyors were changed, and different kinds of instruments used on different sections: the results, owing to Arab hostility, were not checked. The surveyors reported the waters of the Red Sea at high tide to be 32 feet 6 inches above those of the Mediterranean at low tide. The figures, impressively published in Napoleon's monumental *Description d'Egypte*, were accepted without criticism by the world at large. The alleged difference in level was inconsistent with the existence of Amru's canal, but old accounts, which showed that salt water was carried as much as 20 miles up an ancient Nile canal by the tides of the Red Sea, were adduced in support of a thesis which Laplace and Fourier had long ago rejected on theoretical grounds. For thirty years nearly all further projects, and they were numerous, assumed the correctness of the French levels. Among such projects were those of an English engineer, R. H. Galloway,[1] Captain J. B. Seeley,[2] and J. S. Buckingham,[3] the great traveller: all alike assumed the need for locks or sluices.

In 1830 Captain F. R. Chesney[4] went to Egypt with instructions to survey the Isthmus, with a view to reporting on the practicability of carrying out the project of a great ship canal. He reported no essential difference in the levels of the two seas, but his report apparently[5] carried little weight, even in England, where it was duly considered by the Select Committee of the House of Commons.

The main question of a trans-Isthmian canal was now obscured by several new developments. Muhammad Ali had in 1831 contemplated a new canal from Suez to Cairo, a project on which by 1834 the India Board and Foreign Office looked with favour. This project was shelved in favour of a railway from Cairo to Suez which received strong support in Egypt and in Whitehall. Finally, a French engineer in the service of Muhammad Ali, Monsieur Linant, ran fresh levels and confirmed Chesney's conclusions.

In 1833 a Frenchman of good family and some means, the leader of a group of Saint Simonian visionaries, Monsieur Prosper Enfantin, came upon the scene, with a party of twenty technicians[6] with the intention of prosecuting fresh surveys and putting new life into two projects, the Suez Canal and the Nile barrage. He met with Ferdinand

---

[1] *Parliamentary Papers*, 1834, No. 478. *Asiatic Journal*, xx, O.S. 364, 600.
[2] *Asiatic Journal*, xx, O.S. 538; ibid. xviii, O.S. 330.
[3] *Oriental Herald*, v. 9.　　　　　　　　　　　[4] Chesney, Lane-Poole, Rockwell.
[5] There is, however, reason to think that Lord Palmerston was already cognizant of the error in the calculations of the French surveyors.
[6] See Enfantin.

de Lesseps, then Vice-Consul under the French Consul-General, Monsieur Mimaut, who presented Enfantin to the Khedive Muhammad Ali. His schemes were placed before Muhammad Ali's Council. They approved the barrage scheme but not the canal. Enfantin remained till 1837 at work on the barrage; then he returned to France. The hour for the Suez Canal project was not yet ripe. Nevertheless Linant and Chesney's sober reports on a trans-Isthmian canal came to the notice of Ferdinand de Lesseps, whose interest had been aroused by reading the memoirs of the abortive Lepère expedition and, perhaps, by Enfantin's enthusiasm.[1] It was, however, many years before it began to take shape.

During the next few years nothing was done to press forward either a canal or a railway across the Isthmus. From 1841 onwards, projects for a canal were uppermost for a few years. The East India Company favoured a canal, as also the P. and O. S. N. Company, whose Managing Director, Arthur Anderson, made in 1841 a careful study of the whole question. Writing to Palmerston, he estimated the cost at a quarter of a million pounds sterling, but was confident that it would be profitable at ten times the amount, 'since the whole of our political and commercial intercourse with the vast territories of the east would of necessity fall into the Channel and the distance between them and Great Britain for all purposes be reduced by many thousands of miles'. He was confident that all Europe, except Russia, would benefit. He believed that the Pasha would give a concession for such a canal, failing which a right of way could be secured from the Sultan whose approval was in any case essential. Two years later Anderson's views were published in pamphlet form[2] and had considerable influence on public opinion in England. From this time onwards the project of a canal joining the Nile to the Red Sea was by common consent abandoned owing to the increasing size of steamships.

Further unofficial surveys were made, all of them indicating that there was little if any difference in level between the two seas.[3] Expert opinion tended to harden in favour of the practicability of the canal as an engineering project. The British Government were thus compelled to review the whole question, and reach a decision as to the line they should take, on the broadest grounds of expediency, in the national interest. Palmerston was not long in arriving at the conclusion that, however great the commercial advantages, this 'second Bosphorus'

---

[1] Lesseps, 1887.   [2] Anderson, *Asiatic Journal*, 3rd series, ii. 304, 305.

[3] The difference in level between ordinary high and ordinary low water at Suez is 3 feet 9 inches; at Port Said 9 inches. The extreme difference, caused by contrary winds, observed at Suez is 8 feet 6 inches, and at Port Said 4 feet 6 inches (Hartley, op. cit.). These differences are sufficient to prevent stagnation.

might be a source of grave embarrassment. The British Government had refused, in 1834, to give any financial guarantees to an Egyptian railway from Alexandria via Cairo to Suez; Lord Palmerston saw stronger objections still to guaranteeing a Suez canal, and his opposition was strengthened by the willingness of the French Government to sponsor the scheme, and by the belief, frequently avowed by Metternich, that it would largely divert eastern trade to Austria.

By 1843 it was clear that Great Britain must either oppose construction or, by espousing it, embark on a line of conduct which might lead to the annexation of a part, at all events, of Egypt by force of arms and the dismemberment of the Ottoman Empire which, it will be remembered, at this period exercised more than nominal control over greater areas in North Africa than in Asiatic Turkey. The Turkish question was perennial: Palmerston shrank from adding an Egyptian question, and when Palmerston hesitated, his colleagues recoiled from decision.

The French, with the support of their Government, were anxious to proceed with a project disavowed by their English rivals, and the British Government found themselves compelled to descend from aloofness to definite opposition and to advocate, as a counterpoise, the Cairo–Suez Railway. The rest of Europe supported the canal project, as did Muhammad Ali Pasha, the Sultan's Viceroy. England was not popular in Egypt, nor at the Sublime Porte, but she was feared. The occupation of Aden, the war in Syria, and a hostile naval demonstration against Italy were fresh in men's minds. Great Britain was for this reason long able to withstand the weight of hostile influences: her naval supremacy was long a sufficient deterrent to overt action, and her influence at Constantinople tended to increase as the years passed.

Mr. Murray, the British Consul-General in Egypt, wrote in May 1847 that 'a plan for the Suez Canal has been formed, purporting to be complete in all its details; . . . it has been favourably received by the Egyptian Government. . . . In the present state of Science I dare not take it upon myself . . . to assure anyone of its impracticability.' He was instructed, in reply, to remain entirely passive on the subject, and to press the Suez railway scheme as a preferable substitute. Henceforward British authorities both at home and in Egypt consistently displayed an attitude of scepticism and incredulity towards the canal scheme which was wholly unjustified by the available evidence.

In 1846 there had been constituted in Paris a 'Société d'études du Canal de Suez', consisting of Robert Stephenson and Edward Starbuck, of London, Louis Negrelli, of Vienna, MM. Féronce and Sellier, of Liepzig, on behalf of certain German interests, and five Frenchmen MM. Arlès, Enfantin, Jules, Léon, and Paulin Talabot. The *Siège*

Social of this company, which had an initial capital of 150,000 francs, was in the house of Monsieur Enfantin.[1] It was in reality a semi-official commission, whose operations were facilitated in every way by Muhammad Ali Pasha, and by his staff, including the able Monsieur Linant. The Viceroy, too, bore most if not all the cost, a matter of some £4,000. How Robert Stephenson came to be associated with an enterprise, the object of which ran counter to all the views that he had expressed both before and after 1846, remains a mystery. He was urged by Waghorn[2] to have nothing to do with it: he chose a middle course, neither resigning, nor taking an active part in the work. All members of the party agreed that there was no essential difference in the height of the two seas. The Austrian engineers, headed by Negrelli, thought a sea-level canal possible but foresaw difficulties at the termini. The French advocated a canal with locks. Stephenson announced that he had great faith in the project for a sea-level canal so long as the thirty-odd feet of difference in level was believed to exist, for he considered a current of three or four miles an hour necessary, in the light sandy soil of the Isthmus, to keep the channel clear. A long channel deep enough for the largest vessels, without any current flowing through it, would be but a stagnant ditch between tideless seas, enormously costly, wholly unprofitable. A railway alone could adequately serve Britain's need. His convictions corresponded very closely with his interest in the proposed Egyptian railway, and with the known sentiments of the Government of his country. The Post Office was officially 'opposed to steam navigation as a mode of conveyance for the mails'. His views formed the basis of arguments for Lord Palmerston and others, in opposing the canal scheme, long after they had been disproved.

In 1849 the canal scheme received a fresh set-back on the death of Muhammad Ali Pasha, whose successor in the Viceroyalty, Abbas Pasha, was attached to English rather than French interests. During

---

[1] Enfantin, 1869; *Parliamentary Papers*, 1851, No. 605, p. 223.

[2] Thomas Waghorn, son of a Rochester tradesman and a Hugli pilot, was the pioneer of mail communication via the Red Sea. He associated with the Arabs between Cairo and Suez, lived in their tents, and having gained their confidence established a regular caravan service. He built eight stage-houses between Cairo and Suez (still visible from the air) and made what had been a dangerous path beset with robbers a secure highway equipped with horses, vans, and English mail coaches. To his memory in 1869 a bust was erected by de Lesseps at Port Saïd, where it serves to remind us of de Lesseps' magnanimity. (Why is there no statue to Nelson overlooking the Bay of Aboukir?) The impression he made on his contemporaries is referred to by Thackeray, *A Journey from Cornhill to Cairo*: 'The bells are ringing prodigiously; and Lieut. Waghorn is bouncing in and out of the court-yard full of business. He only left Bombay yesterday morning, was seen in the Red Sea on Tuesday, is engaged to dinner this afternoon in the Regent's Park. . . . If any man can be at two places at once, Waghorn is he.'

the six years of his rule little was heard of the canal. Englishmen replaced the French advisers who sought the downfall of Abbas, whose position, as grandson of the hated Muhammad Ali, was precarious, for he could rely on no active support from the British Government. Railway schemes again came to the front; the Alexandria–Cairo section of the Alexandria–Suez railway was commenced in 1851 and completed two years later at a cost of £11,000 per mile for the 140 miles partly double and partly single track covered, including the initial provision of rolling stock. For his services in this connexion Robert Stephenson received £55,000. Scarcely had this section been finished when the short reign of Abbas ended ingloriously in 1854. His successor, Saïd Pasha, restored to his counsels the French advisers whom Abbas had spurned. Work on the Cairo–Suez railway was not, however, stopped and was completed in 1858. But, if British counsels were at a discount in Cairo, they were at a premium in Constantinople, for with the opening of the Crimean War the Sultan of Turkey could not disregard British counsels. The British Cabinet were now more than ever on the defensive, though, as will later be seen, the parliamentary opposition took a different view.

Every circumstance pointed at this time to a permanent French settlement in Egypt, inconsistent with a real neutrality, and likely to lead to grave political difficulty. French newspapers and public men vied with each other in pointing out the extent to which the canal would damage British interests. Events have not taken the course anticipated by the opponents of the Canal, but have not wholly falsified Palmerston's anticipations.

With the accession of Saïd Pasha, a definite French project for the construction of a canal across the Isthmus brought its author, Ferdinand de Lesseps, into prominence. His father had been French Political Agent in Egypt during the rise of Napoleon Bonaparte, and had materially assisted Muhammad Ali Pasha to establish himself in the Viceroyalty. His son Ferdinand spent his early youth in company with Saïd Pasha and other members of Muhammad Ali's household. He had been *élève* in the French Consulate at Cairo, and Vice-Consul at Alexandria; he had, as already mentioned, noted the early efforts of Chesney and of Waghorn. He had been in touch with all the leading personages connected with railway and canal projects. Though his early adult life had been spent in France and in Algeria, he had never ceased to interest himself in the union of the Western and Eastern oceans. He had retired at the age of about 50 from the service of the French Government because he felt unable, as French Ambassador at Rome, to approve the policy of Monsieur de Tocqueville in 1849 of sending a French army to reinstate the Pope. His apprehensions were justified by the event. He would fain have gone to Egypt forthwith, but so long as Muhammad Ali lived nothing could be done and de Lesseps remained on his estate in Algeria till news reached him of Saïd's accession. De Lesseps was a man of action, but also a diplomat by instinct and training.· His first act was to write to his friend of his youth, the new Viceroy, to renew his friendship and assure him of a congratulatory visit. Hurrying out to Egypt, he was soon installed in a mansion, and in the confidence of the new ruler, and within three months had succeeded in transforming his personal intimacy with the Viceroy into a business relationship. His perfect riding won the hearts of men more adept in the saddle than in the office chair. One day he was in the desert with the Viceroy, his tent was pitched upon an eminence covered with loose stones: in one place only was a parapet— it was a dangerous jump. De Lesseps put his horse at it, and cleared it. His hardihood excited the admiration of all, and of none more whole-heartedly than of Saïd Pasha. The great plan was first presented on 15th November 1854 with a confidence and enthusiasm that proved infectious. 'I accept your plan', said he. '. . . Consider the matter settled. You may rely upon me.' Ten days later the preliminary draft of a concession to be issued by the Viceroy, with the consent of his Suzerain, was prepared, approved, and signed on 30th November sub-ject, however, to the consent of the Great Powers, and the great project began to emerge. The Viceroy is said to have signed the document without having read it: it was certainly not scrutinized on his behalf by expert judicial or financial counsellors.

The event was a landmark in the history of the canal. Looking back at an interval of seventy years, one is struck by the fact that the most important single link in the chain of events was the youthful friendship between Saïd Pasha and de Lesseps. But for this fortuitous circum-stance, de Lesseps, or some one else, might have approached the Sultan, not the Khedive. The Sultan might have excluded this barren strip of desert from the control of the Khedive—and a series of contingencies might have culminated in the emergence in very truth of a second Bosphorus—in Turkish hands. Such speculations are unprofitable, but they suggest that Saïd Pasha, with all his failings, deserves more recognition both in Egypt and in Europe than historians have yet seen fit to accord, for though the conditions of his time and his own extravagance were against him, he was in many ways a remarkable man: the youngest son of his father Muhammad Ali, born in 1822, he had been sent to Constantinople at the age of 19 to negotiate with the Porte as to the Egyptian tribute. The intrigues of his predecessor Abbas, who aimed at modifying the law of succession in favour of his own descendants, would probably have succeeded but for his premature death, in which case Saïd Pasha would have been excluded from the throne. Shortly after his accession he created a Council of State; in 1858 he granted to all his subjects freedom to own and dispose of landed property, and he was the first Khedive to attempt to abolish the slave-trade. Shortly after his accession he announced his intention to visit Paris but, as observed by Lord Stratford de Redcliffe in a dispatch of 5th October 1855 (F.O. 78/1087), he was at this time chiefly occupied with his Army, and 'wanted only the opportunity to follow in the footsteps of Mehemet Ali'. Not the least of de Lesseps' titles to the gratitude of the Egyptian people is the fact that he used his influence to divert his august master's wayward energies into more fruitful channels.

BIBLIOGRAPHY

(London, unless otherwise stated, is in all cases the place of publication.)

Anderson, Arthur. *The Practicability and Utility of opening a Communication between the Red Sea and the Mediterranean by a Ship-Canal.* 1843.

Anon. *Le Percement de l'Isthme de Suez.* Enfantin—M. de Lesseps. *Résumé Historique.* Paris, 1869.

Anon. *The Egyptian Railway, or the Interest of England in Egypt.* 1852.

Anon. *The Present Crisis in Egypt in Relation to our Overland Communications with India,* No. 1. 1851.

Asiatic Journal, vols. xviii and xx sqq., 3rd series, vols. ii and xxxix.

Brunlees, J., and Webb, E. B. *Proposed Ship-railway across the Isthmus of Suez.* 1859.

Butler, A. J. *The Arab Conquest of Egypt.* Oxford, 1902.

Calcutta Review, vol. xxiv sqq.

Cameron, D. A. *Egypt in the XIXth Century.* 1898.

Chesney, Francis R., Capt., R.A. *Narrative of the Euphrates Expedition.*

Clarkson, Ed. *The Suez Navigable Canal for Accelerated Communication with India.* 1843.

Diplomatic Review, 1853.

Edinburgh Philosophical Journal, Oct. 1825.

Edinburgh Review, vol. lx sqq., vol. ciii, 1931.

Elgood, P. G. *Bonaparte's Adventure in Egypt.* 2 vols.

Fitzgerald, Percy. *The Great Canal at Suez.* 1876.

Foreign Office Suez Canal Papers, 1833 sqq.

Hallberg, C. W. *The Suez Canal.* P.S. King & Son. 1931.

Hamley, W. G. *A New Sea and an Old Land.* 1871.

Hansard. *Parliamentary Debates.*

Heron, R. M. *The Suez Canal Question.* 1875.

Hoskins, H. L. *British Routes to India.* 1928.

International Scientific Commission, Report and Plan of, 1857.

Lauture, E. de. 'Influence du Canal de Suez sur le commerce.' 1855 (*Bulletin de la Société de Geographie*).

Lane-Poole, S. *Life of General F. R. Chesney.*

Lesseps, F. de. *The Isthmus of Suez Question.* 1855.

—— *Inquiry into the Opinions of the Commercial Classes of Great Britain on the Suez Ship Canal.* 1857.

—— *Résumé Historique.* 1869.

14 BIBLIOGRAPHY

Lesseps, F. de, *The Suez Canal. Letters and Documents descriptive of its Rise and Progress in 1854-6.* 1876.
—— *Recollections of Forty Years.* 1887.
McCoan, J. *Egypt as it is.* New York, 1877.
Nederlands Rijv. Archief. Dispatches, &c. 1855.
Oriental Herald, vol. v sqq.
Public Record Office. F.O. 97/408, *Transit through Egypt: Navigation of the Nile, 1841–8* and F.O. 97/411.
—— F.O. 78, numbers 887, 1156, 1340, 1421, 1489, 1560. *Suez Canal, 1854 to 1860.*
Parliamentary Papers, 478, 1834; 605, 1851.
Price, John Spencer. *The Early History of the Suez Canal.* (N.D.)
Rockwell, C. H. *The Suez Canal.* 1867.
Rose, J. H. *Life of Napoleon.* 1902.
Roux, J. Charles. *L'Isthme et le Canal de Suez.* 2 vols. Paris, 1901.
St. Hilaire (De Lesseps ed.). *New Facts and Figures relative to the Isthmus of the Suez Canal.* 1856.
Seeley, Capt. J. B. See *Asiatic Journal*, xviii, xx, O.S.
Simencourt, A. de. *L'Isthme de Suez*, 1859.
Stephenson, Robert. See *The Engineer*, 15th Feb. 1856.
—— *The Isthmus of Suez Canal.* 1858.
Symons, M. Travers. *The Riddle of Egypt.* (N.D.)
Twiss, Sir Travers. 'Le Canal Maritime de Suez.' 1885. (*Revue de Droit International*.)
Urquhart, D. See *Diplomatic Review* for 1876.
Vetch, Capt. J. R. E., F.R.S. *Inquiry into . . . Ship Navigation between the Mediterranean and Red Seas.* 1843.
Warmington, E. H. *The Commerce between the Roman Empire and India.* 1928.
Willcocks, W. *The Irrigation of Mesopotamia.* 1917.

CHAPTER II

PRELIMINARY NEGOTIATIONS 1854–65

'Marchez à la tête des idées de votre siècle, ces idées vous suivent et vous soutiennent. Marchez à leur suite, elles vous entraînent. Marchez contre elles, elles vous renversent.'

Louis Napoléon, du prison de Ham, 1841.

Draft Concession. Napoleon III's interest. Lord Stratford de Redcliffe. Lord Clarendon. The International Scientific Commission. The Euphrates Valley Railway. Sir Daniel Lange. Disraeli. Gladstone. The Canal Company's capital subscribed in France. Work on the canal begins. Turkish protests. Intervention of Napoleon III. Austrian support. Sir Henry Bulwer. Saïd Pasha is succeeded by Ismaïl Pasha. Arbitration by Napoleon III. The Sultan of Turkey's firman of approval. Lord Palmerston dies. Bibliography.

THE first concession, the text of which was based on railway concessions in France, provided for a company to be organized, not as a French, but as a strictly international enterprise having its origin in Egypt, known as the *Compagnie Universelle du Canal Maritime de Suez*. The concession was to endure for ninety-nine years and the Chairman was always to be appointed by the Egyptian Government, and to be chosen as far as possible from among the shareholders most interested in the enterprise.[1] The canal works were to be executed at the cost of the Company, but all fortifications were to be installed by the Viceroy alone. The route of the canal was not specified. Tariff discrimination was forbidden. The net profits were to be divided as follows:

The founders	10 per cent.
The Egyptian Government . .	15 ,,
The shareholders . . .	75 ,,

Saïd Pasha at once wrote, as in duty bound, to the Sultan of Turkey, seeking his approval both for the canal, and for the Cairo-Suez railway, intending to use the one as a counterpoise to the other. De Lesseps was loth to see these questions thrown afresh to the diplomatic lions of Europe, but the facts were too strong for him. The Viceroy had scarcely presented this application to the Porte, when he was invested with the insignia of the Legion of Honour by the French Consul-General, on behalf of Napoleon III, who thus made clear to the world his peculiar interest in the canal project. In making the presentation, the Consul-General assured Saïd Pasha that, in the glorious but arduous work of reorganization and reform in Egypt, His Highness could rely upon the encouragement, and if need be, the support of Napoleon III.

[1] The Statutes provide that the Board of Directors is to be composed of thirty-two members representing the principal *nationalities* interested in the enterprise.

'The Emperor of Europe' did not even at this early stage reserve
expressions of his approval for such ceremonial occasions. 'His
philanthropy', as Lord Cowley remarked in another connexion, 'far
exceeded his respect for Treaties'. At the Congress of Paris in 1856 he
testified, at the close of a farewell dinner party to the assembled pleni-
potentiaries, to the deep interest he took in a scheme which seemed to
him a universal benefit. He had studied it, he said, in all its aspects,
and acquainted himself with all the documents bearing on it, and
earnestly wished it success. But the enterprise, admirable as it was in
every way, had given rise to certain objections and obstructions,
especially in England. For his part he could not consider that these
objections were well founded, and hoped to see them removed. At the
same time he was not disposed to rush matters for fear of com-
promising their success. Instead, relying upon the happy alliance
which united the two peoples, he looked to the future—and to a very
near future—for an agreement upon this question.[1] In such an
utterance Napoleon III was seen at his best, sustaining a remote and
beneficent design with a statesmanlike appreciation of the proper
method for its attainment, and to this policy he adhered with admirable
good temper. When, three years later, after some particularly dis-
couraging dispatch from London, he told Lesseps not to worry, 'You
can count,' he said, 'on my support and protection', but he added, 'it is
a squall, we must shorten sail'.[2] Would that he had always pursued his
own dreams in the same spirit! As it was, the opening of the Suez
Canal by the Empress was destined to furnish his chequered reign
with almost the last and not the least deserved of its triumphs.

The Suez Canal took the place, at this period, in Louis Napoleon's
mind,[3] of the Nicaragua Canal, the claims of which he had urged, as
against those of Panama, in a pamphlet written, for the most part,
during the period of his captivity at Ham. It was to be called the *Canale
Napoleone de Nicaragua*. With the events of 1848 the whole scheme
was, so far as he was concerned, thrown to the winds. Yet perhaps only
chance, and Lord Palmerston, prevented the canal from the Mediterranean to the Red Sea being called not after an insignificant hamlet
at the southern end, but after Louis Napoleon himself.

---

[1] De Lesseps, *Souvenirs*, ii. 429, 430. Lord Cowley's dispatch of 3rd April 1856,
states that there was at this time no pressure from the French Government, but much
from de Lesseps. Saïd Pasha desired to conciliate France as a means to secure for
himself complete independence. He was at this juncture busy in raising, 'with the utmost
violence and oppression', more than double the 18,000 troops fixed by the firman of 1841.

[2] Ibid. 692, 693, quoted by Simpson.

[3] Louis Napoleon's *Life of Caesar* (i. 163) shows how deeply he was imbued with the
philanthropic urge to bring prosperity to the East by the accomplishment of de Lesseps'
project.

The British Government, whose agents in Cairo made no secret of their opposition, were well represented at Constantinople, where Lord Stratford de Redcliffe was at the height of his power. Vigorous and aggressive, and well acquainted with the guiles and wiles of oriental diplomatists, he was feared by his colleagues, and respected by the Porte. Kinglake, in his *Invasion of the Crimea* (i. 111), speaking of Lord Stratford says: 'he was so gifted by nature that whether men studied his despatches, or whether they listened to his spoken word, or whether they were only bystanders caught and fascinated by the grace of his presence, they could scarcely help thinking that if the English nation was to be maintained in peace or drawn into war by the will of a single mortal, there was no man who looked so worthy to fix its destiny as Sir Stratford Canning. . . . His temper was fierce, and his assertion of self so closely involved in his conflicts, that he followed up his opinions with the whole strength of his imperious nature.' When de Lesseps visited Constantinople in February 1855 he found the Grand Vizier apparently quite favourable to the project, but such was the fear inspired by 'Sultan Stratford', or 'Abdul Canning', as he was often called, that he was refused recognition in any official capacity. Only the Austrian Minister[1] accorded him official support; for the rest he had to rely on such personal influence as he had. So untiring were his efforts that Lord Stratford reported, before the end of the month, that the Turkish Government would confirm the canal concession before long unless he could raise objections on official grounds. He had hitherto acted not 'against' but 'without' instructions, a distinction to which great importance attached in days when communications were slow. De Lesseps' representations to Lord Stratford de Redcliffe were ignored[2] and vigorous oral representations made to the Porte, depicting the perils of severance of Egypt from Turkey and of the interposition of a French colony on the canal between the Asiatic and African possessions of the Porte, culminating in a French protectorate over Egypt. British statesmen could scarcely forget that the Indian Empire was laid by merchants who gradually acquired trading privileges, lands, the management of revenue, and finally sovereign powers. They had no mind to see the same process repeated in Egypt. De Lesseps was foiled for the moment, and returned to Cairo, angry but not beaten.

Opinion in favour of de Lesseps grew in strength, and Lord Stratford realized that without open official interference he could

---

[1] Lord Clarendon, however, wrote to Lord Stratford on 10th December 1857 that the Austrian Government was highly favourable to the canal project, but would not support de Lesseps until all the interested powers of Europe had come to an agreement on the subject. The Ottoman Government took, at this time, the same view.

[2] De Lesseps, *Recollections of Forty Years*, 1887.

not hope indefinitely to postpone the confirmation of the concession. After further sparring, Lord Clarendon, then Secretary of State for Foreign Affairs, summarized in a note to Count Walewski, the French Ambassador, the considered views of the British Government in terms which may be summarized as follows:

(1) The canal project was physically impossible except at a prohibitive cost. If undertaken, it can only be for political objects.

(2) The project would delay if not prevent the Cairo–Suez railway,[1] which was all the British Government required.

(3) The scheme was founded upon an antagonistic policy on the part of France with regard to Egypt;[2] it had survived the policy out of which it arose and should now be dropped.

At this point the canal project as a political issue was temporarily eclipsed in importance by the urgencies of the Crimean War. De Lesseps used the enforced truce between the Quai d'Orsay and Downing Street to initiate a campaign of public education. With implicit confidence in the soundness of his plans he proceeded to place them, over the heads of the British Government, before the English people themselves. Arriving in London at the end of June 1855 he busied himself in interviewing officials and merchants in London. The Prime Minister, Lord Palmerston, was as suspicious and unsympathetic as Lord Clarendon, but mercantile opinion was far more favourable. De Lesseps' pamphlet *The Isthmus of Suez Question* was favourably received: the East India Company adopted a benevolent attitude. The Peninsular and Oriental Company, ignoring the expressed views of the Foreign Office, definitely espoused the scheme. Unofficial opinion in India was equally favourable. On 5th January 1856 de Lesseps secured the signature of the Viceroy to a second Act of Concession, in amplification and completion of the first. To this Act were annexed the Statutes, or Articles of Association, of a Company for making the Concession; these two documents form the Charter of the Suez Canal Company. The grant of the second Act of Concession was followed by no change in the policy of Her Majesty's Government, for, whilst de Lesseps had largely succeeded in converting mercantile and public opinion in England, he had not been able to modify in any way the

---

[1] This argument was weak to the point of falsity, for Saïd Pasha had ordered rails for and ordered work to proceed on the Suez railway regardless of the fate of the canal. M. Walewski assured Lord Cowley (*v.* his dispatch, 4.1.57) that he had warned M. de Lesseps that he was not to expect countenance or assistance from the French Government, so long as H.M. Government were opposed to the scheme. The French Government felt that H.M. Government were masters of the ground at Constantinople and had no desire to come into collision with H.M. Government on such matters.

[2] The *mot d'ordre* of French newspapers had long been 'en perçant l'Isthme de Suez nous perçons le point faible de la cuirasse anglaise'.

official attitude of hostility. Nothing daunted he returned to Paris, after three months in England, to convene, as an International Scientific Commission, a group of leading engineers from the principal countries of Europe, who were to pass a final judgement on his proposals. Great Britain was represented by three eminent engineers, Mr. J. M. Rendel, Mr. J. R. McClean, and Mr. C. Manby, with a representative of the East India Company. Their survey was completed in January 1856, but was only published twelve months later. The report, which was unreservedly favourable to the designs of de Lesseps, concluded with the following pregnant paragraph:

'It is not our province to judge what motives may have retarded the execution of a work of this character. But we believe that we are only echoing the universal opinion in saying that all delay is to be deplored when once a well-matured opinion on the subject has been formed. Our object has been to enlighten, as far as in us lay, the Governments and Nations of the world; with all confidence, we submit to them the final results of our inquiry. May our labour hasten the moment when all impediments, other than those in the actual nature of things, shall be removed, and when the artificial Bosphorus at Suez may be thrown open to the navies of all nations.'

The Report profoundly influenced public opinion, but the British Government refused to be convinced, and even before the Report was published renewed their opposition at Cairo and Constantinople. They were still 'opposed to steam navigation for the conveyance of the mails', and so abhorrent was the idea of trans-Isthmian communication that, on the outbreak of the Indian Mutiny, the War Office sent all reinforcements via the Cape, until compelled by public opinion to ask the concurrence of the Porte and the Khedive to the transport of troops via Suez. The required permission was readily granted.

In vain did de Lesseps, who never failed to maintain his dignity and diplomatic magnanimity, use, with complete success, his influence to secure for Great Britain free telegraphic communication between England and her Eastern possessions across Egypt. He found Palmerston, in his own words, 'defiant and prejudiced', and Saïd Pasha so weary of opposition as to be nearly ready, for the sake of peace, to abandon the enterprise. Behind Lord Palmerston's defiance and Lord Stratford's determination was the knowledge that the reconnaissance of the projected Euphrates Valley railway had demonstrated this project to be in all respects practicable. Though surveys had not begun, the shares of the Company[1] formed to build it were already at a premium. Such a railway would speed up communications with India more than the Suez Canal could hope to do, it would develop the supposed resources of Mesopotamia, then reputed to be a potential granary. Sentiment in Europe was stronger than ever in favour of a canal, but the proposed

---

[1] 'The Association for the Promotion of the Euphrates Valley Railway.'

short cut to the Persian Gulf from Seleucia by Antioch and Aleppo to the Euphrates and thus to Baghdad and Basrah would shorten the passage to India by 1,000 miles for a mere £16,000,000. The plan pleased Lord Palmerston and was supported by Lord Clarendon: the Porte was favourably inclined. But a Government guarantee was necessary, and was not forthcoming. On that rock the project foundered, as it would founder to-day. Professor H. L. Hoskins in his *British Routes to India* tells the whole story with admirable lucidity. It is enough to record here that the project was essentially political, not commercial, and that whilst, for passengers, it was a possible alternative to the canal, it could never have existed along with it.

The brief war with Persia early in 1857, difficulties in China, and the outbreak of the Indian Mutiny in May of that year gave a fresh turn to public discussion. Troops were urgently needed; they all went by way of the Cape. At this juncture de Lesseps made a fresh descent upon England. With the assistance (wholly gratuitous) of Mr. (later Sir) Daniel Lange, a British subject and an old friend, he addressed meetings in the principal mercantile centres of the United Kingdom. His mission was remarkably successful and undermined, while it hardened, the official opposition. Lord Palmerston declared in the House of Commons that the canal would be profitable to France, but hostile to England's interests. This statement, which created a deep sensation, did more to assist de Lesseps in raising capital in his own country than the most energetic support of the French Government could have done. A few months later Robert Stephenson, who had entered the House of Commons, supported Palmerston's views in Parliament. He was waited upon by a representative of de Lesseps with a letter requiring him to name two friends and to furnish a written explanation to de Lesseps who 'placed himself entirely at Mr. Stephenson's disposal'. Explanations followed and the challenge was withdrawn.

In December 1857 Lord Stratford de Redcliffe, the Great Elchi, was on the point of severing his long connexion with Turkey, but the British Government had been at pains to assure the Porte that their policy remained unchanged. On 1st January 1858 Lord Clarendon clinched matters by announcing to the Grand Vizier (Rashid Pasha) that if the Sultan were to give his consent to the Suez Canal Scheme 'the direct and obvious object of which is to separate Egypt from Turkey, the Sultan must not expect that the maintenance and integrity of the Ottoman Empire could thereafter be a principle to guide the policy of the Great Powers of Europe, because the Sultan would himself have been a party to the setting aside of that principle'. The Porte gave way, for the time being, promising not to give assent to the project without the consent of His Majesty's Government. A few days later Rashid Pasha was seized with convulsions after drinking a cup of coffee, and soon expired. De Lesseps lamented his death, as he seemed[1] 'to have shaken himself pretty free of English influence in regard to the canal. He was succeeded by Aali Pasha, an upright man, but timid.

In February 1858 Palmerston fell, but there was no official change in the attitude of the British Government. Indeed Disraeli described the canal project in the House of Commons as 'a most futile attempt and totally impossible to be carried out'.

In June 1858 the matter was again raised in the House of Common, where de Lesseps now had many warm supporters. Lord Palmerston took his customary line: the canal would be a step towards the dismemberment both of the Turkish and British Empires, the arguments by which it was commended to foolish and credulous investors were unsound, if not worse: the railway would always serve British needs more economically than a canal. Never would he be a party to such a sacrifice of British interests.[2]

Mr. Gladstone followed. With close reasoning he argued against the proposition that the canal must tend to sever Turkey from Egypt. As to possible danger to our own interests, was it not a canal that would fall within the control of the strongest maritime power in Europe? And what could that power be but ourselves? What could be more unwise than to present ourselves to the world as the opponents of a scheme on the face of it beneficial to mankind, on no better ground than remote and contingent danger to interests of our own. 'You have engaged', he said, 'in a contest in which you will, in the end, certainly give way. . . . There is not a statesman in Europe who does not denounce the policy of this opposition as unwarrantable and selfish.' 'Let us', he concluded, 'regard the Suez canal as a commercial project, as such let it stand or fall.' His cogent arguments did not at the time commend themselves to his hearers, who were as much against the canal as they were, sixteen years later, in favour of Disraeli's *coup*, but his words were not without effect upon public opinion at home.

Abroad, Palmerston's stormy words had already an effect very different from that intended. The theatre of French action was transferred to Constantinople, where the representatives of other European

---

[1] There is little doubt that a pecuniary bond existed between Rashid Pasha and the Khedive in 1854, and for some years afterwards. On his death his estate was found to be in debt to the Government to the extent of £83,000.

[2] In a holograph note on a dispatch of Lord Cowley, dated 13th October 1859, Lord Palmerston summarized his own views as follows: 'There are three authorities adverse to the execution of this scheme. The English Government, the Turkish Government, and Nature. The two first are not likely to change their views, but the third will be found inflexible.' The note indicates what a heavy responsibility for his attitude rests on the British engineers who had advised him.

nations had official instructions to promote the interests of the Canal Company. There was, however, no immediate prospect of the Sublime Porte reaching a decision, and de Lesseps found himself once again faced with ruin. One course only remained to him; he returned to Paris to constitute his company. Disregarding the advice of expert financiers, ignoring the great banking companies—even Rothschild's—because their terms appeared exorbitant, he appealed direct to the people.

The capital of the Company was fixed at two hundred million francs, divided into 400,000 shares of 500 francs each. On 5th November he opened his subscription lists, on 30th November they were closed. The issue was not a complete success. The French allotment was fully subscribed, but there were no applications from England or the United States, Austria, or Russia. It was the Viceroy of Egypt, Saïd Pasha, prodigal but in this case far-seeing, who came to the rescue and subscribed sixty million francs.[1] The fact that but for him the Company could scarcely have gone to allotment should, in justice to his memory and to his residuary legatees, the Egyptian people, be borne in mind. The whole capital had been subscribed, mostly in small sums, except for some 85,000 shares reserved for investors in England, Austria, Russia, and the United States, in order that the enterprise might be, at all events from the outset, truly international.

In his *Recollections* de Lesseps wrote on this subject (1st January 1859):

'His Highness having wished that the French investments should not much exceed one half of the whole, in order that the company might, so far as possible, maintain its universal character, we have fixed the total number of shares as follows:

France	207,111
Ottoman Empire exclusive of Viceroy's personal investment	96,517
Spain	4,046
Holland	2,615
Tunis	1,714
Piedmont	1,353
Switzerland	460
Belgium	324
Tuscany	176
Naples	97
Rome	54
Prussia	15
Denmark	7
Portugal	5
Sums held in reserve for Austria, Great Britain, Russia, and U.S.A., which the Viceroy authorizes me to guarantee for him should they not be taken	85,506
	400,000

[1] Sir Ian Malcolm in *The National Review*, May 1921 (first edition).

De Lesseps was now the titular head of a strong organization, complete with an administrative council and a vast amount of public and official goodwill in most European countries, to foster and strengthen which he published his own fortnightly *Journal de l'Union des deux Mers* from a Bureau at 52 Rue de Vernueil, Paris, in which the views of the *Canalistes* were propagated and progress recorded. His obligations were, however, no longer to the Viceroy of Egypt, but to his stockholders. As the head of a corporation controlled in France he was a fair target for his enemies. The Sultan was reminded[1] of the danger for a separatist movement in Egypt, fostered by the Canal Company: Saïd Pasha was warned of the peril he had incurred in suffering, without the consent of the Porte, the incorporation under his aegis of a Company endowed with almost sovereign rights.

De Lesseps, now in his fifty-fifth year, was equal to the occasion. He drew, with the skill of a trained lawyer a distinction between the execution of an engineering project and the construction of an international highway. In the Acts of Concession, and in the empty words of approval that had issued from time to time by the Porte, he found sufficient authorization for the construction not of an international highway but of a navigable waterway. He would, he declared, leave to others, preferably to an international congress, the settlement of the political status of the work when completed. He was no longer a diplomat, but a man of business, the president of a commercial corporation charged with works of construction.

In April 1859 the work began at Port Said. Little excavation was done for the first two years, which were devoted to surveys, the erection of storehouses and workshops, the organization of work gangs, and the purchase of dredgers, machinery, tools, timber, iron, lime, cement, &c. Great Britain, strongly seconded now by Austria, made fresh protests at Constantinople and on 1st June 1859 de Lesseps was ordered to suspend operations. The Viceroy did not, however, recall the labourers, and work continued; to the vigorous remonstrances of the British Agents, Saïd Pasha replied that he had no control over the Europeans working on the canal; they must be recalled, if at all, by their own Governments. Never, perhaps, in the history of Egypt, did the Capitulations prove so valuable as at that moment. Fresh protests at Constantinople evoked a note from the Grand Vizier directing the

---

[1] *Vide* Dispatch from the Austrian Ambassador at Constantinople to Count Apponyi dated 30.11.59: 'L'embarras est donc grand à la Porte. Sir H. Bulwer doit lui avoir dit (puisqu'il l'a dit à moi) qu'elle était maîtresse de se prononcer pour le canal mais que, dans ce cas, il s'en suivrait un changement dans les dispositions de l'Angleterre pour l'Empire Ottoman, tandis que, dans l'autre cas, si la Porte prononcerait contre le canal, l'Angleterre la soutiendrait contre quiconque voulût violenter son droit de volonté indépendante . . . L'Ambassadeur de France se tient dans les limites d'une modération très sage.'

Viceroy to stop all work on the canal as altogether unauthorized by the Sultan, and Saïd Pasha announced his intention to carry out the orders of his august master. De Lesseps appeared to have played his last card, and lost.

His only chance was to enlist the open and official support of the Emperor Napoleon who, on Saïd Pasha's accession and on subsequent occasions, had shown himself a good friend of de Lesseps and his schemes, while the political situation in Europe was favourable. De Lesseps returned to Paris in July 1859 and appealed, with success, to the Throne. The Emperor not only promised protection, but instructed the diplomatic corps to give active assistance, while Count Walewski, his envoy at the Court of St. James, was instructed to convey to the British Cabinet the Emperor's hope that they would at last desist from opposition. The Cabinet were unmoved, and reiterated their objections, but excavations continued at Port Said.

It was suggested at about this time to the Porte (Sir H. Bulwer's dispatch of 28th December 1859) that they should refer the whole question of the Suez Canal to the Great Powers of Europe, who were then identical with the Great Maritime Powers, by means of a circular letter. In Congress assembled, their jealousy of each other would protect Turkey: by treating with all the Porte would avoid controversy with any one Power. The idea is as old as Solomon. 'Where no good counsayle is, there the people decaye: but where as many are that can give counsaile, there is wealth.' (Prov. xi. 14, Bible of 1549.) It may be necessary to invoke it before 1968.

Napoleon III was not inactive: in concluding terms of peace with France the Austrian Government pledged its support anew to the canal: Russia followed suit.[1] Finding that nothing could be done at Constantinople the British Government shifted their efforts to Cairo. The application of the *corvée*, or forced labour system, to the construction of the canal was represented as a form of slavery, a catchword which was as popular in England then as now. The Viceroy had indeed been

[1] The pertinacity of the Emperor Louis Napoleon in supporting de Lesseps through all the vicissitudes of fortune is a notable feature of the history of the canal, and one to which more importance perhaps attached than is admitted by some commentators. The interplay of European politics at this period is well shown by the following dispatch to the Austrian Ambassador in London, Count Apponyi, from the Foreign Office at Vienna, dated 14th November 1859: 'L'entente qui subsistait autrefois entre les Cabinets de Vienne et de Londres sur les questions les plus importantes de la politique européenne nous imposait, comme de raison, une certaine mesure dans l'appui que méritait d'ailleurs une œuvre sur l'exécution de laquelle le commerce autrichien fonde de justes espérances. Mais si cette entente ne doit plus subsister, si le Cabinet Britannique s'engage irrévocablement dans une voie qui l'éloigne tous les jours de nous, alors Lord J. Russell ne pourra pas s'étonner de nous voir agir à Constantinople aussi ouvertement contre l'Angleterre que

urged by the British Consul at Cairo to apply the *corvée* to the construction of the Suez railway a few years before, but this did not prevent his successor from utilizing the system to create prejudice.

Sir Henry Bulwer represented to the Porte in June 1860 that the Viceroy had no legal right to employ the funds of Egypt in such an enterprise as the canal project, and that, having forfeited the conditions under which he held the government of Egypt, he might well be deposed by the Sultan. Saïd Pasha's resolution was unshaken. 'I do not know', he said to the British Consul on one occasion, 'if this affair will be commercially advantageous, but of this I am sure, that if the canal project is realized under my reign and with my assistance, my name will be immortalized.' His anticipation has been fulfilled. A high Turkish functionary was sent from the Porte to remonstrate with him, but in vain. He would yield, he said, only to force, and he was satisfied in his own mind that the forces for and against the canal were well balanced.

Nearly two years passed without material change in the diplomatic situation, but the canal continued to make progress, though slowly, and when Sir Henry Bulwer was sent from Constantinople in November, 1862, he was surprised at the forward state of operations on the canal.

On 18th November 1862 M. de Lesseps, emulating Moses at Massah and Meribah, was able to declare at Ismaïliyah 'In the name of His Highness the Viceroy and by the Grace of God, I command the waters of the Mediterranean to enter Lake Timsah'. As with Moses, so with de Lesseps, the flowing water was associated with chiding (*massah*) and provocation (*meribah*).

In January 1863 de Lesseps suffered a severe personal and official loss in the death of Saïd Pasha. He was succeeded by his nephew Ismaïl Pasha, who accepted obligations to the canal enterprise such as he found them, for it was unquestionably popular with his subjects, but was less prepared than his predecessor to make great sacrifices. He was described by Sir H. Bulwer as 'proud, shy, intelligent and to a certain degree timid'; yet the magnitude of the work appealed to his ambition, and its regenerative effect on Egypt to his imagination. He hoped, however, to recover much of the land in the canal zone that his uncle had ceded to the Company. The British Ambassador was not slow to exploit the new situation thus created, and suggested to

l'Angleterre se montre franchement hostile à l'Autriche en Italie. Si le Gouvernement anglais attache quelque prix à notre neutralité dans la question de Suez, qu'il songe bien que sa propre attitude au Congrès qui va s'ouvrir réglera notre conduite à cet égard.'

The point at issue was the restoration of the Arch-dukes in Parma and Modena. Austrian support of de Lesseps at Constantinople was intended to secure French support against Italy in this matter.

the Porte that Ismaïl should be informed that his predecessor's Acts of Concession not having been ratified by the Porte, the Suez Canal Company had no standing in Egypt, and no authority to proceed with construction work. In July 1863 the Porte issued an ultimatum to the Viceroy. He was no longer to permit forced labour:[1] he was to repurchase the alienated lands; the canal itself was to be of a depth which whilst admitting merchant ships would exclude vessels of war. In the event of failure to accept these conditions within six months the Company was to be dissolved, the shareholders compensated, and the canal built under Egyptian auspices.

De Lesseps, however, did not allow these diplomatic difficulties to interfere in any way with the work of construction. The Suez Canal Company had at first decided to entrust M. Hardon with the carrying out of the works, receiving 60 per cent. of the profits on the prices fixed by the original estimates of the International Commission, and reserving to itself merely the general superintendence, the drawing up of the plans, and the furnishing of machinery and stores.

This method was found not to work well, and the agreement with M. Hardon was subsequently cancelled, an indemnity being paid to him of £72,000.

The company next undertook the works for its own account, but eventually entered into agreements with four French contracting firms, who undertook a series of contracts aggregating some £4,600,000, the details of which are given by Rabino.

These large contracts, involving several million pounds sterling, were all granted at the very moment when the diplomatic fate of the canal was hanging in the balance. The political effect in France was very great: de Lesseps was sure, from the outset, of popular support[2] in France in a measure that carried with it the certainty of official support. Faced with the threats implicit in the ultimatum of the Porte, he appealed at once to Napoleon III, with the consent of the Porte, in the name of French investors, to secure better terms from the Sultan. A Commission of Arbitration was nominated in March 1864, and sat until July. The award made by the Emperor was calculated to determine the Company's status in Egypt and to remove any existing grounds for the withholding of approval by the Porte. The Company was to abandon its claim to free labour in return for compensation in the sum of 84 million francs. All lands on the Isthmus, covering

[1] One of the results of the American war was that Egyptian cotton touched 2s. 6d. per lb.; cultivators could earn far more than ever before on the land, and the Viceroy found it cheaper, in practice, to recompense the Company in cash than to provide labour.

[2] French opinion in Egypt was, however, on the whole definitely unfavourable to de Lesseps (Sir H. L. Bulwer to Lord Russell, 3.3.63).

60,000 hectares, the fresh water and all subsidiary canals and navigation rights thereon were likewise to be relinquished against a payment
of 46 million francs, payable in annuities. The total sum of over £3¼
millions was not excessive, and was badly needed by the Company to
finance current construction. The retrocession of the irrigable lands
was unquestionably on political grounds a wise step. It prevented the
Company from acquiring too great political power or local influence
in the immediate vicinity of the waterway: it met the principal, if not
the only, legitimate objection of the British Government which might
well have seized the occasion to reverse its attitude of hostility and
to accept, gracefully, the *fait accompli*, but continued, on the contrary,
a policy of obstruction at Constantinople. The agreement was finally
sealed and documents exchanged in December 1864, but the firman
of the Porte was still not forthcoming. Once more, in February 1865,
de Lesseps appealed to Napoleon. A year later, on 19th March 1866,
the long diplomatic conflict was brought to a close by the promulgation
of the Definitive Firman of Approval by the Sultan. It ran, in part, thus:

'The realization of the great work destined to give new facilities to commerce
and for navigation by the cutting of a Canal between the Mediterranean and the
Red Sea being one of the most desirable events in this age of Science and of progress, conferences have been had for some time past with the Company which asks
authority to execute this work, and they have ended in a manner conformable as
regards the present and the future, with the sacred rights of the Sublime Porte,
as well as with those of the Egyptian Government.

'The agreement... has been drawn up and signed by the Egyptian Government,
in conjunction with the representatives of the Company; it has been submitted for
our Imperial Sanction, and, after having read it, we have given Our assent to it.'[1]

The long duel between de Lesseps and the British Government had
ended. De Lesseps, as Gladstone predicted, had won: the construction
of the canal, moreover, had already reached an advanced state and public
opinion in Europe, and even in England, was ready to welcome the
completion of the great work. The Admiralty, indeed, had already
anticipated the event, and had taken steps, in May 1863, to increase the
harbour and docking facilities at Malta, and to extend the fortifications.
The application to the Maltese Government for funds was supported
by a picture of the prosperity that would result from the piercing of the
Isthmus by de Lesseps. The Peninsular and Oriental Company, too,
had anticipated completion and intended to transfer their shipping to
this route at the earliest possible moment. Similar preparations were
already in progress at Aden and Bombay. The Canal Company was
now certain to succeed.

[1] *Parliamentary Papers*, C. 1415, 1876.

Rabino summarizes the progress achieved during the years 1862-6 as follows:

1862-3

PORT SAID.—Four dredgers, with cranes at work.

MARITIME CANAL—*General Works.*—Second sea water cutting for service of works, 50 feet wide, 3 to 6 feet deep, from Port Said to El Ferdane. Buildings along isthmus: March 1862, 56,500 square yards; April 1863, 96,500 sq. yds.

North of Lake Timsah.—18,000 men at work since November 1862; trench 50 feet by 4 to 6 feet deep, connecting Mediterranean and Lake Timsah; 4,350,000 cubic metres (153,600,000 cubic feet) at 0·68 fr. the cubic metre.

South of Lake Timsah.—From Lake Timsah to Toussoum plateau, canal 190 feet wide and 6 feet below the Mediterranean level, 21,200,000 cubic feet; 21 dredgers at work; 3 dredgers nearly ready, raising each over 353,000 cubic feet per month; 20 other dredgers to be established, raising each 1,050,000 cubic feet.

FRESHWATER CANAL AND WATER SUPPLY.—Canal from Nefiche to Suez begun; 24 miles finished, 64 feet wide at water line, 26 feet at bottom, 6 feet draught of water; cubic feet about 50,000,000.

1863-4

PORT SAID.—Large tract of land reclaimed, area 142,000 yards, to establish works of Compagnie des forges et chantiers de la Méditerranée and those of E. Gouin of Paris; 20 new dredgers, with barges and accessories fitted up; landing stage lengthened 330 feet; about 600 feet quays finished; canal Cheikh Carpouti, 2,000 feet (subsequently 3,300), connecting port with shore of lake and Damietta, and assuring draught of water.

MARITIME CANAL—*General Works.*—Total area built over, 128,000 sq. yds.

North of Lake Timsah.—Excavations from Port Said to El Ferdane, 43,000,000 cubic feet; excavation of gypseous stone along Lake Ballah, 4,500,000 cubic feet.

South of Lake Timsah.—Maritime canal lengthened 4 miles; between Timsah and Serapeum excavations 7,600,000 cubic feet; two cuttings, the one to the Southwater Canal, Ismailia, and the second, east of Lake Timsah, to a stone quarry.

FRESHWATER CANAL AND WATER SUPPLY.—Canal completed from Nefiche to the sea over 55 miles; had taken thirteen months; 118,000,000 cubic feet.

1864

PORT SAID.—530,000 cubic feet of stone taken from the quarries at Mex (Alexandria) for the Port Said quays and embankments; Dussaud frères establish their plant for manufacture and submersion of artificial stone for moles. Tonnage of port, January–July 1864, vessels, 124; tons, 35,220.

MARITIME CANAL—*General Works.*—Telegraph system finished; 13,000 natives at work first three months only; Borel and Lavalley, who afterwards carried out such vast operations, employed in planning their work.

North of Lake Timsah.—Port Said to Timsah; excavation of natives, 23,000,000 cubic feet; Aiton's excavations (with company's plant), Port Said, 1,050,000 cubic feet; in the canal, 8,100,000 cubic feet; Couvreux's excavation, 2,200,000, using 2 excavators, 4 miles of railway, 4 engines, and 30 trucks.

South of Lake Timsah.—South of Chalouf; excavation of natives, 48,000,000 cubic feet; transverse canal to Serapeum, 3,200,000 cubic feet; transverse canal to Chalouf, 425,000 cubic feet.

FRESHWATER CANAL AND WATER SUPPLY.—Junction at Ismailia, 1,300,000 cubic feet; water supplied, Port Said, from 10th April; reservoir, plateau of El Guisr, 110,000 gallons; reservoir, Port Said, 154,000 gallons.

1864–6

PORT SAID.—Plan of harbour modified; instead of two parallel moles, 1,300 feet apart, eastern mole started from shore at a distance of 4,500 feet from western mole, gradually approaching to 1,300 feet, and thus forming a fine port; pass of Port Said 200 to 300 feet wide, 16 feet deep; entry of basin 600 feet wide, 16 to 20 feet deep. Tonnage of port, 15th July 1865 to 15th June 1866; vessels, 595; tons, 108,539. [Work during June 1865 was much hampered by an outbreak of cholera and the consequent flight of 4,000 labourers.]

MARITIME CANAL—*General Works.*—Borel and Lavalley; 32 long trough dredgers at work along 35 miles of canal; native contingents abolished, May 1864, replaced with almost no delay; in 1866, 7,954 European labourers; 10,806 Africans and Asiatics, viz. Arabs, Syrians, &c.

North of Lake Timsah.—Canal from Port Said to Timsah widened to 325 feet, thus allowing formation of strands for the protection of banks from passing vessels, and economizing stone embankments; El Guisr ridge trench widened and deepened by Couvreux, 6 miles, by Gioja, on account of company.

South of Lake Timsah.—Timsah to Suez; first excavations by hand, afterwards by dredgers from Timsah to south of Toussoum; from Toussoum to Bitter Lakes trench opened 5 miles; rock of Chalouf removed,[1] 1,100 feet long; earth, 3,200,000 cubic feet; stone, 1,000,000 cubic feet.

FRESHWATER CANAL AND WATER SUPPLY.—Viceroy set 80,000 men to work at canal from Cairo to Wady; 5th October 1865, 70,000,000 cubic feet; subsequently, 105,000,000; leaving 70,000,000; allowing of the passage of Nile water in all seasons; the company had finished 30,750,000 cubic feet, placed to its charge by the imperial award.

Realizing that success was in sight, the British Government began to consider ways and means whereby the new waterway could subserve imperials needs. On 18th October 1865 Lord Palmerston died at Brocket Hall, his country residence in Hertfordshire; with his death there passed from the scene the most formidable of de Lesseps' antagonists.

---

[1] The Seuil of Chalouf is a hard bank of rock some 2 feet thick at a depth of 6 to 16 feet below sea-level and four miles across. The clay here was full of fossil remains of the elephant and the dog-fish, mixed with layers of bicarbonate of magnesia. Nearly all this section was worked by hand, and fifteen hundred men from Piedmont were specially employed on the work (Nourse, p. 56).

BIBLIOGRAPHY

(London, unless otherwise stated, is in all cases the place of publication.)

Fitzgerald. Op. cit.

Foreign Office, Suez Canal Papers.

Freycinet, C. de. *La Question d'Égypte.* Paris, 1904.

Hansard. *Parliamentary Debates.*

Hoskins, R. L. Op. cit.

Kenney, C. L. *The Gates of the East.* 1857.

De Lesseps, F. *Lettres Journal et Documents pour servir à l'histoire du Canal de Suez, 1854.* Paris, 1875.

—— *Conférences de la rue de la Paix; entretiens sur le canal de Suez.* Paris, 1864.

Morley, John. *Life of Gladstone,* 2 vols. 1903.

Nourse, J. E. *The Maritime Canal of Suez.* Washington, 1884.

Parliamentary Papers, C. 1415, 1876.

Quarterly Review, vol. cii.

Price, J. S. *Early History of the Suez Canal.*

Public Record Office. F.O. 78, numbers 1560, 1715, 1795, 1796, 1849, 1850, 1895, 1896, 1897, 1898, 1951, and F.O. 97/422. *Suez Canal, 1860–5.*

Rabino, J. 'The Statistical Story of the Suez Canal.' *Journal Roy. Stat. Soc.,* 1887.

Roux, Charles. Op. cit.

Simpson, F. A. *The Rise of Louis Napoleon and the Recovery of France.* 1923.

—— *The Rise of Louis Napoleon.* 1925.

State Papers, British and Foreign.

Stephenson, Robert. *A Letter addressed to the Editor of the Austrian Gazette . . . in reply to the statement of M. de Negrelli.*

Wiener Staatsarchiv. Berichte aus London, 1856–9.

CHAPTER III

THE COMPLETION AND OPENING
OF THE CANAL, 1866–1873

'In France, if you venture to tell the public that you are acting for yourself, no one will listen to you. But in England, the man who speaks for himself is always listened to.'

de Lesseps, *Entretiens*, 1864.

Work on the canal progresses. Sir Charles Hartley. Voisin Bey. Dredging machines introduced. Sir John Hawkshaw. Revised Estimates. Immigrant labour. Charles Doughty. Port Said. Ismailia. Port Tewfik. Mishaps at the last moment. The opening ceremonies. The Empress Eugénie. The Prince of Wales. Mail contracts. Effect of Suez Canal on Cape of Good Hope route.

THE Sultan's firman left de Lesseps in almost undisputed possession of the political field, and with his official and personal friendships intact. The work itself was well advanced, for it had been in progress since August 1859, when de Lesseps formally inaugurated the construction of the port on the Mediterranean that has served to immortalize the name of his patron and friend, Saïd Pasha. A vast amount of preliminary work had been done. Machinery had been designed in France, shipped, and erected in position. Machine and repair shops had been provided, workmen's quarters erected, and the details of commissariat, recruitment, and sanitation worked out. The first structures at Port Said were temporary, being replaced gradually by more permanent works as the project advanced. The labourers (*fellahin*) supplied by the Egyptian Government in conformity with the terms of the Concession were paid from 6 to 8 piastres daily (one shilling to 1s. 4d.), though skilled workmen received more. Water had to be brought to them from a distance, usually on camel-back, and when the supply failed, as it occasionally did, men perished. But the allegations, made even by responsible writers, of the heavy loss of life amongst the labourers on the Canal are in no way borne out by the published statistics of the Company's chief medical officer, which give the mortality per thousand

in 1863 as 1·40
,, 1864 ,, 1·36   *average working staff.*
,, 1866 ,, 2·49   .   .   .   18,605
,, 1867 ,, 1·85   .   .   .   25,770
,, 1868 ,, 1·52   .   .   .   34,258

De Lesseps was equally solicitous for the religious welfare of his labour force. Places of worship were provided for Muslims and for Christians of the Roman Catholic and Greek Orthodox Church, and were maintained at his expense.

Early in March 1861 Mr. (later Sir Charles) Hartley, a British engineer of great experience, visited the canal works at the invitation of M. de Lesseps. He expressed the opinion that the scheme was entirely practicable and successful realization only a question of time and money; both could be saved by the substitution of efficient mechanical appliances for hand-labour.

At the time of his visit not one-fiftieth of the earthwork of the canal had been removed—a condition of affairs due to shortage of money, as well as of labour, to difficulties in the supply of water, and to the inefficiency of dredging appliances. The newly dredged entrance at Port Said could not be kept open until the jetties had been built. The Fresh-water Canal from Cairo to Suez by way of Ismailia had to be completed and duplicate iron-pipes laid from Ismailia to Port Said to ensure a constant and ample supply of drinking water for the workmen along the whole length of the canal. Mr. Hartley's report was, however, in general very favourable, but not being published had little immediate effect.

Early in 1862, however, all these works were complete, and 25,000 labourers were in regular employment. The skill and resource of Voisin Bey, the first engineer-in-chief, and his assistants Laroche, Larousse, and Gioia had worked wonders. A French contractor, M. Lavalley, had devised and constructed a fleet of powerful trough-dredgers, the prototype of modern steam excavators which deposited silt by long shoots at some distance from either bank of the canal, without the intervention of barges. These and other mechanical appliances totalling 10,000 h.p., capable of removing two million cubic metres a month, had the effect of reducing by three-fourths the number of workmen needed, while the completion of the Fresh-water Canal in 1863 relieved the company of the vast expense of conveying water on camel-back from the Nile. A rock-breaker was also devised for deepening the canal on the limestone reef under Serapeum, which was found exactly where Sir John Hawkshaw predicted.

The line of work in general was from north to south, but at a later stage, after the issue of the Sultan's firman, operations were carried on at various points simultaneously. Behind Port Said, which in 1861 was simply a collection of hovels on a belt of sandy dunes, separated from the sea by a tongue of land 600 feet wide, lay the great Menzaleh basin, and here dredging began not long after the foundations for a port had been laid. In ancient times this was one of the most fertile parts of Egypt. Beneath the waters are seen the ruins of cities: the base of a large temple, columns of red granite, and masses of brick.

South-west was the city of Touna, on the west Zoan, mentioned in Psalm lxxviii and Isaiah and Ezekiel, and at a later day Mansurah, where Saint Louis was taken captive in the crusade of 1251. To the east is Tineh (*vide* p. 3). The line of the canal here for some 25 miles presented peculiar difficulties until suitable dredgers had been imported, owing to its varying depth. The vigorous race of fishermen on its borders, accustomed to the sun and mud, scooped up the clay in their hands, rolled it into balls on their chests, and then carried it on their backs with the arms crossed behind. In this way they raised some 400,000 cubic metres until the first dredger, let down into the mud by sections, carried forward the work, followed by twenty others. The sulphuric exhalations of the mud were almost unbearable but caused little actual sickness. The men who had toiled all day in the mud with their hands slept on rafts. They were paid at current rates, with free rations of rice, millet, dates, and onions. To these men, unhonoured and unsung, their posterity owes a debt which it has, perhaps fortunately, not attempted to symbolize by any monument of marble or *aes perennis*.

Work next began on cuttings to connect Lake Timsah with the waters of the Mediterranean, and before Saïd Pasha's death on 17th January 1863, at Alexandria, where he was buried, the entire line of the canal was well outlined. On the accession of his nephew Ismaïl almost the entire labour force of 20,000 men was suddenly withdrawn, and for the next two years little was accomplished, but before the end of 1862 boats bearing supplies from the Mediterranean reached Lake Timsah. The event appealed to the public imagination; it marked a definite achievement, and made it easier to obtain labour, even forced labour.

In July 1862 Ismaïl Pasha,[1] who was on a visit to England, had invited a noted English engineer, Mr. (later Sir) John Hawkshaw, then President of the Institution of Civil Engineering, to make a thorough inspection of the canal. He arrived in November, and sent in his report in the February following. He showed that the Company had already constructed at a cost of £28,000 or 700,000 francs so much of the Fresh-water Canal as extends from Ras al Wadi to Timsah, comprising about one million cubic metres. The Company had, partly

[1] Ismaïl son of Ibrahim Pasha was born in 1830 and educated in Paris, Saïd Pasha had employed him on various diplomatic missions, and in 1861 he had suppressed an insurrection in the Sudan. He was the first of the descendants of Muhammad Ali to receive, in 1867, from the Sultan the style and title of Khedive in return for increasing the tribute from £376,000 to £720,000, against permission to change the law of succession in favour of his direct descendants. In 1873 the Sultan made him, by Imperial rescript, in many respects an independent sovereign. He was a man of large ideas, but his extravagance was his undoing. In 1879 he was deposed and died at Constantinople in 1895.

by dredging on Lake Menzaleh, partly by excavating between that lake and Lake Timsah, made a channel between the Mediterranean and Timsah for light draught flat-bottomed boats. They had begun the sea jetty at Port Said and there and elsewhere had built houses and provided plant and machinery 'to a large extent', the total cost to 1st December 1862 being £1,220,000 or 30,500,000 francs.

The extension of the Fresh-water Canals (1) from Timsah to Suez a distance of 50 miles, and (2) from Ras al Wadi a distance of 56 miles, were in hand.[1] The cost of completion was estimated at £140,000 in each case. Of the ship canal between Port Said and Lake Timsah of a total of 32 million cubic metres 6 million had been excavated.

The total cost of the Canal and accessory works, according to the report of the
    International Commission on the plans before them was put at . . £5,750,000
    To this was added:
      Expenses of Administration at 2½ per cent. 150,000
      10 per cent. for contingencies 580,000

                        £6,480,000

For payment of 5 per cent. on the capital during the execution of the work, and for the formation of accessory establishments destined to augment the profits of the Company 1,520,000

                        £8,000,000
            or 200 million francs, which was the total capital of the Company.

Mr. Hawkshaw put forward revised estimates totalling £9,100,000, but suggested that it would be prudent to make provision for certain specified works, and for this reason thought that the total expenditure might reach 250,000,000 francs or £10,000,000. He concluded by stating his conviction that there were no serious engineering difficulties involved or likely to be encountered, and that maintenance, at an estimated cost of £62,800, would present no difficulty.

The report created a deep impression, not least on the new Viceroy. De Lesseps had not exaggerated, and had not misled his predecessor: the very caution displayed by Mr. Hawkshaw, an eminent English engineer with an established reputation, was an additional proof that Saïd Pasha's confidence had not been unwisely accorded.

'Residents in Egypt were more impressed with Mr. Hawkshaw's sound and measured judgements than with those of all the other engineers ever consulted.'[2]

The British Cabinet began to realize that the canal would be com-

---

[1] This section passes near rock quarries at Geneffé, whence great quantities of stone were conveyed for the jetties and other works at Port Said, more cheaply than from stone brought by sea from the quarries of Mex.   [2] *Proc. Instit. Civil Engineers*, vol. cxli, part iii, 1900.

pleted, but there were still those who would not be convinced, and continued to voice their doubts in the public press.

From the beginning of 1865 progress, as will have been gathered from the previous chapter, was rapid. De Lesseps had evaded none of his difficulties; he had surmounted them triumphantly. Diplomatists had ceased from troubling, his finances were assured on the payment by the Egyptian Government to the Company of the sum awarded in the course of arbitration by Napoleon III. De Lesseps was connected by ties of relationship and friendship with very influential circles in France, and he enjoyed the enthusiastic patronage of the Empress. It became the fashion to possess shares, and it was claimed and not denied that de Lesseps owed more to the women of France than to the men.[1]

Public opinion in Egypt was not less favourable than in Europe to de Lesseps and his organization. The wages bill was the strongest argument in his favour: 'Our fathers never saw such things in a dream,' said a Shaikh, as he watched the well-fed fellahin of his village receiving their weekly wages in cash. The standard of living in Egypt was rapidly rising. The construction of the great canal assisted the process, not only by the money it brought into the country, enabling the poorest, if able-bodied, to sell their greatest and only asset—the labour of their hands—but by the developments which followed.

Labourers flocked in from all sides. Doughty learned that as many as two hundred men from Al Qasim in Eastern Nejd were at work at one time.

'Ibrahim had seen, in that enterprise, "the peoples of the Nazara"—French, Italians, Greeks, whom he supposed to speak one language! Some parcels of the canal had been assigned to petty undertakers: Ibrahim wrought in the service of a Frankish woman, and the wife-man, he said, with pistols in her belt, was a stern over-seer of her work-folk. There was a Babel of nations, a concourse of men of every hard and doubtful fortune:—and turbid the tide-rips of such an host of adventuring spirits on the shoals! Moslems and Christians—especially the fanatical Oriental Greeks (*er-Rum*) were mingled together, and peaceable men were afraid to stray from their fellowships.

'He saw in these natural enmities only a war of religions: "It was the Rum, he pretended—they had the most arms—that set upon the Moslemin". . . . These disorders were repressed, Ibrahim said, with impartiality, by the Egyptian soldiery. . . Many a night Ibrahim and his mates stole a balk for their cooking and coffee fire, which they buried in the day time. When I exclaimed, thief! he responded "The Timber, though it cost so much, was no man's, but belonged to the *Kom-*

---

[1] The canal seems to have had a fascination for women from the earliest times. There is a tradition that one of the Pharaoh's opened the first canal between the Nile and Suez to please Sarah, the wife of Abraham, who certainly had influence at court. Cleopatra relied on it as a last resource after the battle of Actium, though her design failed owing to a shortage of water from the Nile.

pania!" Ibrahim returned from this moral quagmire after twelve months' labour; poorer in human heart, richer by a hundred or two of reals. Though not needy at home, he had journeyed seven hundred miles to be a ditcher at Suez!—but such is the natural poverty of the oasis Arabians. Ibrahim was of the illiberal blood, and brother-in-law of Aly the Western traveller. I found their minds yet moved by the remembrance of the Suez Canal, and some of them have said to me, "Might not there be made a canal through Nejd?"—such, they thought, would be for the advantage of their country.'

Port Said took on the appearance of a thriving and populous seaport. The mud flats which had formerly surrounded the squalid mat huts where de Lesseps and his engineer, in earlier days, took shelter from the noonday sun, had been raised by spoil from the great dredgers. The huts had given place to lofty buildings designed to catch the sea breezes. The population to-day exceeds 100,000.

The town might, indeed, have been better planned: more use might have been made of the sea-front: more open spaces might have been provided in the centre of the town. The streets themselves and the buildings might have been designed more specifically to give shade from the sun and to catch the sea-breezes. The eastern bank of the canal might from the outset have been more fully utilized. But these matters were not, for the most part, direct responsibilities of the Canal Company, but of the Egyptian Government or of private individuals. Such was the confusion which reigned in most of the administrative departments of the State that, as Dr. Johnson said of the performing dog, the marvel is not that it was ill-done but that it was done at all.

At the intersection of the Fresh-water Canal with the main channel another new town sprang into existence called, after the reigning Viceroy, Ismailia. Before the canal was opened to traffic the skill of the Canal Company's engineers, worthy successors of the great Muslim town-planners of past ages, had converted it into a pleasant town of six thousand inhabitants. It now boasts of a population nearly ten times as great, with avenues of trees and well-kept gardens, of streets, boulevards, and squares with spacious offices, a cathedral, a hospital, and a large railway station. The Fresh-water Canal, extended to Suez, transformed the filthy village which Napoleon had visited seventy years before into the present Port Tewfik, an industrious town of some 25,000 inhabitants, preferred by many residents there to Port Said or Ismailia. Rabino thus summarizes the work performed during the last two years:

1867-8

PORT SAID.—Western mole, 2,350 yards completed and 100 yards to water edge; eastern mole, 1,830 yards, of which 280 embanked with stone from Plateau of Hyenas; Dussaud frères had submerged all but 57,802 blocks of stone, of which

33,031 had yet to be made; Borel and Lavalley had dredged in passes and basin 123,000,000 cubic feet, out of 165,000,000 cubic feet.

MARITIME CANAL—*General Works.*—On the 15th April there still remained to be excavated a total of over 1,200,000,000 cubic feet. Monthly work:

		Cubic feet.
8 elevator dredgers	. . . .	4,300,000
30 dredgers, with barges .	. . .	21,000,000
22 long trough dredgers .	. . .	31,000,000
		56,300,000
22 inclined planes .	. . . .	4,700,000
7,500 labourers	. . . . .	13,500,000
		74,500,000

North of Lake Timsah.—Couvreux's contract—Port Said to Timsah, 5¼ miles, 156,000,000 cubic feet; at El Ferdane, 3¾ miles, 34,000,000 cubic feet; finished six months in advance of contract. Borel and Lavalley—Dredgings, 306,000,000 cubic feet out of 911,000,000; monthly work, January, 1,700,000, April, 2,400,000. At work—16 long trough dredgers, 6 elevator dredgers, 9 dredgers, with barges.

South of Lake Timsah.—From Lake Timsah to Bitter Lakes, 160,000,000 out of 300,000,000 cubic feet; 11 dredgers at work, doing each 882,500 cubic feet per month; excavated by hand, 24,500,000 cubic feet, out of 45,600,000; excavations by hand going on over 21 miles, from Bitter Lakes to Chalouf. There remained to be finished 248,000,000 cubic feet.

SUEZ.—Borel and Lavalley; dikes and embankments in roadstead, by 15th April, 1,600,000 cubic feet of stone submerged out of 2,300,000.

1868–9

Moles finished at the beginning of 1869. Pass in 1868, 21 to 23 feet deep; now, 29 to 30 feet deep.

MARITIME CANAL—*General Works.*—From Port Said to Bitter Lakes canal open to its full width and length; dredgers at work completing depth.

North of Lake Timsah.—Nil.

South of Lake Timsah.—Flooding of Bitter Lakes commenced in March 1869; Bitter Lakes to Red Sea, 22 miles by hand, 3 miles by dredgers.

SUEZ.—Suez pass finished; breakwater, over 1,600 yards of stonework.

The total excavation work on the canal alone totalled 75 million cubic metres, or nearly 2,650 million cubic feet.

On 19th March 1869, in the presence of the Khedive, the Prince and Princess of Wales, and a brilliant company of Egyptian notables and foreign visitors, the canal sluices were opened to admit into the Bitter Lakes, the ancient Gulf of Heroöpolis, several feet below sea-level, the waters of the Mediterranean. The filling required fifteen hundred million cubic metres of water and was not complete till 24th October. Once full, a single barrier beyond Chalouf was all that restrained the further progress of the water. Final completion of the canal was now in sight, and de Lesseps, whose genius for organization comprehended, as will have been gathered from the preceding pages, the use of publicity on a grand scale[1] now gave notice that the canal would be formally opened on 17th November 1869. For four days the vessels would be permitted to pass free of charge and, thereafter, upon payment of the published dues. This announcement was supplemented by personal invitations to most of the reigning sovereigns of Europe by Ismaïl Pasha, who was making a grand tour of Europe. Never did de Lesseps display greater boldness than in fixing this early date for the inauguration of the principal work of his life: the unexpected obstacles remained till the last moment, but melted before his foresight and courage, and before the skill of his executive staff and the devotion of the whole corps of labourers.

On 2nd November between two soundings, taken at a distance of 130 metres, by means of square shafts holding twelve men, a hard rock was discovered, which broke the buckets of the dredger.[2] It was 5 metres above the bottom of the canal. 'Every one', said de Lesseps afterwards, 'began by declaring there was nothing to be done: "Go and get powder in Cairo"—said I—"powder in masses—and then, if we cannot blow up the rock we will blow ourselves up. The intelligence and energy of our workmen saved us. From the beginning of the work there was not a tent-keeper who did not consider himself an agent of civilization. Hence our success."[3]

On the night of 15th November a fire broke out at Port Said among the fireworks destined for the fêtes. They had been placed in a timber-yard in the middle of the town. Only the timely arrival of 2,000 troops saved the town for, buried hard-by in the sand, lay a great quantity of gunpowder.

On the 16th an abnormally high tide covered the ground destined for the opening ceremony and surrounded the platforms: with difficulty was dry ground made for the visitors. The same evening the *Latif*, an Egyptian frigate, ran aground in the canal, thirty kilometres from Port Said. All efforts to dislodge her failed. The Viceroy repaired to the scene with 1,000 men. 'We agreed', said de Lesseps, 'that there were three methods to be employed—to float her, to beach her on one bank, or—"Blow it up", cried the Prince. "Yes, yes, that's it—It will be magnificent," and I embraced him. Next morning I went

[1] In 1857 the Viceroy had paid some £20,000 in order to ensure that the subject of the canal should be continuously and favourably discussed in the continental press, apart from a sum of some 39,000 francs paid monthly to de Lesseps for similar purposes.

[2] Sir John Hawkshaw had warned them of this danger, declaring that soundings at such intervals did not guarantee the absence of rock.

[3] For an amusing account of a somewhat similar incident in later days see *The Leisure of an Egyptian Official*, by Lord Edward Cecil, 1921, pp. 189 sqq.

on board the *Aigle* without mentioning the accident. I did not wish to change the programme. Logically I was wrong; the results proved me right. We must not be *doctrinaires*. It answers neither in business nor in politics. Five minutes only before reaching the scene I learned by signal that the canal was free, and the brave little *Latif* intact.'

'Within the cabin sat the Empress Eugénie, a prey to the most grievous emotions: every moment she thought she saw the *Aigle* stop, the honour of the French flag compromised, our labours lost. Overcome by her feelings she left the company, and we overheard her sobs —sobs which do her honour—for it was French patriotism overflowing from her heart.' The risk he ran was the measure of his success. 'The canal', he said in a lecture in April, 1870, 'was indeed opened on 17th November, but not without terrible emotions. I have never seen so clearly how near is failure to triumph, but, at the same time, that triumph belongs to him who, marching onward, places his confidence in God and man.' On 17th November the channel was open, and the marriage of the two oceans was celebrated by the slow passage, lasting three days, of the Government fleet through the new waterway.

Sir Ian Malcolm[1] thus describes the scene of de Lesseps' triumph:

'The little harbour at Port Saïd was alive with the ships of many nations, bearing the most eminent representatives of art and science, of commerce and industry, Sovereigns, Princes and Ambassadors, to enjoy the unbounded hospitality of the Khedive and to see with their own eyes this great thing that had actually come to pass. Already on November 13th, His Highness the Khedive had anchored his yacht the *Mahroussa* outside Port Saïd to receive his guests, whose arrivals from over many seas continued for three days and three nights: the Emperor of Austria, the Crown Prince of Prussia, members of other reigning families[2] and finally the Empress Eugénie on board the *Aigle*. It was a gorgeous and a glittering scene at the doorway of the desert, there were fifty men-of-war flying the flags of all nations of Europe, firing salutes, playing their bands, whilst the sandy littoral was covered with tented Arabs and Beduin from far and near who had come with their families, on horseback and camel to join in the greatest festival that Egypt had seen since the days of the Ptolemies. On the foreground were erected three large pavilions or enclosed terraces; in the centre one were massed the illustrious guests of the Khedive; on the right hand was the Muhammadan hierarchy supported by its faithful, and on the left an altar for Christian worship and thanksgiving. When

---

[1] *Quarterly Review*, January 1930.

[2] Others among the six thousand guests invited were the Grand Duke Michael of Russia and the Prince and Princess of Holland, Great Britain was officially represented by Mr. Henry Elliott, British Ambassador at the Sublime Porte, supported by several British men-of-war. The United States was the only Western nation of any considerable size not represented, perhaps because in 1869 the Alabama question was very actively at issue. The principal Christian pontiffs were the Archbishop of Jerusalem, and Monsignor Bauer, the Empress's confessor, who delivered an appropriate eulogium from the pulpit after one of the Ulama had invoked a blessing on the enterprise and on those present.

the rites of all the Churches had been duly celebrated and the Canal blessed, the Civil opening took place in official form. That evening (16th November) there was a display of fireworks, and festivities were prolonged far into the night.

'On the following morning at 6 a.m. all the vessels that had the entrée to the canal were marshalled and paraded. Two hours later the *Aigle*, bearing the Empress of the French and Monsieur de Lesseps, headed the procession and passed in dignified array from the Mediterranean Sea into the waters of the Suez Canal . . . acclaimed by teeming multitudes crowding the arid banks of the burning desert, until they reached Ismailia, the little capital of the canal zone on Lake Timsah . . . and the *Aigle* dropped her anchor. . . .

'On the 19th the journey was renewed, and the *Aigle* with her escort steamed on to the Bitter Lakes, where they anchored for the night and continued on the following morning to Suez, having done the whole journey in sixteen hours . . . without mishap of any kind. The return to Port Saïd was accomplished in fifteen hours by the *Aigle* . . .

'One of the British vessels in the ceremonial procession was the S.S. *Hawk* bound for Suez with the British Indian Telegraph Company's cable.'

The festivities were not restricted to the canal zone. The present roadway leading between rows of trees from Cairo to the Pyramids was built, in the incredibly short time of six weeks, for the convenience of the Viceroy's royal guests, by forced labour urged on by the lash. Verdi composed an opera, *Aïda*, specially for the occasion. It was magnificently presented at Cairo: all the jewels worn on the stage, to the value of several millions, are reputed to have been real.

Great Britain, who almost alone of the Great Powers had steadfastly obstructed the accomplishment of the project, was not backward in offering honourable amends. De Lesseps received at the hands of Queen Victoria the Grand Cross of the Star of India. The Lord Mayor of London, proposing his health at an official banquet in his honour, declared that 'our eminent engineers made a mistake—M. de Lesseps was right, and the Suez Canal is a living fact'. He was made a freeman of the City of London, and the Prince of Wales, in presenting a Gold Medal to him at the Crystal Palace, said:

'Great Britain will never forget that it is to you alone that we owe the success of this great achievement. . . . I hope that since you have been in our midst, our people have shown you how highly they appreciate the advantages that your splendid work has bestowed, and will continue to bestow upon our country.'

The Times apologized for past hostility in a leading article which declared that

'M. de Lesseps has arrived in a country which has done nothing to bring about the Suez Canal but has, since its opening, sent through it more ships than all the rest of the world. This country will furnish the dividends that the shareholders will receive. May they be the compensation for our error.'

The Editor of *The Times*, however, could scarcely have foreseen that the great-grandchildren of his readers would be contributing to pay quite such vast sums as have in fact been received, not only by the shareholders but by the sleepiest of sleeping partners—the Crédit Foncier and descendants of the holders of 'Founder's Shares'. De Lesseps, in the midst of these personal triumphs, retained his dignity, his imperturbability, and above all his generosity. He did not consider the inauguration of the canal complete until he had acknowledged his indebtedness to Thomas Waghorn (vide p. 10), by erecting at Port Said a large bust, executed by M. Vidal-Dubray, of this apostle of the overland route.

The canal had, including harbour works and approaches at either end, a length of over 92 miles. Nowhere was the depth of water less than 26 feet or the width at the bottom of the channel less than 72 feet. Sidings where ships could bank in and allow others to pass had been provided at various points, the whole linked by a system of signals. Docking facilities, and facilities for fuel and water-supplies and lighthouses, had been provided at either end.

In 1869 the Egyptian Government repurchased the Wady Valley, through which the Fresh-water Canal ran, for 10 million francs, and the rights of customs, post office, &c., on the Suez Canal for 30 million francs. This last sum, raised by loan, was secured by the surrender of the right to surplus profits on the 177,642 shares in the Company held by the Egyptian Government. The sums made available were thus:

		Thousand francs.
	Share Capital	200,000
1864	Indemnity for corvée labour	38,000
	Fresh-water Canal and dues, purchased by Egyptian Government .	16,000
	Cultivable Land, do.	30,000
1869	Sale of Wady Valley to Egyptian Government (net) . . .	7,648
	Surrender of Customs &c., do. (net)	29,745
	Profits from Investments	20,103
	Receipts from Services (Health, &c.)	6,871
	Loan	100,000
	Other Receipts	2,807
	Total	451,174

There were creditors for 7,065,000 francs at the end of 1869. Interest at 5 per cent. had been paid from the outset on the share capital.

In spite of the recommendations of the Select Parliamentary Committees, the opening of the Suez Canal did not result in quicker carriage for Her Majesty's mails. Bombay still had in 1870 only two mails a month, four mails, as before, being carried to Madras and Calcutta by the sea-route.[1] Existing mail contracts provided for overland transit by the British owned Alexandria–Suez railway, and till 1874 all mail

[1] See Hoskins, *British Routes to India,* 415 sqq.

steamers stopped at these ports to drop or pick up mails and such passengers as desired to see more of Egypt than they could from the deck of a steamer in the canal. Even after 1874 the accelerated mails via Brindisi were transported by this route. Not till 1888 were all mails carried through the canal.

Nor did the inauguration of the Suez Canal at once involve the abandonment of the Cape of Good Hope route. For technical reasons, as well as considerations of cost and safety, the principal shipping lines did not and could not at once make the necessary consequential changes in their equipment and organization. For some years the channel was not of uniform depth: it was very narrow, and groundings were frequent. Passages were slow, and tended, as traffic increased, to grow slower. Separate fleets had been built for the trade east and west of the Isthmus, the former required high speeds, and quick journeys between adjacent ports, the latter demanded lower speeds, more space for fuel and Lascar crews.

At the same time new and more efficient marine engines were being very rapidly developed, and the older vessels were quickly becoming obsolete. Shipbuilding concerns were swamped with orders.

It was at this moment that the canal was opened. The combination of circumstances heavily handicapped the established shipping lines[1] and favoured the growth of new concerns who could build ships specially designed to meet the new conditions and in particular to navigate the canal. The old mail contracts were a handicap rather than an advantage. The P. and O. ceased to make profits: the British India Steam Navigation Company was hard hit. Professor Hoskins, in his admirable *British Routes to India*, gives a vivid and lucid description of the position during these years. By 1875 the crisis had been successfully surmounted. The P. and O. and the B. I. regained and even increased their predominance. The canal was French, but 75 per cent. of the shipping passing through it was British. This outstanding fact governed the policy of the British Government during the years that followed.

[1] Mr. T. H. Farrer of the Board of Trade wrote in 1882 as follows (*Parliamentary Paper*, Dec. 1882): 'The effect of the Canal ... may not have been on the whole beneficial to the ship-owning interests in the U.K. and to some capitalist interests. The shortening of the voyage is, *pro tanto*, a diminution of the demand for shipping. ... If there had been no Canal, there would have been more ... employment of English capital and labour.' The exports of oriental products, and British entrepôt trade in general, decreased. As late as 1880, however, all jute and rice from India reached England via the Cape. See *Hallberg*, p. 389.

BIBLIOGRAPHY

Calcutta Review, xxxviii. 1863.

Couridon. *Itinéraire du Canal de Suez*. Port Saïd, 1875. (Royal Empire Soc. Collection.)

Denison, Sir W. 'The Suez Canal.' *Proc. Inst. Civil Engineers*, vol. xxvi, 1867.

Doughty. *Arabia Deserta*.

Hallberg. Op. cit.

Hartley, Sir C. 'A Short History of the Engineering Works of the Suez Canal.' *Proc. Inst. Civil Engineer*, vol. cxli, 1900.

Hoskins. Op. cit.

Lesseps, F. de. *History of the Suez Canal. A personal narrative*. London, 1876.

Malcolm, Sir Ian. *Quarterly Review*, January 1930.

Parliamentary Papers.

Public Record Office. F.O. 78/1951 and F.O. 97/422. *Suez Canal, 1860 to 1866* (includes Maps and Plans).

—— F.O. 78, numbers 2014, 2042, 2095, 2142, 2170, 2188, 2234, 2288. *Reports of British Consuls at Suez and Correspondence relating to neutralization of Suez Canal*.

Rabino, J. F. Op. cit.

Steele, John (master mariner). *The Suez Canal, its present and future*, 1872 (Royal Empire Soc. Collection).

'Will the Suez Canal Company rest content with moderate profits? Temptation to extreme exaction is great. . . . England may acquiesce in a grievous wrong while others . . . may be clamorous for amendment. It is the merchant, not the shipowner, who benefits from the canal and, in the long run, pays the dues.'

CHAPTER IV

THE ACQUISITION OF THE KHEDIVE'S SHARE-HOLDING BY THE BRITISH GOVERNMENT

Financial difficulties. Difficulties with shareholders. Proposed International Control. Turkish objections. Proposed purchase by British interests. British grievances. The point of view of the Canal Administration. The consequences of the accession of Disraeli to power. Ismaïl Pasha's debts. Proposed mortgage on or sale of his Suez Canal shares. Lord Derby's views. Disraeli's decision. Sir Stafford Northcote. Parliamentary Discussions.

THE Captains and the Kings had scarcely left the scene of de Lesseps' success when it became clear that the Company was in financial difficulties. The cost of the construction proved to be more than double the original estimate of 200,000,000 francs: it was stated in the balance sheet of 31st December 1869 at 453,645,000 francs.[1] Of the total of nearly £18,000,000 subscribed only £826,000 remained for working capital. The Company had received from various sources over 300,000,000 francs and had to raise a further hundred million. They offered 333,333 bonds of 500 francs each, issued at 300 redeemable in fifteen years, and carrying interest at 5 per cent. They were not underwritten, and proved unattractive until the French Government agreed to the issue of the remaining two-thirds of the issue in the form of *obligations à lots*. In this form they found a ready market.

During 1870 the Company failed to pay dividends, or even the minimum 5 per cent. on the shares, which fell to 208 francs in 1871. A fresh loan of 120,000 'bons trentenaires' was issued at 100 francs, at 8 per cent. redeemable in thirty years at 125 francs secured, with the consent of the Khedive, by a 'temporary' surtax of one franc a ton. This surtax, itself probably illegal, in the absence of the consent of the Porte does not appear to have been levied, but the receipts at this time

---

[1]

	Thousand francs
Cost of construction	291,330
Interest on shares for 11 years, 1859–69	66,849
Sinking Funds on bonds	14,628
Administrative expenses	14,182
Expenses of transit, health, telegraphs, &c., services	13,338
Costs of issue of shares and bonds, &c.	15,472
	415,799
Plant and other Fixed Assets	17,009
Cash, investments, and debtors	20,837
Total	453,645

were far short of requirements. Instead of the expected million net tons of shipping the traffic through the canal in 1870 was only 436,000 tons and in 1871 only 761,000 tons. Expenses exceeded receipts in 1870 by 9,590,000 francs, and in 1871 by 2,650,000 francs, sums which were carried to the cost of 'premier établissement'.

De Lesseps' difficulties were heightened by the Franco-German war, and a little later, at a meeting of dissatisfied shareholders, just after the siege of Paris, a large Communist element clamoured boisterously for directors of their own choosing. De Lesseps was saved from violence only by the personal courage of his friend Sir Daniel Lange, an English director of the canal, who faced a would-be assailant on the platform and threatened in broken but intelligible French to knock him down.

Realizing how insecure was his tenure de Lesseps endeavoured, on Lange's advice, to transfer control to London. The matter was referred in April 1871 to Lord Granville, Secretary of State for Foreign Affairs, who received it very coldly. In June 1871 de Lesseps himself offered to recommend the purchase of the canal by the Maritime Powers for twelve million pounds sterling plus a payment of ten million francs annually for fifty years to the shareholders, as an alternative to acquisition by the Turkish Government. The Foreign Office, supported by the Prime Minister, Mr. Gladstone,[1] were still disinclined to move, though Lord Derby indicated that he favoured the transfer to an International Commission. Lord Farrer, the President of the Board of Trade, suggested that the canal should be placed under a European Commission for purposes of management on the lines of what would now be described as a Public Utility undertaking. 'Complications and difficulties', he said, later, 'would be endless so long as this great highway of nations remains in the hands of a private Company.' The experience of the last fifty years, however, gives little encouragement to such a proposal to-day.

The Sublime Porte, on the other hand, could not admit, even in principle, the sale of the canal, or the creation of an International Administration on its own territory. The Suez Canal Company was an Egyptian company and, as such, subject to the laws and customs of the Turkish Empire, and M. de Lesseps, as *mandataire* of the Viceroy, had no right to raise the question.

The Porte and the Khedive suggested that Great Britain should purchase the canal. General Stanton, then Consul-General at Cairo, pressed the Government to agree: the Duke of Argyll, then at the India

[1] Mr. Childers, who later became Secretary of State for War, and between 1874–80 was chairman of the Royal Mail Steamship Company, had suggested in 1869 to Mr. Gladstone that Great Britain should acquire a large holding. Vide his *Life*, vol. i, p. 230.

Office, lent his support. Mr. Gladstone's Cabinet resolutely shut their eyes to the larger aspects of the matter. They treated it as a purely financial matter and saw no reason why they should 'reimburse the shareholders'. De Lesseps came to England to make a bargain. Lord Granville refused to discuss terms.

The canal might, between 1870 and 1872, have been bought by a private British, as an alternative to an official international group, but proposals to this end, and in particular a combination formed for the purpose by the Duke of Sutherland and Mr. Pender, were discouraged by the Liberal Government and, though the Board of Trade continued to urge international control, no action was taken. Had not France been stricken down and impoverished by her great struggle with Germany immediately after the canal was completed, the attitude of indifference if not of hostility maintained by successive Governments might have cost us dear. Our sailors, at any rate, were quick to realize the importance of the new waterway. Admiral Richards and General Sir Andrew Clarke drew up a report for the Admiralty in 1870, in which they recognized its significance for our commerce and for our sea-power, and the dangers to both which might arise if it fell into the hands of a single State, or even into those of an independent company. But these views, being those of naval experts, carried little weight with the Government of the day.

The arrogance of the Suez Canal officials, their claim that the canal was theirs and they could do what they liked, the open violation of the regulations relating to tonnage measurement, though officially accepted by de Lesseps,[1] had not, however, been without its effect on public and official opinion.

Monsieur de Lesseps was still in a state of half-veiled rebellion delaying and obstructing British ships on various excuses, and worrying both the Porte and the Khedive with extravagant claims for indemnities, and menaces of French intervention. He notified the Egyptian Government that he declined to recognize their jurisdiction, and that in the event of legal proceedings, he would place himself under the protection of France. Everything indicated that the Eastern question would shortly be reopened: there were insurrections in Bosnia and Herzegovina and Panslavist intrigues in Servia. The Suez Canal might in certain circumstances, become, in very truth, a second Bosphorus.

It is none the less important, in fairness to the management of the canal at this period, to try to understand their point of view. The

[1] In April 1874 he went to the length of addressing formal letters to the Admiralty and the Board of Trade notifying them that his agents had received orders 'to enforce the strict observance of the passage dues exacted by the Company, and that vessels refusing to pay these dues would have to take the old route by the Cape'.

British were the leaders of the agitation against the high canal dues: they were also the principal users, and foremost in complaints at the slowness and inefficiency of the service. But they had refused to subscribe either to the original capital of the Company or to subsequent loans. France had just suffered defeat at the hands of Germany but was rapidly retrieving her position. Germany had demanded and obtained a crushing indemnity, but no voice or helping hand was raised. Great Britain had remained inert, though Gladstone was, in fact, the only statesman in high place to urge that Europe should register its protest. For twenty years the British Government, in Whitehall and through its representatives in every capital of Europe, had opposed by every means in their power the inception and completion of a scheme which was sincerely and deliberately regarded in England, and often represented in the French press, as a menace to our preponderant share in Eastern trade. When we accepted the inevitable we did not do so with a good grace. We might have officially guaranteed a loan, to be raised in England, of the amount necessary for completion. The idea was abhorrent to the statesmen of the day under Gladstone, as was the suggestion that England should purchase the canal, though it was Gladstone who in 1883 proposed to lend the Company £8,000,000 at 3½ per cent. We thus forced the Company to meet capital expenditure out of revenue; our opposition had, moreover, already had the effect of almost doubling the cost of construction. The French regarded our statesmen as perfidious, our financiers as hypocritical, and our shippers as unreasonable.

They had, in the diplomatic sphere, scarcely less reason to complain, from their own point of view, of our proceedings. The reputation of Great Britain during the years preceding Disraeli's accession to power on 1st February 1874 had sunk. No longer regarded as a leading power in Europe, Great Britain had been ignored at the time of the Franco-German war. We had permitted Russia to evade compliance with the Black Sea clauses of the Treaty of Paris, and our handling of the United States had been maladroit. The reputation of the British Government was in 1873 not unlike that of its successor exactly sixty years later, for the diplomatic world had only just begun to realize that, with Disraeli as First Minister, observance of British treaties, respect for British rights, and consideration for British opinion was not only expedient but necessary. Only a few months later Disraeli made it clear, as his predecessor would never have brought himself to do, that gratuitous resumption by Germany of hostilities on France would not be regarded by Great Britain with indifference, the statesmen of Europe realized that Great Britain was, for the first time for five years, once more a force to be reckoned with.

Disraeli, too, had always been interested in the East. His old enthusiasm, which had led him in his early youth to make the acquaintance of Muhammad Ali Pasha, the Viceroy of Egypt, at Shubra, and to offer the Caliph his services under the command of the Pasha of Janina, at once led him to study the condition of the Ottoman Empire. He had been borne to the summit of his ambition by a wave of reaction against the domestic activities of Mr. Gladstone. Warned thereby against the dangers of a policy of activity at home, he was encouraged to seek in foreign affairs a diversion for the unspent energies of the nation. In May 1875 he had made up his mind to buy up the Canal Company if he could, and in that month he sent Baron Lionel de Rothschild to Paris to try to reopen the negotiations which Lord Granville had refused to entertain. But time is of the essence of financial transactions, and the favourable moment had passed. De Lesseps was, indeed, in low water, but the tide had turned. In 1872, 1,161,000 net tons of shipping had passed through the canal, and a net profit of 2,071,000 francs was carried forward. Next year 5,000,000 francs was paid on account of the July 1870 coupon and a further 10,000,000 francs was paid in 1874; the carry forward for the next two years was 4,556,000 francs and 2,615,000 francs respectively. In 1874, moreover, the arrears of interest were capitalized at 34,000,000 francs in 400,000 bonds of 85 francs bearing interest at 5 per cent. and redeemable in forty years at par. France was already recovering from the shock of defeat, and Franco-Russian discussions between the Comte de Chaubordy and Prince Gortschakoff at Interlaken in the summer of 1873 had included the defence of French interests in Egypt.

At this juncture a fresh complication arose. Ismaïl Pasha had borrowed, on the security of the revenues of Egypt, nearly seven million pounds a year for the past thirteen years: the public debt had increased during his Viceroyalty from £3,000,000 to over £98,000,000. For practical purposes, the whole had been squandered except £16,000,000 spent on the Suez Canal.[1] The bankruptcy of the Sultan of Turkey in October 1875 rendered Ismaïl Pasha's position hopeless. The crash at Constantinople was followed by a crisis at Alexandria. Unless he could raise a loan and meet the December coupons he would have to tread the same path as his Suzerain. Perhaps that would have been the best solution, but the word *moratorium* had scarcely found its way into the English language,[2] and international debts were not viewed differently from private obligations. The Khedive cared little what he paid provided he could meet the needs of the moment. In urgent need of money, he planned in November 1875 to sell his shares in the Suez

[1] Cromer, i. 11.
[2] The earliest reference in the *O.E.D.* is 28th September 1875 from Belgrade.

Canal to French financiers, or, at least, to use them as security for a fresh loan. He required £4 millions on almost any terms. One group at least was planning to buy the shares, but no one would, even at 18 per cent., lend him more than 50 million francs, and then only with the approval of the French Government, which was not easily obtainable. It was at this time that Mr. Frederick Greenwood, then editor of the *Pall Mall Gazette*, heard on 14th November of the negotiations from Mr. Henry Oppenheim, a well-known financier of Austin Friars, and one of the proprietors of the *Daily News*, in which capacity he found himself debarred from certain political intimacies which Mr. Greenwood fully enjoyed.[1] On 16th November Mr. Greenwood informed Lord Derby of what was in contemplation. The news reached Lord Derby at the Foreign Office on 15th November from unofficial sources, and the suggestion was made that the British Government itself should purchase the shares. Lord Derby was cautious and would probably have temporized, but Disraeli thought otherwise, and at his instance Lord Derby at once informed the British representative in Cairo that Her Majesty's Government would be disposed to purchase if satisfactory terms could be arranged. Ismaïl Pasha was approached, and protested that he had no intention of selling but only of mortgaging the shares. The result would have been the same in either case, and General Stanton, the British Consul-General, insisted on a suspension of negotiations in order to give his Government an opportunity of making a proposal. It was, in effect, from the Khedive's point of view, a question of obtaining a loan of £4 millions, at 5 per cent., on the security of the shares of doubtful value, as the right to 'surplus profits' for the next eighteen years had already been discounted and only the contractual 5 per cent. interest would be paid up to 1894. The political aspect had no interest for him. But he knew what he was doing. 'This is the best investment', he remarked, the day after the arrangements were completed, 'financially and politically, ever made, even by your Government, but a very bad one for us.'

On 27th November the Cabinet, at the initiative of Disraeli, determined in principle to acquire the Khedive's holdings. The decision, though unanimous, was taken with reluctance. The Duke of Argyll, then at the India Office, was however a strong supporter of the scheme.

From the moment that it was made clear that Great Britain was determined that the shares should not fall into French hands, the French Government had to choose between a sale to Great Britain and a serious financial crisis in Paris, where money was scarce. They allowed matters to take their course, and de Lesseps, of all diplomatists the most realistic, hastened to welcome in the most public and official

[1] I have here followed Mr. Lucien Wolf in *The Times* of 26th December 1905.

manner 'the co-operation of Great Britain in the management of the canal'. The phrase indicates the results which de Lesseps anticipated from the investment, but it has not been translated into practice, though the number of directors was at once raised from twenty-one to twenty-four so as to include three British official nominees.[1] The first directors so nominated were Col. (later Sir John) Stokes, R.E., Mr. (later Sir Charles) Rivers-Wilson, and Mr. E. J. Standen, who was to be Resident Director in Paris.

The *coup*, for it was instantly recognized as such throughout the world, was favourably received. The Crown Princess of Germany (later the Empress Frederick) wrote to Queen Victoria, 'Everybody is pleased here, and wishes it may bring England good. . . .' Willy (i.e. Wilhelm II) writes from Cassel, 'Dear Mama, I must write you a line, because I know you will be delighted that England has bought the Suez Canal. How jolly!' M. de Lesseps looked upon the 'close community of interests about to be established between English and French capital . . . as a most fortunate occurrence'. Prince Bismarck congratulated Lord Derby on having 'done the right thing at the right moment in regard to the Suez Canal'. He may have regretted that he had not demanded, in 1871, payment of part of the French indemnity in Suez Canal shares. He might have done so successfully with far-reaching political as well as financial results. The canal had then been open only twelve months: the British Government would doubtless have demanded certain assurances, but would almost certainly not have objected to the transfer. So far as is known the idea was not at any time discussed even in Germany; it is one of the 'might-have-beens' of history.

Lord Derby, however, had at first grave doubts. He wrote on 19th November to Lord Lyons,[2] 'I sincerely hope we may not be driven to that expedient (i.e. to purchase the Khedive's holding). The acquisition would be a bad one financially and the affair might involve us in disagreeable correspondence both with France and the Porte'—a typically departmental view.

The Chancellor of the Exchequer, Sir Stafford Northcote, was at first more outspoken: on 26th November he wrote to Disraeli: 'Our policy, or our proceedings, with regard to the Canal, has not been such as to gain us much credit for magnanimity. We opposed it in its origin, we refused to help de Lesseps in his difficulties: we have used it when it has succeeded, we have fought the battle of our shipowners very stiffly, and now we avail ourselves of our influence with Egypt to get a quiet slice of what promises to be a good thing. . . . I don't like it.'[3]

---

[1] To qualify them for their posts 300 more shares were purchased.
[2] Lord Newton, *Lord Lyons*, ii. 87.   [3] Andrew Lang, *Life of Sir S. Northcote*, ii. 85.

By 26th January, however, he had modified his views, and wrote to Disraeli, 'So far as the purchase of the Suez Canal shares is in question, I think our case is perfect. Subsequent events have strengthened, rather than weakened, the arguments which induced us to decide on it.'

I owe to the courtesy of Professor H. W. V. Temperley of Peterhouse, Cambridge, the following transcripts, which show clearly the grounds on which the leaders of the Liberal Opposition party objected to the purchase when it was first announced.

Private Granville MSS. (Record Office)

W. E. Gladstone to Lord Granville.   Nov. 22, 1875.
    You may like to know how it strikes other friends and even what are the sentiments of a disembodied spirit like myself. Amid the conflicting statements that have appeared I find the meeting point of them all in the version which runs as follows: (*a*) the purchase is immèdiate. (*b*) The payment is immediate. (*c*) For a term of years the Khedive guarantees 5 per cent. upon the money: after which we get the Dividend yielded by the concern. (*d*) In some manner it is subject to the consent of Parliament; and I imagine they are hardly in a condition to pay the four millions themselves outright, though some finance agent may do it on the strength of the pledge to apply to Parliament. (*e*) There is no present sign of an intention to summon the two Houses for the purpose. A storm of approbation seems to swell, almost to rage, on every side.

    I write in mild language, out of respect—such respect as is due—to the sense of what seems an overwhelming majority. But my opinion on the imperfect information before me is this. If the thing has been done in concert with the other Powers, it is an act of folly, fraught with future embarassment. If without such concert, it is an act of folly fraught also with personal danger. I am aware of no cause that could warrant or excuse it, except its being necessary to prevent the closing of the Canal. But that cause I apprehend could not possibly exist. The closing of the London and North Western would be about as probable.

Gladstone to Granville.   Nov. 17, 76.
    Is our real, valuable hold over the S[uez] C[anal] in wartime, any other than our maritime superiority in the Mediterranean? Would Egypt make any real addition to it? If it would not, then the holding of it would be a new military responsibility, a burden and an evil.

Private Granville MSS.

W. E. Gladstone to Lord Granville.   Nov. 22, 1875 (contd.)
    You may remember that in our Cabinet we discussed the neutralization of the Canal and the purchase was suggested or named. As far as I recollect, we peremptorily set aside the purchase, and found no reason then to prosecute the neutralization, partly because it was difficult but principally because we found [?] so well as things are, that there was no motive to desire a change.

                                                            W. E. G.

Idem.   Jan. 19, 1876.

I think Lord Derby's view of the Suez Canal is only *relatively* the right one: right that is in comparison with others that are more and more dangerously wrong. What is the harm which has attended or is likely to attend private proprietorship in this case? Who can say that joint State proprietorship, which by the very force of the terms is all foreign, is either theoretically free from objection, or likely to be free from difficulties in practice.

The Danube Commission is no precedent. There is no joint State enterprise.

Private Gladstone MSS. (British Museum)

Lord Granville to Gladstone.   Nov. 28, 1875.

What do you think of the purchase of less than one-third of the Suez Canal shares? I presume *The Times* got the news from the Rothschilds and the *Telegraph* from Derby.

As regards my first impressions, which I mistrust, it appears to be very foolish.

I presume it is without precedent (is it not?) that the Government should become part shareholder of a private undertaking over which by normal means they can have no control.

Is it not enough of a political measure to induce and justify other countries in taking precautionary measures.

Is it not possible that Lesseps and the Rothschilds have duped the Government into giving this great impetus to the value of Suez Canal shares—by threatening them with a purchase of French capitalists.

Is it the intention of the Government to buy in the open market another 100,000 shares at enhanced prices in order to have an effective control? If they do so cannot the remaining shareholders still get them into endless difficulties? Will it not give rise to all sorts of international difficulties? Is the Canal to remain subject to the discretionary powers which we have always maintained belonged to the Sultan? Ought so great a responsibility to be taken without immediately consulting Parliament?

Private Granville MSS.

Lord Lansdowne to Lord Granville.   Nov. 28, 1875.

What do you say to the Canal coup? I should have thought that we did not require this new and rather sky-sweeperish *locus standi* for interference in Eastern politics so far as they affect our communication with India: but everyone seems to approve and I suppose the result will be to add not inconsiderably to the prestige of Government particularly in the commercial world, and at the seaports.

Yours affectionately,
L[ANSDOWNE]

Halifax, Nov. 28.   Nov. 29.

Gladstone is here and in a state of great excitement about the purchase of the Suez Canal, which he denounces on political, financial and all sorts of grounds.

Berkeley Castle, Gloucester. Lord Hartington to Lord Granville *re* French correspondence in *The Times*. Harcourt's report 'a fair case for the Government'.

Dec. 5, 1875.

According to him the purchase was not made with the intention of ultimately acquiring the whole Canal, nor of increasing our influence in Egypt, nor of announcing to the world what our interest and policy in the Eastern Question would be, but simply to prevent the whole thing falling into French hands. Recommends 'the oracular line' at present.

Brit. Museum F.O. MSS. 38955 *Private Layard MSS. (British Museum).*
From Hammond to Layard.   Nov. 30, 1875.
I suppose you will have been as much astonished as the rest of the world. . . . It is certainly a bold experiment (much appreciated). We stand as a nation in a curious position, bound to conform to the terms of a concession made by the Porte, and in some and that no small degree, exposed to the roguery of the Khedive, which we may be called upon inconveniently to counteract. Wonders if *The Times* can quell insurrection.
                                                            Dec. 22.
Few words from Derby calculated to confirm the suspicion that in purchasing the shares our Government leapt in the dark, they could indeed hardly help doing so.

Private Gladstone MSS. G. MSS.

Lord Hartington to W. E. Gladstone.   Dec. 11, 1875.
Rather approves.
                                                            Dec. 13.
Suggests 'armed neutrality'.
If the Canal had been made through the Isthmus of Panama, should we have allowed America to claim the control of it on the ground that it was (as it would be) vital to her coasting trade?
vide Delane, vol. ii.

Private Granville MSS.

Henry Reeve to Lord Granville.   Dec. 16, 1875.
I have obtained from France very full particulars as to the Constitution and condition of the Suez Canal Company and the result is that I think the case is very strong indeed against the Government for the levity and ignorance of facts with which they acted.
. . . Although I think we have made a very bad bargain and a bad investment, and that the political results may be inconvenient, I think it not impossible that 25 years hence in the next century the country may not be sorry that this purchase was made. But it requires a very *long sight* to see so far.

Private Granville MSS.

John Bright to Lord Granville   Jan. 5, 1876.
Birmingham meeting 22nd.
I agree with you about the 'share' transaction—if but 'a share transaction', it should not have taken place—if anything more—if a great political transaction— then I regard it as the first serious blow at the integrity and independence of the Ottoman Empire. Lord Derby's view of the matter in his despatches seems to me the right one—we ought to invite the 'Powers' to unite in possessing, controlling and guarding the canal. Our interests would be safe and there could be no

jealousy. As it now rests, Russia and Austria are free to do what they like and our power even of remonstrance is greatly weakened. I think also our policy in the Turkish question 1854 to 1876 has been wrong and is terribly humiliating to us as a nation.

The story of the acquisition, and of all the surrounding circumstances, has been told in detail by Mr. Buckle in his *Life of Disraeli* (vol. v). Professor Hallberg in his valuable book, *The Suez Canal*, gives additional details from the French point of view. Professor Hoskins in *British Routes to India* has also marshalled much relevant evidence. Disraeli's success was due, in large measure, to the friendly attitude of the French Government, which was unsympathetic, as were the French bankers, to the purchase of the Khedive's shares by a French syndicate, and anxious to take no steps prejudicial to friendly relations with England, whose support was worth more under Disraeli than it had been under Gladstone. The time for the option passed, and Disraeli, with the assistance of Baron Rothschild, secured the prize. The firm of Rothschilds received a commission of 2½ per cent. upon the purchase price and 5 per cent. interest until the date of repayment. The commission was large, but not disproportionate to the risk.[1] The withdrawal of four millions for an indefinite but considerable period from the resources of the firm necessarily entailed a large derangement of their business; they had to consider possible fluctuations in the value of money and the risk that Parliament would withhold its approval to a transaction for which there was no precedent. Disraeli indeed suggested in the House of Commons[2] that Messrs. Rothschilds had purchased the shares, for resale to the British Government so soon as Parliament had approved the transaction. In fact, however, the British Government were the purchasers, with money borrowed from the Rothschilds. Disraeli's explanation was a constitutional fiction, but a convenient one.

Some months later, when the Suez Canal (Acquisition of Shares) Bill came before Parliament, the principles and methods of a Government shareholding in a commercial company were forcibly criticized. The intention of Government to purchase the shares had, said Lord Hartington, as Leader of the Opposition, become known to certain financiers, who had made use of the information to their own advantage, and the loss of others. 'I do not think', he concluded, 'that we can be proud

---

[1] The actual cost, as reported to Parliament (20th June 1882) was as follows:

Purchase money . . .	3,976,582
Commission @ 2½ per cent. .	99,415
Expenses	625
Total . . .	£4,076,622

[2] Hansard, vol. 327, pp. 99–100.

of the part which our Government has played on the Stock Exchange in Europe: I hope it will be a warning to them to avoid such transactions in future'. It was not clear to critics then, and it is not clear now, what positive advantages the British Government had gained, though it was clearly undesirable that virtually all the shares should be held by French subjects, as it would have made it difficult for the French Government to resist parliamentary pressure in case of any international controversy involving the canal. It would have involved France in responsibility for protecting, in case of disturbances in Egypt such as those of 1882, a canal which was vital to British interests. It was unquestionably to prevent acquisition by France that Disraeli was so quick to make the purchase.

Was there no other means to ensure that the shares so acquired should remain in British hands? That question does not appear to have been seriously considered, and the proposal of Sir John Stokes that the shares should be vested in 706 trustees, each holding 250 shares and thus entitled to 10 votes each and in consequence able to exercise control at the Annual General Meeting of Shareholders, was rejected.

It is often the fate of questions of International Law that action precedes deliberation, with the result that the rule or principle is adduced to explain or defend the action, rather than the action based upon an antecedent inquiry into the extent of the rule of principle.

Disraeli's action was confessedly taken on grounds of political expediency, though he had confidence that it would be justified on commercial grounds. It was, he said, a fallacy to suppose that an institution could not be at once political and commercial: the National Debt, for instance, had that double character. The purchase was made for a high political purpose, but, when made, the Government was found to take every precaution that it should be commercially successful. The juridical aspect scarcely received, at the time, any attention. Yet it created a precedent of the highest significance.

The projectors of the inter-oceanic canal across the Isthmus of Panama protected themselves as early as 1869 by a treaty concluded between the Governments of Colombia and the United States, by which it was agreed that the canal was to be under the control of the United States, and navigation was to be open to all nations in time of peace but closed to belligerents. No such clear-cut stipulations were made in regard to the Suez Canal.

International highways were at this period rapidly developing. The German and Italian Governments had a proprietary interest in the St. Gothard Tunnel. The Belgian Government had an interest in the Rhine Railway. The possibility of the Channel Tunnel was being actively canvassed (*The Times,* 10th Jan. 1876). The Sound, whereby ships enter and leave the Baltic, had just, by the Treaty of 1857, become open to universal navigation. But none of these enterprises had anything in common with the Suez Canal. They were the outcome of engineering and commercial enterprises to which the doctrines of free international intercourse had given free scope, and embodied the recognition that they were impossible of achievement without the cognizance and the patronage of governments, or, in many cases, without the consent of the Governments of different States.

National proprietorship in any foreign commercial enterprise necessarily differs in its commercial and political consequences from such proprietorship on the part of individual persons. In the case of every joint-stock enterprise there are at least three local jurisdictions which may be concerned.

(1) That of the legal domicile of the enterprise, which will probably determine the court in which the Company itself must be sued by all outside persons for alleged injuries or breaches of contract. In the case of the Suez Canal Company this domicile is Egyptian.

(2) That of the domicile of the shareholders of the Company in that capacity. This depends on the Statutes, Charter of Incorporation, or Articles of Association. It is this jurisdiction to which the shareholders, in their litigation with each other, are amenable. In the case of the Suez Canal Company this domicile is French.

(3) That of the domicile of all outside persons, to which those persons are amenable in the case of their committing a breach of contract or an injury against the Company. This may be anywhere.

The British Government is thus obliged, in its capacity of shareholder, to abide by the decision of an Egyptian or a French court, as the case may be, and would be so obliged even if owning a majority, or the whole, of the shares. The status of the Suez Canal is of vast importance not only or principally to Great Britain but to India and to the Dominions. In the ultimate resort, Great Britain must rely for the defence of her claims on the purity and impartiality of foreign Courts of Justice. Circumstances may well arise (as have arisen elsewhere) when she will be tempted to choose between defiance of the law, as administered, or peacefully foregoing acquired rights the maintenance of which she believes to be essential to the integrity of the British Empire.

There is, indeed, a Permanent Court of International Justice at The Hague, sometimes, but not always, competent to deal with such questions, but it would be folly to rely on it, and the conciliation procedure of the League of Nations is not adequate on such cases.

The fact is that a State cannot become a proprietor in a commercial enterprise, the seat of which is in the territory of another State, without incurring the necessity of inventing new securities and guarantees which would be superfluous in the case of private subscribers.

In the case of an enterprise like that of the Suez Canal the main object of the national proprietors (the British Government) is strategical and political, that of the other shareholders and royalty owners, including the Egyptian Government, is wholly commercial. The interest of the British Government is or should be to ensure that the canal does not exact more from users than is needed to pay a fair remuneration to the shareholders. The interest of the other shareholders is the opposite.

'It is', wrote Mr. Sheldon Amos in 1876, 'the duty and interest of England to treat the question of profits as one of no concern whatever if a conflict arises.' The admission of a State like Great Britain into the body of shareholders is in fact the admission of a member whose interests and duties are never identical with and usually opposed to those of the other proprietors, and once a State has purchased shares they are generally for ever out of the market.

It was clear from the outset that the canal could not in the interests of the world be wholly subject to the sovereignty of a weak nation such as Egypt, and its international importance made and still makes exclusive control by any one power undesirable. Equally objectionable, in a world which is striving, however feebly, to remove obstacles to international trade, is the continuance of effective and unfettered commercial control by a Company whose primary object is to make as large a profit as possible out of the movement of commerce between Europe and Asia, even at the risk of diverting a large proportion, as at the present moment, to the longer routes via the Cape or the Panama Canal.

BIBLIOGRAPHY

Amos, Sheldon. *The Purchase of the Suez Canal Shares and International Law*. 1876.
Arrow, Sir Frederick. *J. Roy. Soc. Arts*, 11th March 1870.
Lang, Andrew, *Life of Sir Stafford Northcote*.
Magniac, Charles, *J. Roy. Soc. Arts*, 25th February 1876.
Newton, Lord, [*Life of*] *Lord Lyons*.
Public Record Office. F.O. 78, numbers 2256, 2257, 2310–19, 2368–73, 2430–2, 2538, 2540–4, 2690–3, 2925–6. *Suez Canal, 1870–8*, including suit of Messageries Maritimes against Suez Canal, and Mr. Cave's Mission.
Wolf, Lucien. 'The Story of the Khedive's Shares.' *The Times*, 26th December 1905.

I

APPENDIX TO CHAPTER IV
THE BRITISH GOVERNMENT'S SHARE

In 1875 the British Government bought 176,602 shares from the Khedive for £3,976,580.[1] The 500 fr. shares were later divided into shares of 250 fr. and on 31st March 1932 the British Government held 298,526 of an estimated market value of £52,947,640 and certificates for the drawn shares in respect of which £406,977 had been received and applied towards the reduction of the National Debt. Until the mortgage on the shares expired in 1894 only interest at 5 per cent. was received—£3,833,484 in all. The following table, compiled from the Finance Accounts of the United Kingdom, shows the amounts received in interest and dividends for each financial year to 31st March.

Year.	Amount.	Year.	Amount.	Year.	Amount.	Year.	Amount.
	£		£		£		£
1894/5	279,011	1904/5	990,199	1914/15	1,154,276	1924/25	1,090,264
1895/6	673,418	1905/6	1,053,323	1915/16	858,152	1925/26	1,115,161
1896/7	694,075	1906/7	1,054,028	1916/17	773,486	1926/27	1,099,751
1897/8	698,684	1907/8	1,127,821	1917/18	524,319	1927/28	1,546,272
1898/9	678,856	1908/9	1,058,374	1918/19	617,215	1928/29	1,696,932
1899/1900	801,818	1909/10	1,056,208	1919/20	682,497	1929/30	1,834,140
1900/1	814,767	1910/11	1,129,260	1920/21	798,566	1930/31	1,870,697
1901/2	847,570	1911/12	1,187,935	1921/22	1,094,303	1931/32	2,238,879
1902/3	933,778	1912/13	1,318,686	1922/23	919,754		
1903/4	936,151	1913/14	1,246,370	1923/24	878,203		

Altogether, from 1876 to 1932, the British Government has received in dividends and interest the sum of £43,206,683.

[1] The Suez Canal (Acquisition of Shares) Bill, 1876, received the Royal Assent on 15th Aug. 1876.

CHAPTER V

THE QUESTION OF CANAL DUES, 1870–84

Financial Situation, 1870–2. System of Measurement. Gross Tonnage. Net Registered Tonnage. Suez Canal Measurement. Decision of International Commission of 1873, de Lesseps refuses to comply. Sultan insists. Prevarications. Principle established. Arabi Pasha's Rebellion. Agitation in 1883 for second canal. View of Law Officers. Official Negotiations with de Lesseps. Agreement of 10th July 1883. View of British Directors. Discussion in Commons. Mr. Childers. Mr. Gladstone. Public disapproval. Agreement withdrawn. De Lesseps' attitude. Lord Salisbury's views. Mr. Gladstone's announcement. Sir Stafford Northcote's arguments. Debate in House of Commons. Conclusions to be drawn. De Lesseps resumes negotiations with shipowners. Agreement of 30th November 1883. Lord Granville's approval. Attitude of Her Majesty's Government, relations with France. De Lesseps' satisfaction. Appendix (A) Agreement of 30th November 1883 and connected correspondence. (B) Summary of public discussions, &c., in regard to the Suez Canal, 1883.

THE completion of the Suez Canal was the consummation of the marriage of the two oceans: it was followed by the birth of a hydra-headed brood of problems, political, strategical, commercial, and financial. This chapter is devoted solely to the disputes that arose, very shortly after the opening of the canal, on the question of dues.

The financial situation of the Suez Canal Company in 1870 was, as will be shown in a later chapter, far from encouraging, and by the beginning of 1872 it became clear that, unless means could be found for increasing the traffic or the receipts, the Company would be unable to pay its way. The first and second concessions had given it the right to levy tolls on vessels and on passengers passing through the canal, and Article 17 (3) of the second concession stipulated that the rate charged should not exceed 10 francs 'par tonneau de capacité des navires et par tête de passager'. In October 1868 de Lesseps appointed a Commission to examine the question. It reported on 14th November[1] that the English official tonnage system was the best, but in the absence of any uniform systems the Company should accept the tonnage shown on the ship's papers, and their recommendation was adopted in the Navigation Rules of 17th August 1869. An additional ruling of 1st February 1870 declared that dues would be levied on the official net tonnage.

The Company soon realized the evil effects on their finances of this ruling, which incidentally involved unfair, if involuntary, discrimina-

[1] Voisin Bey, ii. 58; Roux, ii. 11.

tion, and appointed an international commission of investigation. Its advice was that no attempt should be made to impose a uniform system till a test case arose, and that the Company should be prepared to suffer a temporary financial loss in order to popularize the canal. The Company now petitioned the French Government to negotiate with the other Powers. It was a false step; they should have addressed the Sultan. In the event, the Franco-Prussian War intervened and de Lesseps appointed yet another commission of engineers and representatives of shipping to study the problem. This Commission advocated the adoption of the British or Moorsom system; holding however that it allowed too much space for machinery and coal, they suggested that 30 per cent. should be added to the gross tonnage, and from this new figure 25 per cent. should be deducted to get the net tonnage. A ruling to this effect was issued on 18th March 1872, and was at first accepted without objection and approved by the British and French Governments. It soon transpired that the immediate effect of this ruling was to increase tolls on British ships by about 30 per cent. at a moment when the canal was rapidly becoming essential; at a moment, also, when it was becoming clear that the Mediterranean Powers would before long bring Indian produce direct to their own ports under their own flag and not, as formerly, via London. Complaints poured into the Board of Trade, the first being from the New-castle Chamber of Commerce. A French shipping company, the Messageries Maritimes, raised the question in the French courts, claiming that tolls should be determined by the official tonnage on the ship's papers. The case was given against de Lesseps in the Tribunal of Commerce, but overruled on appeal. Meanwhile, the controversy had aroused great interest in England; it is necessary for our purpose to give some account of it here.

Since the year 1854 England has applied a scientific rule to the measurement of ships according to a system established by Captain Moorsom, based upon Newton's laws for the measurement of curvilinear bodies. The interior capacity of every British ship since 1854 is accurately measured by this rule in cubic feet. The total capacity thus obtained is called the gross tonnage, and from it is deducted the space, similarly measured, occupied by the engines and fuel; the remainder gives the number of cubic feet utilizable for carrying cargo; this figure divided by 100 gives the net registered tonnage. This is the only certain method of ascertaining correctly the 'dead weight' cargo capacity of a ship. Some nations had adopted it, others adhered to their old plans, which were mostly empirical, having been converted from some certain basis by a rule of thumb upon no basis at all, to suit the exigencies of the moment, the general principle of all being to discover some system by which to save port dues by enlarging the registered ton upon which they are habitually charged.

Of all these systems the French was probably the least scientific. It affected aristocratic airs of antiquity, professing to date from the time of Colbert, and ostensibly was a ton having a cubic measurement of 1·44 metres, equal to 51 cubic feet English.

The Canal Company said that the concession was in French—that the French ton of 1·44 metres was therefore intended. They added that experience showed that, as a rule, the number of tons of this magnitude in English ships was equal to the whole contents or gross tonnage of the ship before deduction of engine and coal space as ascertained by the Moorsom rule, and that, therefore, to save trouble, they would charge 10 francs per ton on the gross tonnage.

The case as thus shown was plausible, but in order to succeed it had to be shown that a *tonneau de capacité des navires* meant something definite; otherwise the contention of the Company for a small ton was as good as that of the shipowners for a large one. De Lesseps declared that the expression meant 'the real capacity of the ship'. The Porte, appealed to by de Lesseps, declined to permit the Company to be withdrawn from the jurisdiction to which it was amenable by the Act of Concession, and invited the principal Maritime Powers to send delegates to a conference at Constantinople to consider and settle the tonnage question.

The Commission met and the whole case crumbled away at the first touch. An ardent partisan of the Canal Company represented France. He stated his case, and it at once appeared that although the French legal maritime ton was ascertained by using 42 French feet, or 1·44 metres as a divisor of the supposed total capacity, the ingenious device had been adopted of reducing this total capacity so as to minimize the product. Instead of ascertaining the real contents of the ship by the Moorsom, or some equally correct mode, by the use of an arithmetical formula, constructed for the purpose, the bulk of every ship was systematically reduced. For instance, by the mode of gross measurement, a ship of 60,000 cubic feet was reduced to 44,000, and although the ton was apparently one of 1·44 cubic metres, the gross capacity was so reduced that the legal ton of capacity actually became one of 2·82 metres, or very nearly double the ostensible ton.

Though put forward as the commercial ton, it was admitted that the ton varied in France even according to the ship and the article, the French Messageries charging for the ton of 1 metre, which might with equal justice have been put forward.

The Commission, composed of representatives of twelve countries, on 18th December, decided by a majority of 11 to 1, the French delegate dissenting, that the British or Moorsom system of measuring gross tonnage capacity was the best, and that in order to ascertain the 'useful capacity' of a vessel certain deductions should be made, of which the chief were crew-space, engine-space, bunkers, and shaft tunnel. All closed-in spaces are measured, but the Suez Canal measurement is greater than the British net tonnage measurement. One main difference is that bridge decks and certain other spaces are liable to dues for the life of the vessel if goods have *once* been carried in them, whether goods are subsequently carried in them or not. The Commission also recommended that, in view of the financial position of the Company, vessels, whose capacity had been measured as above, should pay a surtax of 3 francs and other vessels of 4 francs; when the shipping using the canal reached 2,100,000 net tons the surtax was to be reduced to 3·50 francs, and further reductions of 50 centimes were to be made for every increase of 100,000 tons in traffic, so that the surtax would be abolished when the shipping passing through the Canal in a year reached 2,600,000 tons.

The award was accepted by the Porte and made mandatory upon the Company by a decree, which was backed by a circular to Turkish representatives at foreign courts announcing the decision.

De Lesseps did not accept the award with good grace. He proposed an alternative plan whereby the Company should accept the new system of measurement, but that the surtax of 3 francs per ton should be maintained till the shareholders had received their arrears, and till the net revenue reached 8 per cent.

The Porte was adamant, and warned de Lesseps that failure to comply within three months would involve reversion to the original toll of 10 francs, without surtax. De Lesseps declared he would hold the Porte responsible for the losses that would ensue, some 700,000 francs a month. Finding that this made no impression he threatened to close and abandon the canal.[1] 'I shall oppose', he telegraphed to the Porte, 'as President of a Universal Financial Company and as a French citizen, an absolute resistance to the violation of a bilateral contract accepted and fulfilled by 40,000 French shareholders. In the absence of any responsible plaintiff, and of any sentence or judgement of the Porte, the Powers have no rights to interfere in our affairs when we strictly observe the terms of our contract.' To this telegram no reply was sent, but on 29th April 1874, the Khedive, under orders from the Porte, sent 10,000 men under an American officer, General Stone, who was Chief of Staff of Ismaïl Pasha's army, from Cairo to strategic points on the canal, and a frigate commanded by a British officer in Egyptian service to Port Said. De Lesseps, on

[1] The documents are given in full in Fitzgerald, vol. ii.

the advice of the French Government, bowed to force and reserved his protests for a further hearing. This done he proceeded to put into practice new and unlawful devices of measurement. The decisions of the Conference were openly ignored and stigmatized in official correspondence as 'international robbery' and, notwithstanding strong protests by the British Ambassador at Constantinople, these illegal exactions continued, and a monthly letter of protest and claim for damages was sent to the Porte by de Lesseps. Every vessel paying dues on the new scale was served with a protest and a claim for the amount due under the old scale, couched in offensive language. The high-handed methods of the canal officials provoked a demand in Great Britain for a second canal which was actively maintained until 1876, when the acquisition by Great Britain of the Khedive's holding threw the project, for a time, into the shade and was followed by a period of peace. The outcome of the controversy was to establish that the Suez Canal Company was more than the property of a Company incorporated under a Charter of the Viceroy of Egypt with the approval of the Sultan of Turkey. De Lesseps was a *mandataire* rather than a *concessionaire*, and had not the sole right to interpret the Company's Statutes: those Statutes were subject to interpretation and to challenge in the Mixed Courts. The Sultan of Turkey had exercised his sovereign right to place his own interpretation *ex aequo et bono* upon the Statutes. He had called into consultation the representatives of the Maritime Powers, and had made their recommendations mandatory upon the Company. There is no reason why, on due cause being shown, the same procedure should not be adopted, *mutatis mutandis*, by the King of Egypt, so far as he is the inheritor of the sovereign rights of his suzerain.

Through the good services of Colonel (afterwards Sir) John Stokes the terms of the Commission's recommendations as to dues were modified and, with the consent of the British Government, a slower rate of reduction was conceded to M. de Lesseps who, in turn, agreed to spend a million francs a year in improvements. The normal rate of ten francs was not again reached till 1884 instead of in 1880, as originally contemplated. This new income, outside the terms of the Concession, saved the canal from ruin and made it a profitable concern, all at the expense, mainly, of the British shipowner—a fact generally forgotten to-day.

In 1878 we leased Cyprus from Turkey, and in the same year over 8,500 Indian troops and followers passed through the canal on their way to Malta. In June 1882 came the military rebellion of Arabi Pasha. France and Great Britain had, for the previous six years, worked hand in hand to repair the damage caused by the extravagance of Ismaïl Pasha and to restore the finances of Egypt without, however, repudiating any portion of the vast indebtedness of His Highness. France was pressed by Great Britain to co-operate in the bombardment of Alexandria and in operations from the banks of the canal at Ismaïliyah. She declined to do either. The victory of Tel el Kebir followed; Cairo was occupied by British troops, and the rebellion was quelled. De Lesseps showed himself at this juncture more of a Frenchman and less of a diplomatist than was his wont. If not a partisan of Arabi, he displayed a confidence in him which is not easy to understand, even in the light of Wilfrid Blunt's *Secret History*. He protested emphatically (his language was always vigorous and his outspokenness perhaps his greatest diplomatic asset) against the use of the canal as a base of military and naval activities, invoking the firmans of 1856 and 1866 which declared the Canal Zone to be 'neutral'. Great Britain took the view that this could not be secured by a unilateral act, and that her military and naval activities were in fact in aid of the Civil Power. During hostilities the canal services were taken over by the British Admiral in command; but only for forty-eight hours, whereafter the Company resumed charge.

De Lesseps had, however, overplayed his hand, and the agitation in England, begun in 1872, for a second canal assumed great prominence. British forces had just saved the canal from Arabi Pasha. Nearly four-fifths of the traffic through the canal was British,[1] but the management was exclusively French, the staff in Egypt French, and the control French. There were many complaints against the pilots; it was claimed that they were often inexpert, and that almost no British-born pilots were employed. The strict adherence to the letter of the Company's regulations, regardless of inconvenience, the autocratic attitude of the senior officials, and the absence of any Englishmen in the higher ranks of the hierarchy, either in London or in Paris, were made matters of loud complaint, both publicly and privately, by shipowners and others. In the early 'seventies, transit had been fairly rapid, but as the tonnage using the canal increased, so did the time lost in passing. Moreover in 1883 the canal was available only in daylight,[2] so that the average time of transit rose, by the year 1883, to nearly fifty hours, and was frequently as much as three days. The scheme for a new ship canal under

---

[1] A Board of Trade inquiry in 1882 showed that a little over 40 per cent. of shipping entering British ports from the East and Australia came through the canal: and a little under 40 per cent. of vessels clearing for these destinations. Jute, rice, and some cotton still came by the Cape. Only 17 per cent. of our imports from and 2 per cent. of our exports to Australia came through the canal. In 1887, however, the proportion reached 30 per cent. Exports from India, however, doubled between 1870 and 1880, but the Mediterranean ports gained more than those of the United Kingdom.

[2] Navigation by electric light was introduced in 1887 simultaneously with lighted buoys and other aids to navigation.

purely Egyptian auspices from Alexandria via Cairo to Suez, sponsored by Sir John Fowler, chief Engineer to the Khedive, was revived, as also a quaint project of one Captain W. Allen, R.N., to cut a channel from Haifa, whereby the waters of the Mediterranean would flood the Dead Sea valley, raising its level by 1,300 feet, whence traffic would continue over the mountains to Akaba. More seriously, demands for a second canal under British control, parallel to the existing canal, were pressed upon Lord Granville from many directions with the support[1] of some members of the Cabinet, who in 1882 had maintained that Great Britain should take such steps as would enable her to secure an effective preponderance in the Council of the Canal Company. De Lesseps, on the other hand, asserted that the Act of Concession gave his Company the monopoly of canal construction from sea to sea. This claim was, somewhat surprisingly, upheld by the Law Officers of the Crown, Sir Henry James and Sir Farrer Herschell. It was not unreasonably maintained by many very eminent English lawyers that the word 'exclusive' in the concession applied only to the geographical limits of the areas conceded to the Company. It was urged that in every case of such a grant of exclusive privileges, the grantee is rigorously confined by all courts of justice to the strict terms of the grant which, in case of ambiguity, are not to be construed in his favour to the public prejudice; every such grant being in the nature of a monopoly was therefore to be construed strictly against the grantee, and the greater and more universal the subject matter of the grant, the stricter the scrutiny to which its terms should be subject. Sir C. Dilke wrote as follows in his diary:

'On July 4th there was a meeting of Mr. Gladstone, Lord Granville, Childers, Chamberlain and myself, as to the Suez Canal, and we decided to ask de Lesseps to come over and meet us. Childers had a scheme in regard to the Canal, to which only Chamberlain and I in the Cabinet were opposed.

'On July 19th there was another Cabinet, Chamberlain and I tried to get them to drop Childers's Canal scheme, but they would not. The Cabinet was adjourned to the 23rd, and on Monday the 23rd they dropped it.'

Childers, on the other hand, when Chancellor of the Exchequer (*Life*, ii. 151) wrote to Lord Granville (9th May 1883):

'I am not one of those who believe that we should encourage a second canal; although by not snubbing those who promote this project we may in the end obtain better terms from M. de Lessep. . . . "We should", he continued, "aim at a further reduction of the tariff and equal control with the French, our claim to which is very strong." '

De Lesseps, however, did not adopt a merely negative attitude. He empowered his son Charles to enter into negotiations with the British

---

[1] *Life of Sir Charles Dilke*, i. 553; *Life of Mr. Childers*, ii. 151.

Directors of the Company, Sir John Stokes and Sir Charles Rivers Wilson, and on 10th July 1883 they signed an Agreement,[1] subject to ratification by Parliament, in the following terms:

Heads of Agreement between the Representatives of Her Majesty's Government and the President of the Suez Canal Company.

1. The Company to construct a second Canal as far as possible parallel to the present Canal, of width and depth sufficient to meet the requirements of maritime construction, settled in agreement with the English Directors.

2. The second Canal to be completed, if possible, by the end of 1888.

3. The Company to reduce the dues and tolls as follows:

From the 1st Jan., 1884, ships in ballast to pay $2\frac{1}{2}$ fr. per ton less than laden ships.
After the profits (interest and dividend) have been distributed at the rate of 21 per cent., half the pilotage dues to be remitted from the following 1st January.
After the profits are 23 per cent., the rest of the pilotage dues to be remitted.
After the profits, as above, are 25 per cent., the transit dues of 10 fr. per ton to be reduced by 50 centimes to 9 fr. 50 c.
After the profits are $27\frac{1}{2}$ per cent., a further 50 centimes to be taken off.
After the profits, as above, are 30 per cent., a further 50 centimes to be taken off.
For every additional 3 per cent. of distributed profits, 50 centimes to be taken off, to a minimum of 5 fr. per ton.

4. No two reductions of pilotage or transit dues to take place in the same year.

5. If the distributed profits should fall off, an increase of transit dues to take place according to the same scale, but no two increases to take place in one year.

6. On the first occasion of a vacancy one of the English Directors to be nominated by the President for election as Vice-President, and thereafter one of the English Directors to be always a Vice-President.

7. The English Director now acting as honorary member of the Comité de Direction to become a regular member when vacancies permit, and thereafter one of the English Directors to be always a member of the Comité.

8. Two of the English Directors to be always on the Finance Commission.

9. An English officer, selected by Her Majesty's Government, to be appointed by the Board 'Inspecteur de la Navigation'. His functions to be determined in agreement with the English Directors.

10. The Company to engage, in future, a fair proportion of English pilots.

11. Her Majesty's Government to use their good offices to obtain a Concession—

(a) For the land required for the new Canal and its approaches.

(b) For the Sweet-water Canal between Ismailia and Port Said, on the basis already accepted by Her Majesty's Government.

(c) For the extension of the term of the original Concession for so many years as will make a new term of ninety-nine years from the date of the completion of the second Canal. In consideration of such extension the Company to pay annually to the Egyptian Treasury 1 per cent. of the total net profits, after the statutory reserve.

[1] Egypt, No. 17, 1883, pp. 44–5.

12. Her Majesty's Government to lend to the Company, by instalments, as required for the construction of the works, including the Sweet-water Canal, not more than 8,000,000*l.* at 3¼ per cent. interest, with a sinking fund calculated to repay the capital in fifty years, such sinking fund not to commence until after the completion of the works.

13. These Heads of Agreement to be at once communicated to the House of Commons. They will be developed in full detail in a Resolution of the Council of Administration of the Company, the terms of which will have been settled in accord with Her Majesty's Government. That Resolution will be communicated to Her Majesty's Government for formal acceptance. The Agreement, however, and the acceptance of the Resolution, will have no effect until the necessary authority has been obtained from Parliament.

Pour le Président,
(*Signed*) CH. A. DE LESSEPS.

(*Signed*) C. RIVERS WILSON.
　　　J. STOKES.
London, July 10th, 1883.

The draft Agreement was confirmed by the Board of the Company, though not without demur. The French directors disliked the idea of a loan, even on such favourable terms, from the British Treasury; they resented the stipulations regarding an Inspector of Navigation (who was to be an Admiral or post-Captain), and additional British pilots.

In submitting the heads of agreement on 11th July 1883 to Lord Granville, the British directors observed, in a letter presented to Parliament a few days later, that from 1st January 1884 M. de Lesseps would have power to charge 10 francs per ton on all vessels, laden or in ballast, in addition to pilotage dues, and it was therefore imperative to reach an agreement which should embrace a substantial reduction of charges from 1888 onwards. M. de Lesseps and his son Charles further agreed that pilotage dues should be abolished by 1887, and that dues on ships in ballast should continue to be at least 2½ francs lower than on laden vessels. A sliding scale was clearly desirable: it might be regulated by annual tonnage, or by fixed periods, or by a combination of both, but neither system was practicable so long as additional capital works had to be met from revenue. For this reason de Lesseps proposed, and the British directors agreed, that successive reductions should depend on the net profits realized by shareholders. The actual scale, as set forth, provided for a reduction of tolls to the stipulated minimum toll of 5 francs when the shareholders received not less than 51 per cent. on the par value of their investment.

As regards the acquisition of a large share of authority on the Board of the Company in Paris, a power to which great importance was attached in England, the directors (following Mr. Childers's views) observed that the addition of more British directors, unless in numbers sufficient to secure an actual majority, would weaken rather than increase the authority of the Government directors, who were already consulted in advance on all matters of real importance.

'if it were stipulated that a certain number of seats were to be reserved for Englishmen not having an official status by reason of their nationality alone, we cannot but think that the result would be the creation on the Board of separate parties, leading to a system of constant voting on the questions presented, with the disadvantage to English interests that the English members would be in a minority.'

The loan would hasten reductions of dues and be of great value to British commerce, making possible the immediate construction of a second canal.

The British directors concluded by expressing the belief that short of a complete reconstruction of the scheme of management of the Company on the basis of an entirely British administration, the arrangements proposed were adequate to protect British interests.

The text of the Agreement was communicated on the following day to the House of Commons by the Chancellor of the Exchequer (Mr. Childers), who emphasized the importance he attached to the fact that the Senior British Director was a very distinguished engineer and that the works ultimately decided on would be approved by him. It was not favourably received, and both Mr. Childers, Mr. Chamberlain (President of the Board of Trade), and the Prime Minister, Mr. Gladstone, were strongly criticized, and not only by the Opposition. It was widely felt that if a second canal were to be constructed it should not be under the control of de Lesseps, but of the British Government or a British Company. Mr. Gladstone replied that the Law Officers of the Crown held M. de Lesseps to be in possession of an exclusive right to make a canal through the Isthmus of Suez and that the Egyptian Government had been similarly advised. On general grounds of equity he agreed with them and had no hesitation in following their advice, in preference to that of other lawyers, however eminent for, he claimed, our policy from 1875 onwards had been founded on that assumption, which formed the basis of all negotiations between M. de Lesseps and the British Government. This was energetically contested, for the Opposition, by Lord Salisbury, who reminded the House that Disraeli's purchase was primarily political, not commercial, and was not properly susceptible of such interpretations or deductions.

It was also felt the provisions as to British pilots[1] were inadequate and that the Agreement failed to protect British shipping from excessive charges. It was suggested that the finances of the Company might

---

[1] There were at the time in the service of the Canal Company 17 sea pilots at Port Said and 97 canal pilots. Of the Port Said pilots 12 were Greek, 2 French, 1 Maltese, 1 Austrian,

be so manipulated as to keep surplus divisible profits at a figure which would minimize the remissions of tolls due under the agreement. Mr. Childers replied that the Founders, the holders of the 15 per cent. profits purchased from the Egyptian Government, the Directors, and the employés, were all interested in dividends being as high as possible and naïvely referred to 'a famous case a good many years ago, when a Scotch Company declared dividends below what were earned, were convicted of fraud and very severely punished'.

These and other attempts to commend the Agreement to public approval met with little success. That it had so little support, either in Parliament or in business circles, was due in part to the manner in which it was presented. The Command Papers presented to Parliament were incomplete, and did not deal with the main point, viz., the claim of de Lesseps to an exclusive right in any new canal that might be made from sea to sea. The Prime Minister had the support of the Lord Chancellor as well as of the Law Officers, but the Lord Chancellor spoke as a member of the Government, and the opinions of the Law Officer could not be adduced without creating an undesirable precedent.

The British Directors thereupon approached M. de Lesseps afresh. They pointed out that the British Government were bound, if he desired, to submit the Agreement to Parliament; the result would, however, probably be unfavourable, and to force such an agreement through Parliament without more or less general approval was undesirable. De Lesseps, always the gentleman, when thus approached, declared that he quite understood the difficulty and would not press the matter. He would go ahead with the second canal, raising the capital by other means, and he would maintain the proposed reduction of dues *pari passu* with increased profits. He addressed his reply, dated 20th July, to the representations of the British Directors not to them but to his 'dear and honourable friend' Mr. Gladstone.

'In France', he wrote, 'public opinion, forgetful of the past, has unanimously approved this Agreement; in England, it seems to me that a section of public opinion, which has, perhaps, pronounced itself hastily, has not understood the full scope of the equitable arrangement arrived at. Unfortunate discussions between the two friendly nations have resulted which, I fear, are capable of injuring deeply, and for a long period, the necessary sentiments of cordial friendship which united the two nations.

'Personally, I should much regret that the work of peace carried out in Egypt by French capital, in the interests of universal commerce, should become a pretext of disunion, and that Europe should witness the development in the Parliament

1 Italian, of whom 8 could make themselves understood in English. Of the canal pilots 27 were French, 24 Italian, 19 Greek, 17 Austrian, 7 Maltese, 3 English. All could make themselves understood in English.

of England, and under your liberal Ministry, of an error of judgement, leading to a failure of justice.

'In the interests of general peace, in the interests of the Franco-English alliance, indispensable to the civilization of the world, I beg you not to consider yourself bound, towards the ship-owners and towards myself, by the terms of the Agreement which we have signed.

'Our Council of Administration holds, under the Statutes of the Company, sufficient powers to decide upon the excavation of a second maritime channel, and to settle the tariff to be levied, and our shareholders are in a position to provide us with the means of excavating the second Canal.

'Consequently, I formally declare that if our Agreement should be suspended, or even cancelled, the excavation of the second Maritime Canal will be immediately carried out, and all the reductions of tolls provided for in that Agreement will take effect.

'We shall thus continue peaceably and amicably as heretofore, in agreement with the representatives of the Queen's Government on the Council, to carry on and improve the Maritime Canal, according to the requirements of a work designed to remain freely open and available to the fleets of all nations, without exclusion or favour, according to the terms of our Concession.'

This letter and Mr. Gladstone's acknowledgement were presented to Parliament a day or two later,[1] and Lord Granville announced on 23rd July that Parliament would not be asked to assent to the Agreement.

Lord Salisbury, as Leader of the Opposition in the House of Lords, in congratulating Lord Granville on the decision, summarized the widespread dislike of the proposed arrangement in the following language:

'M. de Lesseps proposed to cut a new Canal without the assistance of the British Government, but with the approval of the Egyptian Government, which presupposes the consent of the British Government. Upon what terms will that consent be given?

'Shall we be prepared to give M. de Lesseps another Canal without security that the passage of British commerce will be more free, the administration more impartial, and the facilities more complete than they are now? Shall we accept such bad terms as those which have driven the shipping interest to so marked a demonstration of dissatisfaction?

'[Lord Granville] spoke as if the Company was in some sort a representative of France. I cannot admit that doctrine for a single moment. It is a private Company, and nothing more, in which England is nearly as large a shareholder as France, it is entitled to just, equitable, and considerable treatment, but that does not extend to recognition of a monopoly not justified on the surface of the Acts of Concession, not assigned by any unanimity of legal opinion, refused to them by many distinguished authorities, and obviously inconsistent with the first interests of this country. Now the scheme has been abandoned I hope that all those gravely

[1] Egypt, No. 15, 1883, C. 3695.

imprudent admissions are to be banished from our recollection as if they were a dream, and that the admission of that monopoly shall not be held to have been established by certain unfortunate expressions of Ministers of the Crown, drawn from them only by the exigencies of debate, which appear in this instance to have severely compromised the interests of England.'

At the same hour Mr. Gladstone announced in the Commons that Government proposed to take no further action on the Agreement.

'We think it our duty', he said, 'to do justice, as far as lies in our power, to this Great Canal Company, and to its eminent, sagacious and energetic projectors. . . . We will not be parties to employing influence which may attach to our temporary and exceptional position in Egypt, for the purpose of procuring any abatement of any right lawfully enjoyed. . . . We cannot undertake to do any act inconsistent with the acknowledgement that the Canal has been made for the benefit of all nations at large, and that the rights connected with it are of common European interest.'

'We think', he added later, 'that the Company's methods should be improved; that is by no means confined to the Suez Canal, because our methods of management are not quite the same as on the Continent, and wherever we go we are apt to think we can improve just a little on the arrangements. . . . We feel that so far as this is a commercial question, it is hopeless to expect that it can be dealt with so long as it is entangled with political complications. We desire that the commercial and shipping interests should have time to consider the question, and arrive at a matured conclusion.'

Sir Stafford Northcote replied for the Opposition:

'No one can go beyond myself in admiration of the character and energy and work of M. de Lesseps, whose friendship I have enjoyed for many years. Every respect is due to him, but that is no reason why we should give in to exorbitant demands. . . . Lord Granville in 1872 laid down the principle that we could not agree that the Company should be the judges or interpreters of their own concession: so we say here that the Company ought not to be the sole judges, and we should be extremely careful not to give colour to those claims beyond what those claims can be proved to be.'

An entry in Sir C. Dilke's diary of 22nd November, 1883, gives an insight, unobtainable elsewhere, into the attitude at this moment of the Cabinet.

'Another matter which was active at this moment was the position of Lesseps, with whom we had now made peace, and to whom we had given our permission for the widening of the first Canal. We supported him against the Turkish Government, who wanted to screw money out of him for their assent, and got the opinion of the law officers of the Crown to show that no Turkish assent was needed. On a former occasion we had contended that his privileges must be construed strictly, as he was a monopolist. On this occasion the law officers took a more liberal view. The fact is that the questions referred to the law officers for opinions by the Foreign Office have very often much more connexion with policy than with law, and their opinions are elastic.'

A few days later, on 30th July, Sir S. Northcote returned to the charge. In an exceedingly able speech he quoted from published correspondence to show that de Lesseps was not only a *concessionaire*, but *mandataire* of the Khedive who was, in the words of de Lesseps, 'the master of the house', but, in the speaker's view, never intended to part with his own power of making a new canal when he gave M. de Lesseps authority to form a company for the execution of a particular project. Of a monopoly there was no suggestion in any published documents, nor was it claimed until September, 1883, it was indeed supported by the law officers, but rebutted by legal opinions of equal weight. He quoted Lord Granville's dispatch to the Porte on 3rd March 1873:

'Her Majesty's Government do not in the slightest degree impugn the right of the Porte to increase the dues.... The Company is, as Her Majesty's Government consider, Egyptian, and the rights over it of the Porte are undoubted. Her Majesty's Government, however, feel confident that the Turkish Government cannot but be sensible of the equitable consideration which is due from the Porte to the maritime interests which are concerned in relation to traffic through the Canal which has thus become one of the highways of the world, the obstruction of which, by the imposition of an excessive toll, would be an injury to commerce, ... against which every nation would be driven to protest.'

The matter could not be laid at rest as being entirely between the Egyptian Government and the Suez Canal Company, irrespective of the interests of the maritime nations. The sooner it was cleared up, and the less it was trifled with, the better.

Mr. Norwood, who represented a constituency of merchants and shipowners, urged that time should be allowed for misunderstanding to be removed, and for mercantile men of both countries to reach a solution. He would not willingly follow Sir S. Northcote in challenging unnecessarily, except on the clearest reasons, the validity of the Concession. It was more important to uphold a standard of highest commercial morality than to secure a temporary advantage over the Suez Canal Company. The Government would have done better to consult mercantile opinion in the first instance, before negotiating through the Government directors, who were better aware of the feelings of de Lesseps than of the merchants of this country, who were not without hope of reaching a rational and satisfactory agreement.

Mr. Norwood believed that de Lesseps would admit the British Government into full partnership, with one-half of the administration and one-half of the responsibility, with alternate French and British Presidents after the decease of M. de Lesseps. He reminded the House that though four-fifths of the shipping was under the British flag, the cargo was very differently owned.

The debate, which lasted for some ten hours, was continued by Mr. Charles Palmer, who pointed out that, whereas the Concession required that the nations principally interested should be represented on the Board, they were, in fact, excluded. If we paid a bounty to ships that went round the Cape we could soon almost empty the canal. The matter was ripe for international consideration.

Baron Henry de Worms considered the principal defect of the Agreement was the absence of specific reductions of tolls to take effect at definite periods; he regarded the provision of a London Office of the Canal Company as another essential condition. Mr. Ashmead Bartlett adduced detailed arguments against the monopoly claimed by de Lesseps. We were justified, not merely in our own interests, but in those of Her Majesty's subjects overseas, in examining thoroughly what the Company had obtained in return for benefits conferred. He considered that M. de Lesseps and his coadjutors were already adequately rewarded without giving them a monopoly of all Suez Canals for all time. The more the Government yielded, the more they asserted the delicacy and difficulty of the diplomatic issues at stake, the bigger would be the demands of France, the greater the irritation, and the greater the certainty of future trouble.

Mr. Arthur Cohen said that it was established by incontestable authority that in every grant made by a sovereign there was reserved the right of domain, viz. the right of resumption of possession of the thing granted on the ground of public utility or expediency. The Canal Company could not impose arbitrary terms upon the world. M. de Lesseps knew very well that he could not abuse the power granted him, and after negotiation he would doubtless yield.

Mr. T. C. Bruce held that the Act of Concession required the Directors of the Company to be chosen from the nationalities principally interested. Had that condition been observed, the interests of Great Britain and of other countries would have been adequately secured, but it had been ignored and the Company had obstinately refused to grant other nationalities their just share in the administration. To hand over the traffic of the East to a single company for a hundred years would be too dear a price to pay even for M. de Lesseps and his French associates, who had contributed only £6 millions against the £16 millions, apart from the forced labour of innumerable peasants, contributed by Egypt, which to-day had no financial interest whatever in the Company.

Mr. Horace Davey (later Lord Davey), a lawyer of high repute, alluded to the legal considerations already mentioned, which he had expounded elsewhere. He deprecated the elaboration of legal arguments in the House of Commons: if the monopoly of the Company was challenged, it would be before a judicial tribunal in Egypt, and no good could come of a discussion in the Commons. The question did not in his view, turn on the nice consideration of the exact meaning of a curiously worded document, but on business interests to be determined by men of business. The best course was not to commit ourselves to a particular view, and to resume negotiations with our hands free.

Mr. Giles, member for Southampton, introduced a very practical note. Speaking as an engineer, he observed that one canal double the present width would be more useful than two narrow ones. The present traffic of twelve ships daily and talk of the necessity for two canals was idle. The existing canal could be widened for less than half the cost of making a new channel. As to tolls, from the Cape to Bombay was 4,450 miles longer than via Suez—equivalent at 10 knots to $18\frac{1}{2}$ days. Deducting two and a half days—the average time taken in making the transit between Port Said and Suez, the extra time was reduced to 16 days. The question was one of figures. Traffic was being driven away because the tolls often cost more than 16 days' steaming; the sooner the Canal Company realized this the better for all concerned.

On this very practical and prophetic note the debate might well have ended. But the Chancellor of the Exchequer replied that the unanimous opinion of the mercantile world was in favour of two canals. The Government Directors were inclined to the same view, as were, on the whole, a majority of the French Directors, headed by M. de Lesseps who, on his part, demanded an extension of the concession and financial assistance in return for committing himself to so vast an undertaking.

It was clear that the movement within the Company for a new canal was not unaffected by the agitation in England directed to the same end, which is summarized in an Appendix to this chapter. The United Chamber of Shipping, the General Shipowners' Society, the North Shields Shipowners' Society, and the Associated Shipowners' Society had, among others, petitioned Government to promote the construction (under British control) of a new canal. The petitioners included more than half the aggregate tonnage using the canal. It was in the light of these representations that de Lesseps and the British directors had entered upon their negotiations. The debate culminated in a learned duel between two lawyers, Sir Hardinge Giffard and Sir Henry James, the Attorney-General, and was wound up in a full house in the early hours of the morning by Sir Stafford Northcote, on the Opposition side. 282 votes were cast for the Government, and 183 against.

I have thought it well to give a full summary of this debate, firstly, because it is almost the last occasion on which the Suez Canal was seriously discussed in Parliament, and many of the arguments used, on either side, may with equal propriety be employed to-day. Secondly, because the debate throws much light upon the sentiments entertained in England, both in official and mercantile circles, towards the Canal Company. Thirdly, as illustrating the fact that in advocating or assuming the necessity for a second canal not only did the British Directors, with de Lesseps and the majority of his colleagues, prove to be wrong in their estimate of the expediency of widening the existing canal, but also the almost unanimous opinion of shipowning circles, and of many eminent engineers associated with them, was shown by events to be equally erroneous.

The civil engineers, headed by Robert Stephenson, had been wrong in their estimate of the feasibility of the canal in the 'forties and later: Lord Palmerston had, perhaps not unwillingly, been misled by them, and Disraeli had followed his lead, though mercantile and marine opinion had supported de Lesseps. Now, nearly thirty years later, almost the only voice raised in favour of the scheme eventually adopted, of widening the existing channel, was that of the member for Southampton, Mr. Giles. Her Majesty's Government had been induced, on expert representations that proved wholly erroneous, to offer no less a sum than £8 millions for the execution of an engineering work that would, as Major-General Sir Andrew Clarke anticipated and as events have shown, have been wholly superfluous. De Lesseps and his colleagues had been likewise misled into sponsoring a scheme which, had it been executed, would have been technically unsatisfactory and would almost certainly have involved the retention in perpetuity of tolls at the maximum permissible level. Both canals would have had to be widened, and in later years deepened, to accommodate larger vessels; both individually would require almost as much maintenance as a single enlarged channel. The British Parliament did a great service to de Lesseps, the world, and the British mercantile marine when, in conformity with public opinion, it forced Mr. Gladstone to drop the projected Agreement.

On reconsidering the question in the light of the rebuff he had received Mr. Gladstone (*vide* Childers, *Life*, ii. 154) took the view that the dual character of the British directors, and consequently of the Cabinet, as business men and politicians, was fatal to the success of such negotiations. He was consequently well pleased when M. de Lesseps, accompanied by his son Charles Aimé, came on his own initiative to London, and a series of interviews between him and Lord Granville removed previous misunderstandings. De Lesseps saw that he had no alternative but to seek a good understanding with Great Britain, and forthwith entered into negotiations with a body consisting of British shipowners and others most interested in the navigation of the canal. Under the immediate auspices of Mr. Joseph Chamberlain,[1] then President of the Board of Trade, a voluntary arrangement was drawn up. In addition to the three existing official directors who had occupied seats on the Board since the purchase of the Khedive's shares, seven new directors, chosen from among English shipowners and merchants, were to be admitted to the Board and to the enjoyment of emoluments of office.

Arrangements were made for paying shipping dues in London, and for the increase of the number of English-speaking officials (not necessarily of British birth) employed in the transit service of the Company. Above all, it was agreed that transit dues should be at once reduced and that all net profits above 25 per cent. should be applied to the reduction of dues until such dues fell to 5 francs. This Agreement, afterwards known as the 'London Programme', is printed,[2] together with relevant correspondence, as an Appendix to this chapter.

This Agreement was not universally welcomed; the North of England Steam Shipowners Association complained they had been ignored, and the Liverpool Chamber of Commerce held that steps should be taken to obtain full voting power for the Government shareholding. It was further suggested that the agreement was not in fact more than 'a temporary arrangement, requiring to be completed by considerable and indispensable additions before it could be acceptable from a national point of view'. It was, however, submitted to and approved by Lord Granville in his capacity as Secretary of State for Foreign Affairs, but the Foreign Office was at pains to emphasize, in correspondence simultaneously presented to Parliament, that the arrangement arrived at was the result of direct negotiations between the Association of Steamship Owners trading with the East and M. de Lesseps, 'in which Her Majesty's Government took no part'.

The attitude of Her Majesty's Government at this juncture towards all questions affecting the management and finance of the canal appears, from the correspondence presented to Parliament, to have been very different from that adopted in 1883. In 1883 Gladstone was ready to offer de Lesseps a loan of £8 millions at 3¼ per cent. to enable the Company to build a second canal. Finding public opinion unfavourable to their proposals, the Government of the day proceeded to abdicate their functions in relation to the canal, and to encourage direct negotiations, in which the Government directors officially took no part, between de Lesseps and a self-constituted and only partially representative body. An arrangement—which can scarcely be regarded as, and was not in form, a binding contract—was reached, and formally

[1] Lord Edmond Fitzmaurice, *Life of Granville*, 1905, ii. 313. See also Garvin, *Life of Joseph Chamberlain*, 1933, i. 432.   [2] See Egypt, No. 3, 1884, C. 3850.

approved by Lord Granville. Yet both he and his successors in office insisted that, the intervention of Mr. Joseph Chamberlain notwithstanding, Her Majesty's Government were not responsible for it.

The change of attitude was due almost certainly to considerations of high policy. The agreement left much to be desired, but it was regarded by public opinion as on the whole a fairly satisfactory solution of a controversy which was felt to be wearisome. On the other hand, the maintenance of good relations with France was becoming daily a matter of greater difficulty.

Admiral Pierre, commanding the French fleet in the East Indies, had just attacked Madagascar, and had grossly insulted the British flag in the person of Mr. Pakenham, the British Consul, who lay dying in the Consulate. He had demanded the consular dispatches, and placed sentries on board British mail steamers, and finally arrested and treated with indignity and brutality a Nonconformist missionary. The Admiral was probably suffering from the incipient stages of the disease of which he died before his return to France,[1] but his actions were none the less a source of diplomatic embarrassment. There was trouble over French adventures in China, friction over French claims in Newfoundland, and French enterprise in Central Africa was a further source of anxiety. 'The Egyptian question', writes Sir C. Grant Robertson (*Bismarck*, 1918, p. 413), 'with all the embarrassments arising out of the tangle or created by ministerial policy in Great Britain, was just what Bismarck could have wished. It made Great Britain more dependent on German good will and, properly handled with the requisite air of impartiality, could separate France and Great Britain.' In the circumstances it may readily be understood that the Foreign Office viewed with complacency any means whereby even one major issue could be settled out of court without official intervention.

De Lesseps, too, was well pleased. Public opinion in England, which had set strongly against him, had been placated. He on his part had said, at the annual meeting of the Company in June 1883, many hard things of 'this sterile agitation' and of those who were responsible for it, but throughout his career de Lesseps successfully maintained the dual role of President of the Company and the champion of its rights on the one hand, and on the other of an agile and pliant negotiator, ever ready to 'agree with his adversary quickly, whiles he was in the way with him'. The acrimonious tone of some of the speeches delivered in both Houses of Parliament, the violent language of the Press on both sides of the Channel, which accurately reflected public opinion, were not reflected in the actual conduct of negotiations on either side. The discussions were not public, and were not prolonged.

[1] Fitzmaurice, op. cit., ii. 314.

'Since the signature of "The London Programme",' writes Sir Ian Malcolm,[1] 'there has been nothing to disturb the harmony that has ever since existed in that international board room.' He does not mention that this instrument, though formally approved by Her Majesty's Government, was gratuitously abrogated, as to its financial provisions, in 1900, but he emphasizes the point that most mattered. Seven British merchants had secured directorships, that point once conceded, harmony has reigned, though the British directors have remained permanently in a minority on the Board.

The London Agreement met with strong opposition among the shareholders of the Company, who wanted their ten francs, and de Lesseps only carried his proposals in the General Meeting of 12th March 1884 by 843 votes to 761. The opposition still continued. He had said at that meeting: 'On a donné à tort à ce document le nom de contrat ou de convention. C'est un programme que la Compagnie a préparé dans sa pleine indépendance, après s'être assurée qu'il donnait satisfaction aux désirs exprimés par les armateurs.' And again 'Ce ne sera que lorsque le revenu aura atteint 25% que ce calcul cessera et que la partie de vos bénéfices supérieure à 125 francs par action servira intégralement de base à la réduction de la taxe de transit jusqu'au moment où elle sera descendue à 5 francs par tonne.' The words *de base* are important as they seem to infer the possibility of a modification. In the Report for 1883, presented at the General Meeting on 29th May 1884 it was specifically said:

'Le revenu de 125 francs, au delà duquel le *surplus* acquis servira de base au calcul des détaxes, ne sera pas un maximum, puisque ce surplus sera en entier distribué aux actionnaires et que les détaxes ne continueront que si ce *surplus* se produit au bénéfice des actionnaires.

'Le formule du programme peut se simplifier en cette proposition exacte:
Participation des clients du Canal Maritime aux bénéfices du Canal, sous la forme de diminutions de taxe proportionnées à l'accroissement des recettes, à partir du revenu de 90 francs par action et jusqu'au moment où la taxe de transit se trouvera ramenée à 5 francs par tonne.

'Nous vous disions en 1882: " Nous déclarons hautement que les actionnaires du Canal Maritime de Suez ne doivent pas seulement jouir d'un brillant revenu, mais qu'ils doivent s'enrichir comme tout industriel en a le droit lorsqu'il a rendu au monde un service comparable au percement de l'Isthme égyptien".'

The truth seems to be that de Lesseps originally thought a maximum revenue of 125 francs per share (25 per cent.) to his shareholders until the dues were reduced to 5 francs was fair, but had to modify his views in deference to the claims of the shareholders, whose approval of reduction of dues was necessary.

[1] *Quarterly Review*, January 1931.

On this point it is worthy of note that the preliminary scheme of MM. Linant Bey and Mougel Bey, engineers to the Viceroy of Egypt, dated 20th March 1855, contained the following passage:

'We propose to the Company to have a clause inserted in the Statutes by which tariffs shall be lowered as soon as dividends exceed 20 per cent. (De Lesseps, *The Isthmus of Suez Question*, 1855, p. 167).

The memorial of de Lesseps to Saïd Pasha of 15th November 1854 also states that the proposed dues of 10 francs per ton 'might be reduced in proportion to the increase of navigation' (de Lesseps' *Recollections*, i. 174). He appealed in particular to the coal-mining interests for support.

De Lesseps' next step was to summon a second International Consultative Commission consisting of eight Frenchmen, eight Englishmen, and six members of other nationalities.[1] It met at Paris in June 1884 and thereafter sent a Sub-Commission of eight members under the presidency of Mr. Dirks to make investigations on the spot, and in particular to examine the proposal of the engineer-in-chief of the Company, M. Lemasson, for an enlargement of the existing canal, as an alternative to the excavation of a new waterway. M. Lemasson contended that the channel should be wide enough for two steamers in motion to pass anywhere. This meant a channel 230 feet broad at the bottom on the straight, 262 feet broad on the curves. For a depth of 8 metres (26¼ feet) the cost was put at £8,118,000; for 9 metres (29½ feet) £9,750,000, as against £11,150,000 for a new canal of the same size as the existing one. This scheme had from the outset been supported by Major-General Sir Andrew Clarke, who was at this time Inspector-General of Fortifications at the War Office (vide Childers, *Life*, ii. 154). It was also strongly supported by American engineers.

This scheme was, with a few modifications, eventually adopted, after it had been submitted, with a *questionnaire*, to nine captains of the largest size steamers navigating the canal and to twenty-five of the

---

[1] The actual composition of the Commission was as follows:

French.	*British.*	*Others.*
De Lesseps	Maj.-Gen. Sir Andrew	Peschek* (Germany)
Lefébure de Fourcy	Clarke	Crillanovitch* (Austria-
Vice-Amiral Jurien de la	Sir Charles Hartley*	Hungary)
Gravière	Sir John Coode*	Saavedra (Spain)
Pascal	Capt. Chitty, R.N.	Gioia* (Italy)
Voisin Bey*	Thomas Sutherland	Dirks* (Netherlands)
Laroche	James Laing	Alexeiff (Russia)
Tillier*	William Mackinnon	
Dupont	R. Alexander	

* Members of the sub-committee which visited the canal.

(Hartley, *Proc. Instit. Civil Eng.*, 1900.)

most skilful pilots of the Company. The largest steamer which had at that time passed through the canal was the Orient Company's s.s. *Austral* which had a length of 456 feet, a beam of 48 feet, gross tonnage of 5,665 tons, and a draught of 27 feet when fully loaded. (The maximum depth permitted at the time was 24 feet 6 inches.) The sub-committee made a careful examination of the revetments and the effect thereon of the wash from passing vessels, of the effect of plantations of tamarisks, reeds, and similar plants, and of the best type of cross-section at various points. They also witnessed experiments then being made in the use of electric light.

A steamer was fitted with a 1,600 candle-light lamp at a height of 18 feet, and lighted buoys were disposed in pairs at intervals of 500 metres. The trials were inconclusive, and no one ventured to predict that in less than five years' time the result of these early experiments would have the effect of virtually doubling the carrying capacity of the canal.

It was unanimously agreed that the widening of the canal was preferable to the construction of a second waterway. Enlargement would be more rapidly accomplished, and shipping would benefit at once from the work as it progressed. The greater breadth would render possible a greater speed of individual ships when not passing each other: the cost of maintenance would be no greater, and it would be possible to effect further improvements by increasing the width at the curves.

There was some difference of opinion as to the depth to be aimed at. Sir Charles Hartley favoured 31 feet (9½ metres) to provide for steamers of 28 feet: the British delegates as a whole were emphatically in favour of 9 metres, to accommodate ships of 27 feet draught. The majority of the sub-committee consisting of representatives of nations who had no considerable mercantile marine were content with 8 metres. The question of depth was, of course, all important, as insufficient width could always be met by using the *gares* or sidings, and it was stressed particularly by the German engineers, as the German ship-owners were using ships of greater capacity than the English lines. The British view eventually prevailed, and the plans and estimates of M. Lemasson[1] were accepted almost in their entirety.

This Commission was reconstituted in 1887 as a *Commission Consultative International des Travaux* and has since, with few intermissions, met annually in Paris to record its agreement with all important proposals for the improvement of the canal.

From 1885 dues remained at 9.50 fr. per ton Suez Canal measure-

[1] After a residence of nearly thirty years in Egypt M. Lemasson was assassinated in 1894 by a discontented workman. He was succeeded by M. Quellenec.

ment and dividends, after a drop in the depression year, 1886, to 15 per cent., rose steadily till in 1901 the expected limit of 25 per cent. Next year the dividend was at the same rate, and again in 1903, when the dues were reduced to 8.50 fr. per ton. At this figure they remained for three years, but the dividend was raised to 28.2 per cent. Discontent again broke out in the shipping world, and the Chamber of Shipping of the United Kingdom stated in their Report for 1905 that: 'Your Council dealt in their last three Annual Reports with the varying phases of the lengthy controversy in which they have been engaged with the Suez Canal Company upon (1) the charging of Suez Canal Tonnage Dues on partially enclosed spaces; (2) the unsatisfactory nature of the composition of the 'London Committee' of the Suez Canal Company, and (3) the increased dividends paid to the share-holders of the Suez Canal Company in contravention of the 'London Agreement'. Appeals were made to the Foreign Office, and after long delays a conclusive reply was received on behalf of Lord Lansdowne, showing that in 1900 the London Committee had surrendered what-ever control they had over dues and that the Government approved. It is probable that the 25 per cent. limit could not have been main-tained in face of the opposition of the shareholders; indeed, M. de Lesseps showed in 1884 that the limit did not exist. But British shipowners did believe it was a reality, and it was a shock to find it had been secretly given up. However, indignation was forgotten in growing prosperity.

BIBLIOGRAPHY

Allen, Capt. W., R.N. *The Dead Sea, a new route to India.* 1855.
Gwynn and Tuckwell. *Life of Sir C. Dilke.* 1917.
Sargent, A. J. *Seaways of the Empire.* 1918.

APPENDIX A

(Reprinted from Egypt, No. 3, 1884, C. 3850)

No. 24.

Mr. Westray to Earl Granville (Received December 1.)

Association of Steam-ship Owners Trading with the East,
112, Fenchurch Street, London,
November 30, 1883.

My Lord,

REFERRING to the correspondence which has passed between your Lordship and this Association, I have now the honour to submit the following statement:

Sir Julian Pauncefote writing to the Association on your Lordship's behalf, under date of the 30th October last, stated that it was indisputable that any operations for the construction of the Canal, having their seat in the Isthmus of Suez, would be far more cheaply and expeditiously conducted by the present Compagnie Universelle than by any other Company, and that the Government, therefore, recommended this Association to enter into direct communication with the Suez Canal Company, in order to ascertain what prospects there might be of obtaining through that medium the necessary facilities for British shipping and commerce. As your Lordship is aware, the MM. de Lesseps have recently paid a visit to this country for the purpose of ascertaining the views of the different shipping and commercial bodies in regard to the present and future position of the Suez Canal. Accordingly, several interviews having taken place between these gentlemen and the Association, at which the decision was very fully and exhaustively discussed, I have now the honour to inform your Lordship that certain conditions for the future administration of the Canal have been this day agreed upon between M. A. Charles de Lesseps and the Committee of this Association, and I beg respectfully to hand your Lordship herewith a copy of the particulars in question. Your Lordship and Her Majesty's Government will observe that the conditions agreed upon provide for important reductions in the charges of the Suez Canal Company in the interest of shipping and commerce; also for an immediate increase in the number of British Directors on the Board of that Company, and for other valuable arrangements, especially such as that of the establishment by the Company of an office in London, in which the British Directors will form a Comité Consultatif.

In transmitting this document, I have, on behalf of the Association, to express the hope that Her Majesty's Government will consider that the arrangements entered into are satisfactory.

I have, &c.
(Signed) J. B. WESTRAY.

Conditions for the future Administration of the Suez Canal.

MEETING of the 30th November, 1883, at the offices of the Peninsular and Oriental Steam Navigation Company; present, the members of the Association of Steam-ship Owners engaged in the Eastern trade. Mr. James Laing in the Chair.

M. Charles Aimé de Lesseps, Vice-President of the Council of Administration of the Compagnie Universelle du Canal Maritime de Suez, being also present at the meeting, moved from the gentlemen present an expression of their opinion upon the matters relating to the Suez Canal, whereupon, a discussion and an exchange of views having taken place, it was agreed that the twelve following points should constitute the views desirable for the future administration of the Suez Canal:—

1. To prevent delays in the transit between the Mediterranean and the Red Sea, and *vice versa*, and also to provide for the expansion of trade, the Company shall either sufficiently enlarge the present Canal, or construct a second channel, as may be hereafter determined; and that, in order to arrive at a proper decision as to the course which should be pursued in this respect, a Commission of engineers and ship-owners shall be appointed to examine the question, of which not fewer than one-half of the members shall consist of English engineers and ship-owners.

2. In addition to the three Directors designated by the English Government, seven new Directors, chosen from amongst English ship-owners and merchants, shall at once be admitted as members of the Board. In order to confer upon these seven Directors the power of voting which attaches to the present Directors, the Administration will propose to the shareholders to modify the Statutes, and to revert to the figure at first fixed for the number of Directors, namely, thirty-two. In the meantime, and until the necessary formalities shall be accomplished, the Administration will invite these seven Directors, as soon as they have been chosen, to be present at the meetings of the Board.

3. A Committee ('Comité Consultatif') shall be formed in London, consisting of English Directors. The Company will open an office in London. Arrangements will be made for the payment of dues in London.

4. In future, appointments in the transit service of the Company will increase to a large extent the number of officials speaking English.

5. It is understood that the last surtax of 50 centimes shall definitely disappear from the 1st January, 1884.

6. All expenses resulting from groundings and accidents in the Canal shall, for the future, be borne by the Company. From this, however, are to be excepted collisions which may occur between vessels passing through the Canal. The Canal Company also except damage which may be caused to the craft and other appliances of the Canal by ships passing, providing that the ships are to blame for such accidents.

7. That from the 1st July, 1884, the Company will entirely extinguish the pilotage dues.

8. From the 1st January, 1885, the Company will diminish the transit dues by 50 centimes, thus reducing the charge from 10 fr. to 9 fr. 50 centimes, and should the dividend for 1883 amount to more than 18 per cent., a further reduction in the transit dues over and above the 50 centimes referred to shall be made from the same date, namely, the 1st January, 1885, on the basis of one-half of such dividend above 18 per cent. That the Company will thereafter divide with the ship-owners on every succeeding 1st January to the extent of half the profits, whatever the amount of such profits may be in excess of the amount of profit last previously divided with the ship-owners, which moiety is to be applied to a reduction of dues

determined upon the basis of the tonnage which has passed through the Canal in the year for which such profit is ascertained. For example, if the accounts for 1884 show profits at the rate of 20 per cent. the ship-owners would be entitled to a reduction in the Tariff equal to the net profits of the Company corresponding to 1 per cent. (about 2,800,000 fr.) for the year commencing the 1st January, 1886, over and above the previous reduction. And, again, if the profit on the revenue of 1885 should be 21 per cent., a half-share of the difference between 20 per cent. and 21 per cent., viz., ½ per cent.—say, in round figures, 1,400,000 fr.—will go towards the reduction of dues from the 1st January, 1887, over and above the previous reduction, and this division, by moieties, will continue until a profit of 25 per cent. is reached; above such profit of 25 per cent. all the net profits of the Company shall be applied to the reduction of dues until such dues are reduced to 5 fr.

9. It is understood that in the foregoing clauses the profit on which the reduction of dues is to be calculated shall include the 5 per cent. paid in the first instance to the shareholders.

10. The reduction already agreed to in favour of ships in ballast is to be confirmed.

11. As to the statutory reserve, the Council of the Suez Canal Company will propose that when such reserve shall have reached the sum of 5,000,000 fr., the deductions thereafter to be made from the net profits for the benefit of such reserve, and which are now at the rate of 5 per cent., shall in no case exceed a maximum of 3 per cent. on such net profits.

12. It is understood that the calculations on which the afore-mentioned reductions in the Tariff are to be arranged are based upon the present capital of 200,000,000 fr. In the event of any change being made in the amount of such share capital the basis for the reduction of dues shall be readjusted, so that the diminution in the Tariff shall not be adversely affected.

(*Signed*) James Laing, Chairman.

Thomas Sutherland, Chairman of the Peninsular and Oriental Steam Navigation Company.

William Mackinnon, Chairman of the British India Steam Navigation Company.

J. G. S. Anderson, Orient Steam Navigation Company, Limited.

J. B. Westray, Honorary Secretary of the Association of Steam-ship Owners, trading with the East, and (by authority) for the City Line, the Hall, the Clan, the Glen, the Shire, the Harrison and Ducal Line.

John Glover

R. S. Donkin.

Ch. A. de Lesseps.

The foregoing points having been agreed upon with M. Charles A. de Lesseps, the Committee expressed the opinion that the shares held by the British Government should be made to carry adequate voting power at the meetings of the shareholders, to which M. Charles A. de Lesseps, whilst reserving his opinion upon this question in its legal aspect, and as regards the principles on which the Suez Canal Company has been constituted, replied that he is not in a position to share this point of view.

(*Signed*) JAMES LAING, Chairman.

Earl Granville to the British Suez Canal Directors.

Foreign Office,
January 15, 1884.

Gentlemen,

HER Majesty's Government have had under consideration the proposed conditions for the future administration of the Suez Canal, as agreed to on the 30th November last between the Association of Steam-ship Owners trading with the East and M. de Lesseps.

These conditions were laid down in twelve Articles, the execution of which will no doubt confer great benefits on British shipping and commerce.

With reference, however, to the 1st Article, under which a Commission is to be appointed for the purpose of advising the Company as to the changes necessary for the improvement of the transit, Her Majesty's Government are of opinion that nautical men experienced in the navigation of the Canal should be admitted as members of the Commission on the recommendation of Her Majesty's Government.

They are also of opinion that the official Directors appointed by Her Majesty's Government should be members of the London Consultative Committee provided in Article 3.

Her Majesty's Government, who possess as shareholders a very large interest in the undertaking, consider that the Agreement affords a satisfactory solution of the differences which have arisen between the Company and its customers; and on the understanding that no difficulty will be made with regard to the two points above-mentioned, they approve of the scheme of proposed measures as putting an end to the differences which have arisen, and insuring the development of the undertaking in the interest of the trade of the world.

I authorize you to communicate a copy of this despatch to M. de Lesseps.

I am, &c.
(*Signed*) GRANVILLE.

APPENDIX B

SUMMARY OF PUBLIC DISCUSSIONS ETC. WITH REGARD TO THE SUEZ CANAL, 1883

(From *The Times Register of Events, 1883*)

France, May 11th. M. de Lesseps, speaking at the annual banquet of the Suez Canal Company, said there was no need for apprehensions from a second canal.

Meeting of Shipowners at the Cannon Street Hotel on the proposed new Suez Canal. Resolutions adopted in favour of it.

Leader in *The Times* on the projected Suez Canal.

May 22nd. The projected Suez Canal. Text of opinion of the Egyptian Judicial Committee published.

May 24th. Leader in *The Times* on Egypt.

June 2nd. Meeting of Dutch Shipowners declared their confidence in M. de Lesseps and his Suez Canal policy.

Leader in *The Times* on the Suez Canal.

June 5th. France. The Suez Canal Company held their Annual Meeting in Paris. M. de Lesseps spoke, reviewing the general situation.

June 6th. The Suez Canal. Text of the Shipowners' Memorial to Lord Granville published.

July 10th. Leader in *The Times* on the Suez Canal.

July 12th. Leader in *The Times* on the Suez Canal.

July 13th. The Suez Canal Directors approved of the new Canal arrangement.

The second Suez Canal Conference of industrial representatives in Aldgate. Meeting of merchants and shipowners in the City, and Meeting of the Council of London Chamber of Commerce.

Leader in *The Times* on the New Suez Canal.

July 14th. House of Commons. At morning sitting numerous questions asked in reference to the New Suez Canal. Strong expression of public opinion against the New Suez Canal scheme. Meeting of merchants, &c., at Lloyd's. Deputation of Associated Chambers of Commerce to Mr. Childers.

Leader in *The Times* on the Suez Canal.

July 16th. Leader in *The Times* on the Ministry and the Canal scheme.

July 17th. Turkey. Strong representations made by the Porte that no change can be made in the status of the Suez Canal without its consent.

House of Commons. Many questions on the Suez Canal scheme, most of which the Ministry declined to answer at present.

July 18th. House of Lords. After several questions had been discussed, Lord Granville made a statement on the Suez Canal negotiations. Lord Salisbury and the Lord Chancellor also spoke.

House of Commons. Questions on Suez Canal Company. Leader in *The Times* on the Suez Canal Agreement.

July 19th. The Suez Canal. Meeting of the London Chamber of Commerce; resolutions passed condemning the Agreement.

July 20th. House of Commons. A number of questions asked on the Suez Canal scheme.

Leader in *The Times* on the Government and the Session.

July 21st. France. The Suez Canal Company's Managing Committee had a special meeting.

July 23rd. Egypt. Mr. Royle drew up an indictment against the Suez Canal Company.

Leader in *The Times* on the Suez Canal Convention.

July 24th. House of Lords. Lord Granville announced the abandonment of the Suez Canal Agreement.

House of Commons. Mr. Gladstone made his statement on the Suez Canal Agreement.

Leader in *The Times* on the abandoned Agreement.

July 25th. House of Commons. Several questions on the Suez Canal negotiations. Leader in *The Times* on the Government and the Canal question.

July 26th. Mr. Gibson spoke at Portsmouth on the Suez Canal question. Leader in *The Times* on England, Egypt and the Canal.

July 27th. Leader in *The Times* on the Suez Canal question.

July 31st. France. M. de Lesseps had a long interview with M. Ferry.

House of Commons. Debate on Sir S. Northcote's motion on the Suez Canal. Mr. Gladstone, Mr. T. Bruce, Mr. Davey, Sir H. Giffard, the Attorney-General, and others spoke. The motion was rejected by 282 to 183, and Mr. Norwood's amendment agreed to. The House adjourned at 4.40 a.m. Leader in *The Times* on the Suez Canal Debate.

August 4th. House of Lords. Lord de la Warr moved for papers on the new Suez Canal.

August 7th. House of Lords. Lord Stratheden reviewed the Egyptian question, and moved for papers. Lord Granville replied.

House of Commons. Mr. Gladstone made a long reply to questions as to the occupation of Egypt. Leader in *The Times* on England and Egypt.

August 8th. France. French papers criticize British Rule in Egypt.

August 9th. France. The Suez Canal Company held their Monthly Meeting, M. de Lesseps and the three English members being present.

September 12th. Leader in *The Times* on Egypt.

September 20th. Leader in *The Times* on the Suez Canal.

September 27th. Leader in *The Times* on Egypt.

October 4th. Associated Chamber of Commerce, Autumn Session, opened at Derby. Discussion on the Suez Canal.

October 10th. Leader in *The Times* on Egypt.

October 12th. Professor Leone Levi delivered a lecture at King's College on the Suez Canal and the Channel Tunnel.

November 6th. Leader in *The Times* on M. de Lesseps in England.

November 10th. At the Guildhall Banquet Mr. Gladstone, M. Waddington, and M. de Lesseps made speeches. Leaders in *The Times* on the speeches at Guildhall and on Frenchmen at Guildhall.

November 15th. Trinity House Corporation entertained Mr. Chamberlain and M. de Lesseps. Leader in *The Times* on the Trinity House Banquet.

November 16th. M. de Lesseps visited Liverpool.

November 17th. M. de Lesseps, at a meeting of Liverpool Merchants, spoke on the Suez Canal. Leader in *The Times* on the Suez Canal.

November 19th. Egypt. The Government sent a note to the English Government asserting its right to be heard in any negotiations on the Suez Canal question.

M. de Lesseps addressed meetings at Manchester on the Suez Canal. He was entertained at luncheon by the Mayor.

November 20th. M. de Lesseps and his sons visited Newcastle.

November 21st. M. de Lesseps addressed a meeting of the Newcastle Chamber of Commerce, and also spoke at a banquet given in his honour in Newcastle.

Leader in *The Times* on M. de Lesseps.

November 22nd. M. de Lesseps spoke at a banquet in his honour at Jarrow.

November 25th. M. de Lesseps had an interview with the London Chamber of Commerce on the Suez Canal question.

November 26th. The Shipowners' Association held a meeting on the Suez Canal scheme. MM. Waddington and de Lesseps spoke. Lord Northbrook received a deputation in connexion with the movement to raise a memorial to the late Lieutenant Waghorn, the pioneer of the Overland Route.

Leader in *The Times* on the situation in Egypt.

November 30th. M. Charles de Lesseps had a long interview with the Shipowners' Association on the Suez Canal question.

December 1st. At a meeting of the Shipowners' Association an agreement was settled with M. Charles de Lesseps as desirable for the future administration of the Suez Canal.

Leader in *The Times* on the Suez Canal.

December 4th. France. Box sent by post containing dynamite to M. de Lesseps. No one injured, M. de Lesseps having been warned in time.

December 12th. The North of England Steamship Owners' Association declines to accept the Suez Canal agreement conducted in London.

December 13th. Leader in *The Times* on Egypt.

December 15th. Leader in *The Times* on Egyptian affairs.

December 19th. Lord R. Churchill, in a speech at Edinburgh, attacked the Egyptian policy of the Government.

December 21st. *The Times* officially contradicts the statement that Government had ordered increase of British troops in Egypt.

December 22nd. The Hull Chamber of Shipping passed a Resolution condemning the Suez Canal Agreement.

December 24th. Leader in *The Times* on the Egyptian question.

CHAPTER VI

THE NEUTRALIZATION OF THE SUEZ CANAL

Origin of idea. Definition of term. Status of neutrality. Proposals of Metternich and de Lesseps. Events of 1882. Proposals of British Government. Proposed Conference at Cairo. Convention of Constantinople, 1889. Tests of Convention in 1904. Anglo-French Agreement of 1906.

THE democratization of Western Governments during the past century has often made it necessary for statesmen and publicists, in order to win popular approval, to epitomize their policies in words and phrases marked less by lucidity than by brevity. The battle is half won if an epigrammatic label can be devised, and popularized. The word 'neutralization' was, until quite recently, such a label and, in its application to the Suez Canal, it was broad enough to hide the true facts of the situation and to shelter much fallacious reasoning.

Hallberg, whose treatment of the subject of this chapter in his *Suez Canal* is both comprehensive and lucid, ascribes the genesis of the idea of 'neutralizing' the Suez Canal to Prince Metternich, who suggested it to Muhammad Ali in 1838, and in a more definite form in 1841. The word itself appears for the first time in French in 1797, in a political sense not in English until 1875. The definition of the term is important. 'Lord Granville', writes Cromer (ii. 384), 'was evidently apprehensive lest the mere use of the word "neutrality" should carry him farther than he intended.' With commendable prudence therefore, he directed that, in dealing with this subject, its use should be avoided, and that the words 'freedom' or 'free navigation' should be substituted in its place.

A status of neutrality can only be conferred by international agreement, not by a unilateral act, and the fact that Article 14 of the second Act of Concession states that the canal shall always be open as a neutral passage has, of itself, no juridical validity.

De Lesseps submitted in 1856 to the Congress of Paris a formula whereby the signatory Powers guaranteed the neutrality of the canal, and agreed that no vessel could be seized therein or within four leagues of either end, nor could foreign troops be stationed on its banks without the consent of the territorial government. It was opposed by Lord Clarendon, and dropped.

Prince Metternich then suggested that the Viceroy of Egypt should himself propose a conference at Constantinople to provide for the neutrality of the canal. The Viceroy would not hear of it, regarding the proposal as dangerous to Egyptian interests. De Lesseps returned to the charge eight years later, suggesting an international agreement which should:

1. Proclaim the complete neutrality of the canal and freedom of passage for all merchant vessels at all times.
2. Prohibit war vessels not specially authorized by the territorial Power.
3. Prohibit the landing of troops in the Isthmus by ships passing through the canal, and the erection by the Company of any fortifications.

Nothing came at the time of this proposal, but the French Government raised it again in 1869, as did also an International Trade Conference at Cairo and in 1870, during the Franco-Prussian War, the Admiralty expressed a belief in the need for international agreement in the matter of neutrality.[1] No action was however taken.

In 1873, at the Tonnage Conference, a declaration (dated 14th Dec.) was adopted which recognized the right of warships and transports to employ the canal. What might happen to merchant vessels in case Turkey was at war was not discussed, but the principle that the navigation of the canal was under the protection of all Europe was, in principle, admitted. But this fell far short of 'neutralization'. In 1877 war broke out between Russia and Turkey: Russia would legally have been justified in landing troops on the Isthmus, as being Turkish territory. Lord Derby warned Russia that any attempt on the part of either belligerent to blockade or interfere with the canal would be inconsistent with the maintenance by the British Government of an attitude of passive neutrality. The Russian Government gave the desired undertaking, but the question remained open, and the Institute of International Law in 1878 and 1879 urged that the navigation of the canal 'should be placed by an international Act outside of all hostile acts during the war'. Nothing was done.

In 1882 the revolt of Arabi Pasha against the Khedive of Egypt imperilled the safety of the canal. During the period which preceded the battle of Tel-el-Kebir Lord Wolseley used the canal as his base of operations. Troops were landed at Suez and Port Said, and strong naval forces were stationed at Port Said under Admiral Hewett. Kantara, Ismailiya, and other stations on the canal were occupied. All ships in the canal or entering Suez were stopped: the entrance to the Fresh-water Canal was held and access to the railway and telegraph lines prevented. For three days the canal was in British hands, the staff of the canal having been ordered by de Lesseps to abandon their

[1] The presence of French warships at the approaches of the canal was the cause of their anxiety.

work, though all these actions were based upon a decree of the Khedive, dated 15th August, which recognized 'the military occupation charged to re-establish order in Egypt, and authorized them to occupy all the points necessary'. The occupation of the canal secured the closing of the campaign and of the war (see Nourse, p. 127). De Lesseps protested, but vainly, for British troops were in fact in Egypt for the benefit of and at the invitation of the territorial power of which de Lesseps was merely a subordinate *mandataire*. In 1883, after some preliminary conversations, the British Government suggested[1] to the principal European Powers that

1. The canal should be free for the passage of all ships in any circumstances.
2. In time of war, a limitation of time as to ships of war of a belligerent remaining in the canal should be fixed, and no troops or munitions of war should be disembarked in the canal.
3. No hostilities should take place in the canal or its approaches, or elsewhere in the territorial waters of Egypt, even in the event of Turkey being one of the belligerents.
4. (2) and (3) above not to apply to measures necessary for the defence of Egypt.
5. Any Power whose vessels of war happen to do any damage to the canal should be bound to bear the cost of its immediate repair.
6. Egypt to take all measures within its power to enforce the conditions imposed on the transit of belligerent vessels through the canal in time of war.
7. No fortifications should be erected on the canal or in its vicinity.
8. Nothing in the agreement shall be deemed to abridge or affect the territorial rights of Egypt further than is therein expressly provided.

Two years passed and nothing was done. Then, in February 1885, the French Government suggested a conference at Cairo. Lord Granville described the proposed conference as 'a useless excrescence', but agreed to a Committee of Experts to draft an agreement on the basis of the Circular. The British representatives were Sir Julian Pauncefote and Sir C. Rivers Wilson: they held that Lord Granville's Circular was the sole basis of the conference. The French delegates, with Russian and German support, propounded an alternative scheme for an International Commission to secure the protection of the canal—a method which really entailed its internationalization.

The Proceedings of the Conference[2] (covering over 300 foolscap closely printed pages) dragged on for over ten weeks and ended without agreement on 13th June. A draft Treaty was however elaborated, subject however to a general reservation by the British Delegation, 'as to the application of its provisions in so far as they would not be compatible with the present transitory and exceptional condition of Egypt,

---

[1] Dispatch dated 3rd January 1883. Egypt, No. 10, 1883, C. 4305.
[2] Egypt, No. 19, 1885.

and might fetter the liberty of action of Her Majesty's Government during the occupation of Egypt by the forces of Her Britannic Majesty'.

A few days later Mr. Gladstone's Government fell, and the question of neutralizing the canal was put aside for a time. Till 1887, when the question of free navigation of the canal was raised at Constantinople by Sir Henry Drummond Wolff, and a Convention drafted which embodied the views which had been maintained two years earlier by Sir Julian Pauncefote. This Convention was not ratified by the Sultan owing to strong protests from several Great Powers. Lord Salisbury, however, returned to the charge, and after lengthy negotiations a Convention[1] was signed at Constantinople on 29th October 1888, subject to the proviso, among others, that it was not to become effective during the British occupation of Egypt.

But the canal was not 'neutralized'—rather was it 'universalized'. The Convention forbade acts of hostility within its waters, but made it a corridor for all belligerents. As in the case of the Panama Canal, a single Power remains responsible for the protection of the Suez Canal, and that the Power interested more than any other in keeping it open. The first serious test of the British attitude was in 1904, when Russian warships passed through the canal on their way to fight Japan, then our ally, and one of the Russian vessels grossly violated the 'Egyptian Rules regarding coaling by belligerent warships in the Suez Canal'. *Exceptio probat legem*. The position was strengthened by our passivity on this occasion.

Nothing further was done in this matter until 1904. Under the Anglo-French Agreement, signed on 8th April of that year, the British Government agreed to give effect to the Suez Canal Convention of 1888 with the exception of those portions which established a Local International Board at Cairo to watch over the execution of the Convention. The relevant provision reads as follows:[2]

'In order to insure the free passage of the Suez Canal, H.B.M.'s Government declare that they adhere to the stipulations of the Treaty of 29th Oct. 1888, and that they agree to their being put into force. The free passage of the Canal being thus guaranteed, the execution of the last sentence of paragraph 1 as well as paragraph 2 of Article VIII of that Treaty will remain in abeyance.'

Lord Cromer adds:[3] 'The actual working of the Canal Convention was put to the test during the Russo-Japanese war. On the whole it may be said that it worked well but, as usually happens in such cases,

[1] Commercial No. 2, 1889, C. 3623.
[2] Treaty Series, 1911, No. 24, Cd. 5969. See also *British Documents on the Origins of the War*, vol: ii, p. 333, quoted by Hallberg, p. 307.
[3] *Modern Egypt*, ii. 387.

a number of questions of detail arose in respect to which the wording of the Convention was wanting in precision. It would be desirable that an opportunity should be taken to revise the Convention by the light of the experience which has now been gained.'

The actual effect of the Agreement of 1904 made no real difference to the status of Great Britain in relation to the canal or to Egypt. The authority conferred upon the Egyptian Government by Article IX of the Convention of 1888, to take the necessary measures for ensuring the execution of the said Treaty, necessarily entailed a delegation of this duty to Great Britain, whose relation thereto differs but little from that of the United States in the case of the Panama Canal, though in practice it is so unobtrusive as to be unobservable in time of peace.

The happy issue of the Algeciras Conference in January 1906 was followed by a sharp crisis in which Mr. Asquith's Cabinet had to show its teeth to the Turkish Government which had occupied a key position in the Gulf of Akabah whence it would be easy to bring the Turkish frontier up to the eastern bank of the Suez Canal. The measures adopted by the Cabinet were prompt, warlike, and effective, and resulted in an early settlement, and the present eastern frontier of Egypt follows the line then laid down. 'Some members of the Cabinet', writes Mr. Spender (op. cit. i. 180), 'were doubtful what their colleagues might say . . .', but where Abdul Hamid was concerned there was unanimity that force, or the threat of it, was the right remedy. The wisdom of the attitude adopted in 1907 was vindicated by the events of 1914. Abdul Hamid is dead, but his spirit lives on. 'Force is no remedy,' said Trevelyan; but Lyall comments, 'Had he lived in the East, he would have learned that it is sometimes the only remedy.'

BIBLIOGRAPHY

Hallberg. Op. cit.
Lawrence, T. J. *Principles of International Law*, 1910, pp. 198 sqq.
Parliamentary Papers. See volumes quoted *supra* in footnotes.
Public Record Office. F.O. 78/2170, 1869 to 1870. *Neutralization of Suez Canal.*
Spender, J. A., *Life of Lord Asquith.*
Zetland, The Marquess of, *Life of Lord Cromer*, 1932.

CHAPTER VII

THE SUEZ CANAL FROM 1889 TO 1914, AND THE ATTEMPT TO RENEW THE CONCESSION IN 1910

Growth of Prosperity: Increase of Traffic. Application for renewal of Concession. Sir Edward Grey's view. Sir Eldon Gorst's attitude. Preliminary discussion in the General Assembly of Egypt. Assassination of Boutros Pasha Ghali. Committee of Assembly recommends rejection of project. Discussion of Report. Zaghlul Pasha's views. Sidky Pasha's support. Rejection of Egyptian Government's proposals. Hostility to Great Britain. Discussion in House of Commons. Mr. G. J. Sandys. Sir E. Grey. Anomalous position of British Government.

THE conclusion of the Convention of 1888 removed the Suez Canal from the list of unsettled international questions. The Suez Canal Company itself, little affected by the diplomatic problems which it had created, continued a now well-established career of prosperity. The passenger traffic, which in 1881 had been 90,000, was doubled by 1889, and trebled by 1911, though subject to wide fluctuations during intervening years. The number of transits, 2,727, in 1881, was doubled by 1912 (5,373), and in the same year the total net tonnage of $5\frac{3}{4}$ millions in 1881 reached $20\frac{1}{4}$ millions. The proportion of British tonnage averaged about 78·6 per cent. during the five years 1881–5, but tended to fall slowly, and by 1912 was only 63·5 per cent.: it was, however, still four times as great as that of Germany, which held second place with $2\frac{3}{4}$ million tons, the Netherlands being third with $1\frac{1}{4}$ million tons, and France fourth on the list with 800,000 tons. The increase in British tonnage was, however, between the years 1875 and 1905, 37 per cent. greater than that of all other flags put together. Between 1908 and 1913 the number of ships bound for Australia and New Zealand more than doubled, and amounted in 1913 to nearly 10 per cent. of the total traffic through the canal. Ships bound for Europe from Australia, New Zealand, were, however, in 1908 more than twice as numerous as those bound in the opposite direction: this proportion has tended to increase, and over 75 per cent. of the outward bound shipping from Europe to Australia now goes via the Cape, as the saving of 1,000 miles between London and Melbourne is more than outweighed by the burden of canal dues.

The period with which this chapter deals was one of increasing commercial prosperity in almost every country in the world. The Canal Company's gross receipts rose from 55 million francs in 1881 to nearly 140 million francs in 1912, and the market price of the 500-franc shares rose from about 2,000 francs in 1881 to 2,600 francs in 1891, 3,700 francs in 1901, and 6,100 francs in 1912. During the same period the Canal Company greatly improved its properties, widened and deepened the canal, and shortened the time taken in transit. Most efficient bunkering and repair services grew up under private enterprise, and shipowners were thus encouraged to acquire a subsidiary and indirect interest in the working of the canal. The position of the British directors, whether appointed by Government or nominated by the London Committee, in the proportion that it became more remunerative, became less responsible, and Sir John Stokes and Sir Charles Rivers Wilson, a former Consul-General at Alexandria, were succeeded by men whose distinction in official life was greater than their qualifications to represent His Majesty's Treasury or the British Empire on the board of a great commercial concern. When a Government directorship became vacant by death the Government of the day nominated men[1] whose past services it was desired to recognize by the grant of a substantial old-age pension.

In 1909 the Suez Canal Company applied to the Egyptian Government for an extension of their concession for a further period of forty years, from 1968 to 2008. Their proposal, in the form finally put forward,[2] provided for the payment by the Company of a capital sum of £E 4 millions and a share of the annual receipts rising from 4 per cent. in 1922 to 12 per cent. in 1961. From 1968 onwards the profits were to be shared equally by the Company and the Egyptian Government. The Egyptian Government would nominate a maximum of three directors to the Board.

The proposal was undoubtedly profitable to Egypt, but it was even more profitable to the Company. The Company's title to charge as much as the traffic would bear, subject to a maximum of 10 francs per ton plus pilotage and other charges, was not to be restricted. The right of the 'fondateurs ou ayant droit' (M. de Lesseps' descendants or coadjutors) to 10 per cent. of the profits was to be perpetuated, as also that of the directors to 2 per cent. of the profits. (Their individual share would not have been appreciably diminished by the addition of three Egyptians to their number.) The Concession was to be textually renewed, without revision, though both in substance and in form it was, as was to be expected after a lapse of over forty years, defective and ambiguous, and in many respects obsolete. No attempt was to be made to revise the statutes of the Company in conformity with generally accepted models, or to define the Company's responsibilities,

---

[1] See Appendix B to this chapter.
[2] The draft concession and the note attached thereto, as submitted to the General Assembly in Egypt, are reproduced in full as Appendix A to this chapter.

liabilities, and immunities in the light of modern conditions. The status of the Company as holders till 1968 of the right conferred on them by the Territorial Power in 1854 to levy, for services rendered, sums sufficient to yield a dividend of 100 per cent. per annum or so would remain inviolate;[1] the interests of international commerce were at no time publicly mentioned, nor, as far as can be ascertained from published records, even officially discussed.

The great Maritime Powers do not seem to have realized the magnitude of the issues at stake: and, so far as is known, made no representations to the British or Egyptian Governments on the subject in 1909 when the question was first raised. Sir Edward Grey, as Secretary of State for Foreign Affairs, announced in Parliament on 4th November 1909 that the proposed extension of the Suez Canal Company's concession would be brought before the General Assembly in Egypt, and that in the meantime it was inadvisable that any discussion should take place. On 25th November he definitely refused facilities for a discussion. Even after the project had been laid before the General Assembly he declined to lay papers on the subject before Parliament, 'as the question was not under the control of His Majesty's Government'. Though Sir Eldon Gorst, the British Agent and Consul-General at Cairo, had described it as 'of exceptional importance to present and future generations' [of Egyptians] it was not considered proper to permit the House of Commons, representing a nation under whose flag 70 per cent. of the shipping using the canal sailed, to express any opinion on the subject of the extension of the Concession until the General Assembly of Egypt had approved, or rejected it—that is to say until it was too late to take effective action. The immediate domestic interests of Egypt alone carried weight.

The proposal was submitted on the morning of 9th February 1910 to the General Assembly in its second session by the Khedive Abbas Hilmi with an explanatory memorandum and a note[2] which indicated the alterations demanded by the Egyptian Government and accepted by the Company.

These documents included a long explanatory memorandum which expressed the fear that the eventual interests of Egypt in the canal, and its potential value, might be affected by the following factors:

(1) a reduction of the canal dues to 5 francs, 'in conformity with an undertaking given by the Company' (no such clause appears in the Convention),

(2) the known intention of the Company to reduce the dues before

---

[1] Zaghlul Pasha's admissions on this subject (see p. 99) are of particular interest.

[2] Vide appendix to this chapter. I have not reproduced the note of the British Adviser, which was marked 'Confidential'.

the end of the Concession in a manner designed to damage the interests of the Egyptian Government, in the event of failure to agree upon terms of renewal,

(3) competition of the Panama Canal (see Chap. X),

(4) diminished importance of the canal as a result of scientific discoveries and the creation of new ways and means of communication,

(5) the possibility that when the canal reverted to the Egyptian Government it might be compelled to permit ships to pass through the canal free of charge or at a greatly reduced rate.

It is scarcely a matter of surprise that a proposal, however financially advantageous, supported by such arguments should have been examined in a spirit of criticism, and ultimately rejected with contumely.

In recommending the project for acceptance the Khedive observed that the General Assembly had been convened for the sole purpose of considering the proposed agreement with the Suez Canal Company. Although the matter did not come within the category of questions which should be submitted to the Assembly for advice, yet, owing to its exceptional importance to present as well as future generations, the Council of Ministers had decided to withhold ratification, pending consideration by the Assembly, of the project, which was recommended by their financial advisers, headed by Sir Paul Harvey.

Having thus spoken the Khedive left the Chamber, amidst the cheers of the Deputies led, as President of the Assembly, by his uncle H.H. Prince Husain Kamal, the present King, and business was adjourned till the afternoon of the same day, when Muhammad Shawarby Pasha and Amin el Shamsy Pasha pressed for the appointment of a committee to investigate the project. Abdu Latif Bey el Sufany, on the other hand, proposed to adjourn the discussion till the following day: this was approved.

On 10th February the debate was resumed by Amin el Shamsy Pasha, who commenced to speak on lines unfavourable to the Agreement. He was, however, cut short, and a committee[1] was appointed to consider the documents laid before them by the Khedive.

This done a Deputy (Ismail Pasha Abaza) asked whether the decision of the General Assembly would be conclusive or regarded

[1] The Committee consisted of nineteen members of whom four, shown in brackets, resigned: [Mohammed Eloui Pasha, Ahmed Afify Pasha, Morcos Semaika Bey Pasha, Tolba Seudi Pasha], Mahmoud Soliman Pasha (Chairman) Ismail Abaza Pasha, Hassan Madkur Pasha, Ibrahim Murad Pasha, Ahmed Yehya Pasha, Aly Sha'rawy Pasha, Mahmoud Bey Abd El Ghaffar, Hassan Bey Bakry, Fathallah Barakat Bey Pasha, Abdel Latif El-Sufany Bey, Gad Moustapha Bey, Saad Makram, Diab Effendi Mohammed Selim, Amin Bey El-Aaref, and Ismail Effendi Kerim.

merely as advisory. The Premier, Boutros Pasha Ghali, evaded the question by declaring that Government could add nothing to the khedivial speech and, though strongly pressed by Abdul Latif Bey Sufany and Ismail Abaza Pasha, declined to commit his Government. The debate, which became heated, lasted a little more than an hour and was adjourned by the President. On 21st February, before the discussion could be resumed, the Premier was murdered on the steps of the Ministry of Justice as he stepped into his carriage. The crime was purely political. The assassin, a young Egyptian, possessed just the kind of character to be influenced by the violent tirades in the Cairo press against 'the betrayal of the Nation in the interests of the Canal Company's shareholders'. He had just completed a medical course in London and did the deed under the direct instructions of certain men who were never brought to justice. Boutros Pasha Ghali was an able and upright Egyptian, devoted to the interests of his country. He was also a Coptic Christian: as such, and as the Prime Minister of a Government which had, on the unanimous recommendation of its British advisers, urged acceptance of the Convention, he was a natural target for the arrows of fanaticism. He had, moreover, been compelled in 1906 by Lord Cromer to sit as a member of the Special Tribunal which tried the Denshawi case, though he was wholly without judicial experience.

The decision to refer the matter to the General Assembly, which thus cost the Premier his life, was, of course, taken at the instance of Sir Eldon Gorst, who misjudged its probable attitude and rated too highly the influence that the Khedive and his Ministers could exercise. Lord Cromer would scarcely have fallen into such a trap; he would have scented the strength of the opposition (as in the case of his proposed reform of the Capitulations) and dropped the scheme.

On 15th March the Committee submitted its report to the General Assembly, advising rejection of the scheme on the following grounds:

(1) The scheme should not have been submitted to the General Assembly till approved by the Company's shareholders.

(2) The Assembly had no power to modify the scheme.

(3) It would entail upon Egypt a loss of over £130 millions.

(4) The fears of the Government as to possible scientific discoveries and inventions in methods of transit and the establishment of overland routes, &c., were not well-founded, and the Company might in the future be inclined to offer better terms.

(5) There was no urgent financial necessity for renewing the Concession in consideration of a cash payment. To do so was to mortgage the future to the detriment of posterity.

(6) There was no provision for financial control of the Company.

On 4th April the General Assembly met to receive and consider this Report. The visitors' galleries were crowded to overflowing. All the Ministers were present and two Under-Secretaries of State, Fathy Zaghlul Pasha—Zaghlul's brother and Sidky Pasha—sat behind the members of the Assembly. Public interest had been aroused, and a crowd had already assembled to watch the arrival of leading political figures.

Mohammed Saïd Pasha, the new Prime Minister, began by re-capitulating the history of the project which the Government had modified after careful study; before taking a decision it was desired to ascertain the views of the Assembly, which had accordingly been con-voked, although this was not legally necessary. The Assembly had heard the proposal and memorandum of the Financial Adviser on the question and had appointed a Committee which had duly reported. On its report the Government had made certain observations which were commended to the consideration of the Assembly by the Prime Minister, who concluded by announcing that the decision of the As-sembly would, without creating a precedent, be regarded as final and binding. The announcement was loudly applauded.

Saad Zaghlul Pasha, Minister of Justice, followed in support of the scheme. He expounded the memorandum in detail, emphasizing that the scheme was purely financial and non-political. It did not entail the loss of the canal, but was merely an extension of an already existing lease which could in no way affect the future status of Egypt. Zaghlul Pasha then proceeded to make comment in detail on the Report of the Committee. After speaking for an hour he showed signs of fatigue and asked his colleague Sirry Pasha to read a certain part of his remarks which were based on a printed memorandum. After some time he resumed his speech, explaining at great length that Egypt would in all probability be forced to make the passage in the canal free when it reverted to her; unless the administration was conducted by a com-mercial company it would be impossible to induce the Powers to submit to the continued imposition of dues on a scale sufficient to yield large commercial profits. The proposals of the Company entailed a large cash payment which could be used for various projects. Sirry Pasha here read a statement on irrigation and drainage schemes, involving the expenditure of £E 16,000,000, destined to bring under the plough no less than 1,600,000 acres of desert or lake.

Zaghlul Pasha concluded his great speech by urging acceptance of the scheme. He deprecated the idea of rejection on the ground that the nation had no control over public expenditure; it was wrong to refuse benefits merely because Egypt had as yet no Constitution.

Abaza Pasha and Sufany Bey expressed satisfaction at the intention of the Government to accept the decision of the Assembly, but urged rejection in speeches of considerable length. After other speeches the discussion was adjourned to Thursday, 7th April.

When the Assembly resumed its deliberations the debate was opened by Abaza Pasha, who reiterated his conviction that the Government had not proved its case. He was followed by Zaghlul's nephew, Barakat Bey, who announced that the Committee of General Assembly had prepared a reply to the Government. He moved that it be read and the vote of the Assembly taken afterwards.

The reply of the Committee was duly read: though couched in sympathetic terms it again advised the rejection of the scheme. It was loudly applauded from the public galleries, crowded with boys of all ages between 5 and 20 years. About 50 members of the Assembly then rose in their seats and declared amidst wild applause that they would reject the canal scheme. Zaghlul Pasha, the spokesman of the Ministry, who had been taking notes and shaking his head disapprovingly during the reading of the Committee's reply, rose to speak; it was some time before his voice could be heard. But he had hardly began to speak when Abaza Pasha rose to ask him why he wished to continue the debate.

Zaghlul Pasha answered that he wished to comment on the last statement of the Committee, but Abaza Pasha declared that the debate on the subject had been finally closed and that the vote should be taken at once. Zaghlul refused indignantly to submit to the behest of any private member and insisted upon his right to answer for the Government. Abaza Pasha again interrupted, claiming that the Assembly having accepted the motion of Barakat Bey there should be no further discussion.

Some forty or fifty members of the Assembly supported Abaza Pasha in his endeavour to silence Zaghlul; who at last managed to make his voice heard. 'Why do you interrupt me?' he shouted, 'By what right do you endeavour to prevent a member of the Government from making his statement? Have I no right to speak here, and is this how you mean to carry future motions or conduct serious affairs? Gentlemen, you are acting against fair play and right, and also against your best interests by trying to silence me; the very procedure you are now employing against me will be used against you yourselves. It is clear that you wish to make this grave decision without hearing the explanation of the Government, which has given it most careful study! I deeply regret the fact, for it has always been my desire to see your opinion respected; that is possible only when you make your decisions after hearing all that can be said on the subject. You are committing a great error, as the Government is not your enemy and we are not the other party in a lawsuit. We, the members of the Government and the members of your Assembly, are one and the same company working for one and the same end. We are members of the same body and no member has the right to enforce silence upon another member. We are here to act upon the principle of liberty, not to stifle and oppose liberty of speech.'

Abaza Pasha retorted, at great length, that every discussion should end somewhere. If they were to allow the Government now to study this last report and make a new statement in reply, there would be no end to the matter, and the present Suez Canal concession would have expired before the last word was said. (Cheers.)

Zaghlul Pasha urged that a reply by the Government was imperative seeing that the report in question had been kept secret to the last minute. 'Before entering this hall', declared the Minister, 'I asked the President about this new report, and he said that he had not seen it. I am therefore asking to make my observations on a document which I had no means of seeing before this moment. Why should you try to silence me? By vindicating the principle of the liberty of speech in your Assembly, I am serving you better than those who pretend to be the advocates of your rights.'

Several members here tried to speak on either side, but were not heard in the general uproar.

At last the Minister abandoned his attempt to speak; the discussion was closed, and the whole Assembly, with the exception of the Ministers and Semaika Bey,[1] thereupon voted for the summary rejection of the scheme amidst deafening applause.

Members, visitors, employees of the Assembly, journalists, and others were seen embracing one another and exchanging congratulations on the outcome of the debate, while a crowd of some 15,000 persons, mostly youths of school age, proceeded to parade the town with music and banners. For almost the first time the streets of Cairo resounded with the cry of 'Down with the Army of Occupation' and 'Down with England'.

The opinion was widely expressed at the time that the scheme, thus unequivocally condemned, had been inadequately studied and had never received impartial consideration at the hands of experts. It is difficult to resist the conclusion that the General Assembly decided rightly in rejecting the Convention although, in fact, the vote was intended to be an indication of hostility to Great Britain, and of the intention of the Notables to condemn every scheme, irrespective of its merits, proposed by the Government. It was, however, as observed

---

[1] Semaika Bey's acceptance of the project was subject to certain conditions which he had expounded and distributed to all members in pamphlet form, doubtless with a view to inclusion in the procès-verbal of this momentous Assembly.

twenty years later by Abbas Hilmi II,[1] greatly to be regretted that no counter proposition was put forward.

Some months later the matter was raised again in the House of Commons when Sir J. D. Rees asked the Secretary of State for Foreign Affairs whether measures would be taken to support the British financial and commercial interests adversely affected by the rejection of the proposed extension of the Suez Canal Company's concession which, he said, was stigmatized by Sir E. Gorst as displaying an entire lack of confidence in the intentions and good faith of the Government on the part of the Egyptian General Assembly. Sir E. Grey replied that it was a matter which primarily concerned the Egyptian Government and the Suez Canal Company. There was no reason for intervention in British interests; if His Majesty's Government did exert their influence in Egypt in a case of this kind, it must be from the point of view of the Egyptian interests. He had no knowledge of any correspondence that had passed between the Company and Sir E. Gorst, or between Sir E. Gorst and the Egyptian Government, nor did he possess copies of correspondence between the Company and the Government of Egypt.

A fortnight later the question of the Suez Canal Convention was raised, on 21st July, by Capt. G. J. Sandys (M.P. for Wells), who regretted that no discussion on the subject in the Commons had been permitted until the matter had been settled one way or another. 'I have come to the conclusion', he said, 'that there has been a tendency to treat this matter as one concerning Egypt alone, in which the people of this country are not deeply interested. . . . In view of the attitude adopted by the Government, we should insist on the fact that the Suez Canal is of great national importance to us as well as to Egypt. . . . Anything that effects its future must be of the greatest importance to this country and to the Empire.' The proposed extension of the Concession, he continued, to 2008 was, as Sir E. Gorst said, a satisfactory bargain from the Egyptian point of view, but on the subject of British representation on the board of directors, and on the matter of canal dues, the Report was silent. He considered that any extension of the Convention should provide for representation more in keeping with our shareholding. As to canal dues, he observed that the Agreement of 1883 had not been kept, though dividends reached 28 per cent. in 1909, dues were still 7·75 francs, instead of 5 francs.

Sir Edward Grey replied that he regarded the question as one for the Egyptian Government, which should have a free hand in dealing with the Suez Canal Company, to make the best bargain in the interests of Egypt. The bargain having been made, it was for the British

[1] *A few Words on the Anglo-Egyptian Settlement*, 1930.

Government to review the proposed Convention to see whether, regarded impartially, it was a good bargain or not in the interests of Egypt. If not, we should point out in what respect it required amendment, otherwise, he was bound to let the Egyptian Government proceed, and keep the matter of British interests for separate consideration. He believed it to have been a good bargain, but it was not essential to Egypt that the Concession should be renewed.

Continuing, Sir E. Grey said:

'We have also to look at any question of the extension of the Suez Canal Concession from the point of view of British interests. That, I think, we ought to reserve, and we did partly reserve, for discussion between the British directors and their colleagues on the Board of Directors. That was the natural place for us to bring forward our interests, and, as a matter of fact, considerable discussion took place. First of all, there is the point of view of the shareholders, which is the Treasury point of view, and then there is the point of view of the shipowners, which the Board of Trade had carefully to consider. We had to consider these great interests, and they were very carefully considered by the Treasury and the Board of Trade, as well as by the Foreign Office, in conjunction with those two Departments, and in consultation, too, with the official directors of the Suez Canal Company. Our directors on the Board of the Company are, and always have been, on terms of the utmost cordiality with their colleagues on the Board, and the discussions which took place between them would, I believe, have resulted in such conclusions with regard to the future administration of the Company, that the prolongation of the Concession might well have been recommended to this country from the point of view of British interests. But a good deal more had to be discussed. There was the question of representation on the Suez Canal Board which has been under discussion here for many years. It has been carefully considered by the Board of Trade. Considerable difficulties attach to it.

'Then, again, there is the question of the reduction of the Canal dues. These are matters of the utmost importance, and had the negotiations proceeded, undoubtedly the prolongation of the Suez Canal Concession would have been discussed and criticized from both those points in this House. But in my opinion these are matters to be considered by the Treasury and the Board of Trade when the question of the extension of the Concession again comes up, both from the point of view of the reduction of the dues and that of representation on the Board. Undoubtedly, if the negotiations are resumed and reach a conclusion, the question will be discussed in this House, and the Government of the day will have to put before the House the considerations which guided them in instructing the official directors as to the vote they may give either for or against the prolongation of the Concession. From the point of view of British interests I think it is our duty to put these matters before the Company through our official directors, although, of course, in any future action the Government of the day will be responsible for the instructions given to and votes given by the official directors. I trust I have made this complicated question somewhat clearer than it was when the Debate first began. It is extremely difficult for any one in my position to deal with this question, having both points of view to consider; I have endeavoured to steer a perfectly straight course and to be fair to the interests of Egypt, while giving due consideration at the same time to British interests. . . . The question of the Suez Canal concession is a complicated matter, and requires to be elucidated.'

On this note the debate concluded. The interests of the British Empire were scarcely mentioned in the debate; the interests of the other great Maritime Powers were not discussed, nor the inevitable repercussions of the Panama Canal, the completion of which was by this time assured. No papers were laid on the table: a question on which, thirty years earlier, voluminous papers had been presented to Parliament was declared to be 'not under the control of His Majesty's Government', which was, as in Mr. Gladstone's day, deeply embarrassed by the anomalous position in which it was placed as

(1) owner of 46 per cent. of the shares,
(2) guardian of the interests of Egypt,
(3) protector of the Canal Zone in the event of war,
(4) guardian of the interests of British shipping then constituting 70 per cent. of the total canal traffic,
(5) responsible for instructing its three directors on the Board whose existence made it convenient and indeed necessary that the views of the British Government should be made through them, though they had no power to enforce their views.

British shipping interests seem to have taken little or no interest in the matter. The view generally taken was that 'the Company could do what it liked and no one could say anything'—in any event it was useless to expect the British Government to move, as they held nearly half the shares and wanted to make as big a profit as possible. It was the first instance of participation on a large scale by the British Government in commercial undertakings on foreign soil: financial success obscured the political and commercial evils entailed.

BIBLIOGRAPHY

Abbas Hilmi II. *A few words on the Anglo-Egyptian Settlement.* 1930.
M. Travers Symons. *The Riddle of Egypt.* (n.d.)
Official Publications of Egyptian Government. 1910.
Contemporary journals published in Cairo during 1910, and the files of *The Times,* have also been consulted.

APPENDIX A

The French official Texts of the Draft Convention with the Suez Canal Company for the Prolongation of its Concession and the Note attached thereto, as submitted to the General Assembly of the Egyptian Government and read during the debate of Wednesday, 9th February 1910.

NOTE

A L'Assemblée Générale relative au Project de Convention avec la Compagnie du Canal de Suez.

La Compagnie du Canal de Suez a fait au Gouvernement des propositions pour la prolongation de sa concession. Après de longs pourparlers, le project de convention ci-annexé fut rédigé et soumis au Conseil des Ministres. Le Conseil en sa séance du jeudi 27 janvier 1910, présidé par S. A. le Khédive, a unanimement été d'avis que le projet en question en sa forme primitive devrait être écarté; qu'il pourrait toutefois être accepté à condition que les modifications suivantes y soient apportées:

1° La garantie de Frs. 50,000,000 par an accordée à la Compagnie pour la période de la prolongation d'après l'art. 11. Elle doit être entièrement supprimée; en d'autres termes le partage des bénéfices de 1969 à 2008 devra s'effectuer absolument par moitiés, sans aucun prélèvement privilégié de la Compagnie.

2° La participation de 50% ainsi assurée au Gouvernement doit commencer non pas à partir du 1er janvier 1969, mais bien à partir du 17 novembre 1968, point de départ de la prolongation.

3° L'art. 8, aux termes duquel le Gouvernement devrait assumer la charge des pensions, retraites et secours des employés de la Compagnie, à partir du 2009, date de l'expiration de la concession, doit être supprimé.

Toutefois comme c'est uniquement en raison de la charge des pensions et de retraites assumée par le Gouvernement égyptien que la Compagnie acceptait de payer à ce dernier la somme de £E90,000 stipulés à l'art. 9 du projet, et comme d'autre part le Gouvernement égyptien se trouvera exonéré de la charge ci-dessus, le Conseil des Ministres serait disposé à faire, par contre, abandon de la dite somme de £E90,000.

Le Conseil serait également disposé à régler à cette occasion la question soulevée par la Compagnie de l'attribution des terrains qui viendraient à être éventuellement conquis sur la mer à Port Saïd par suite de l'exécution de travaux que la Compagnie effectuerait à ses frais.

Le Conseil n'est pas d'avis d'attribuer des terrains à la Compagnie, mais accepterait de stipuler qu'ils soient consignés au Domaine Commun.

PROJET DE CONVENTION

Article Premier

La concession de la Compagnie Universelle du Canal Maritime de Suez qui devait, à défaut d'entente entre le Gouvernement égyptien et la Compagnie, expirer le 17 décembre, 1968 est prolongée jusqu'au 31 décembre, 2008.

Article 2

Pour la période comprise entre le 1er janvier 1969 et le 31 décembre 2008, le partage des produits nets ou bénéfices annuels de l'entreprise sera effectué à raison de 50% attribués au Gouvernement égyptien et 50% à la Compagnie, sous réserve des stipulations ci-après:

1° Au cas où le montant des produits nets ou bénéfices serait, pour une année quelconque de la dite période, inférieur à cent millions de francs, la Compagnie prélèverait par privilège une somme de cinquante millions et le Gouvernement égyptien ne recevrait que le surplus.

2° S'il advenait que le montant des produits nets ou bénéfices fût, pour une année quelconque, égal ou inférieur à cinquante millions de francs, la totalité de ces produits nets ou bénéfices de l'exercice serait attribuée à la Compagnie.

La participation ainsi reservée au Gouvernement égyptien implique l'abandon par lui, à partir du 1er janvier 1969, des 15 % qui lui sont attribués aux termes de l'article 63 des Statuts de la Compagnie.

Art. 3

En échange de la prolongation de la concession, la Compagnie s'engage à verser au Gouvernement égyptien, au Caire, une somme de £E4,000,000 (Frs. 103,694,000) en quatre termes égaux payables les 15 décembre 1910, 15 décembre 1911, 15 décembre 1912, et 15 décembre 1913.

Art. 4

La Compagnie s'engage en outre à opérer au profit du Gouvernement égyptien, sur les produits nets ou bénéfices de l'entreprise, un prélèvement, qui commencera à s'exercer à compter de l'exercice 1921 et dont les taux sont fixés d'après l'échelle ci-après:

de 4% de 1921 à 1930   de 6% de 1931 à 1940
de 8% de 1941 à 1950   de 10% de 1951 à 1960
de 12% de 1961 à 1968

La part de la bénéfice ainsi attribuée au Gouvernement égyptien sera déterminée dans les mêmes conditions que le dividende des actionnaires et sans distinction d'aucune sorte; elle sera payée aux même dates.

La Société civile bénéficiaire jusqu'au 17 novembre 1968 du 15 % attribué au Gouvernement par l'art. 18 de l'acte de concession du 5 janvier 1856, ne devra pas participer aux charges résultant pour la Compagnie de l'art. 3 ci-dessus ainsi que du présent article.

Art. 5

Dans le règlement des comptes des exercices postérieurs à 1968 pour la détermination de la part revenant au Gouvernement en vertu des stipulations de l'article 2 de la présente convention, les seuls emprunts dont les charges entreront en ligne de compte seront ceux contractés postérieurement à 1910, en vue des travaux d'amélioration du Canal et de ses ports d'accès exécutés à partir de 1911, sous réserve que les charges d'intérêts et l'amortissement soient répartis à l'aide d'une annuité égale sur toute la durée de ces emprunts.

La part revenant au Gouvernement sera déterminée dans les mêmes conditions que le dividende des actionnaires, mais seulement tout autant qu'il n'y aura pas lieu de faire des applications des réserves contenues à l'alinéa précédent.
Elle sera dans tous les cas payée aux mêmes dates.

Art. 6

Il est specifié que la participation du Gouvernement s'éxercera, dans la proportion de 50 %, à la fin de la concession sur tout reliquat de l'actif social après retour au Gouvernement du Canal Maritime dans les conditions prévues par l'acte de concession du 5 janvier 1856.

Art. 7

La Compagnie admet qu'il y aura lieu, à partir de 1969, d'assurer la représentation des intérêts égyptiens au sein du Conseil d'Administration, en raison de la participation importante qui sera alors reservée au Gouvernement dans les bénéfices de l'entreprise.

Il est dès à present stipulé qu'à la demande du Gouvernement égyptien, trois sièges, au maximum, seront attribués à des administrateurs désignés par lui, présentés par le Conseil d'Administration et nommés par l'assemblée Générale dans les formes usitées.

Art. 8

A la demande de la Compagnie, le Gouvernement accepte d'assumer, lorsque la concession prendra fin, la charge du service de retraites, pensions et secours, tel qu'il résultera de l'application des règlements actuellement en vigueur concernant les employés, pilotes et ouvriers, règlements dont des exemplaires ont été remis au Gouvernement.

Art. 9

La Compagnie s'engage, pour l'avenir, à exécuter elle-même et à ses frais les travaux d'entretien et d'amélioration qu'elle jugera utiles pour maintenir en bonne condition les accès du Canal Maritime de la côte de Suez. Elle accepte en outre de prendre à sa charge, jusqu'à concurrence de £E90,000 (Frs. 2,333,070) la dépense des dragages en cours dans la rade de Suez, entreprise par le Gouvernement égyptien pour l'approfondissement de la passe donnant accès au Canal.

Art. 10

Il est spécifié que dans tous les actes, Conventions ou Accords intervenus antérieurement entre le Gouvernement et la Compagnie, les dispositions se rapportant directement ou indirectement à la durée ou s'appliquant à la durée ou à l'expiration de la concession telle quelle seront prolongées par la présente Convention.

Art. 11

La présente Convention ne sera définitive et ne produira ses effets que lorsqu'elle aura été ratifiée par l'Assemblée Générale des Actionnaires de la Compagnie.

APPENDIX B

LIST OF BRITISH DIRECTORS

Representing His Majesty's Government

1876 {
- Colonel (afterwards Sir) John Stokes, R.E.
- (Sir) C. Rivers Wilson, K.C.B.
- E. J. Standen

1891	(Sir) Henry Austin Lee	vice E. J. Standen.
1896	Sir C. W. Fremantle	„ Sir C. Rivers Wilson.
1902	General Sir John Ardagh	„ Sir John Stokes.
1903	H. T. Anstruther	„ Sir C. W. Fremantle.
1917	Sir W. Garstin	„ Sir John Ardagh.
1919	Lord Downham	„ Sir W. Garstin.[1]
1920	*Sir Ian Malcolm*	„ Sir H. A. Lee.
1922	*Sir J. T. Davies*	„ Lord Downham.
1926	*Earl of Cromer*	„ H. T. Anstruther.

Nominated by 'The London Committee'.

1884 {
- Robert Alexander
- (Sir) James Laing
- (Sir) Wm. Mackinnon, M.P.
- C. J. Monk, M.P.
- Sir C. M. Palmer, M.P.
- John Stagg, M.P.
- (Sir) Thomas Sutherland, M.P.

Lord Brassey
R. S. Donkin
Sir E. S. Dawes
Sir Henry Calcraft
Lord Rathmore
Sir Fred. Greene
J. B. Westray
Sir J. L. Mackay
   (Lord Inchcape)
J. W. Hughes.
Oswald Sanderson.
Lord Kylsant.
Sir Aubrey Brocklebank.
T. Harrison Hughes, vice-chairman.
Sir Alan Anderson.
Sir John Cadman.
Sir Robert Horne, M.P.
Sir Thomas Royden.
Sir E. Wyldbore-Smith.
Sir A. Cayzer.

NOTE. Those in italics were in office in October 1933.

[1] A question was asked in Parliament in 1919, but never answered, as to the circumstances attending the involuntary resignation of Sir William Garstin and his replacement by Lord Downham, who, as Mr. Hayes Fisher, was President of the Local Government Board from 1917–19 and later Chairman of the L.C.C. With this exception all Government directorships have been for life.

CHAPTER VIII

THE FINANCES OF THE SUEZ CANAL COMPANY

First allotment of profits in 1875. Financial situation, 1870–83. Cost of improvements. Increase of traffic. Dues levied, 1884–1913. Dividends, 1883–1903. Dividends, 1904–13. Cost of improvements, 1884–1913. Loans in 1887. Suez Canal Accounts, 1884–1914. Surplus profits, 1884–1913. Causes of variation in traffic figures. Suez Canal Traffic, 1890–1912. Cargoes, 1911–13.

Canal traffic receipts, 1914–31. Fluctuations during war period. Suez Canal Accounts, 1914–19. Surplus profits, 1914–19. Traffic variations. Suez Canal Accounts, 1920–7. Surplus profits, 1920–7. Dividends, 1920–7. Suez Canal Accounts, 1928–31. Surplus profits, 1928–31. Remuneration of Directors. Cost of improvements, 1914–19. How met. Summary of Balance Sheet of 31st December 1931. Summary of net profits, 1870–1931, and discussion of principles. Dues and goods, comparative figures: classes of goods carried: incidence of dues of various commodities and per cargo ton.

Table I. Suez Canal Receipts. Table II. Suez Canal Payments. Table III. Suez Canal Division of Surplus Profits. Table IV. Suez Canal Traffic—by Nationalities. Table V. Traffic through Suez Canal with countries east and south.

AFTER the increase in dues and the funding of arrears of interest the Company began to pay its way, and the first allotment of 'surplus profits' was made in 1875. According to the Statutes, after meeting the general and administrative expenses of the canal, the service of the bonds, and 5 per cent. (plus 0·04 per cent. sinking fund) on the unredeemed capital, 5 per cent. was to be allotted to the statutory reserve till it reached 5 million francs, and the remainder was to be distributed as follows: 71 per cent. to the original shares, redeemed or not, 15 per cent. to the Egyptian Government, 10 per cent. to the holders of founders' shares (originally 100 of no par value, then divided into 1,000 for 1876–9 and then into 100,000), 2 per cent. to the directors, and 2 per cent. to the staff (for pensions, &c.). 'Actes de jouissance' are issued in respect of redeemed shares, and different rates are paid on these and the other shares according as they are 'to bearer' or not, and tax is deducted. In 1880 the Egyptian Government share was transferred to the Crédit Foncier de France in part satisfaction of debt, and was by them sold to a French Société Civile (administered by the Comptoir National d'Escompte) for 22 million francs.

The financial situation of the Company from the beginning of 1870 to the end of 1883 may be summarized as follows:

RECEIPTS	Thousand francs.	PAYMENTS	Thousand francs.
Dues: Shipping . . .	409·142	Administration . . .	15·254
Passenger . . .	11·435	Transit	23·489
Other . . .	31·639	Maintenance . . .	30·974
		Lands, water, &c. . .	13·320
Total . .	452·216	Bond Interest, &c.[1] . .	161·088
Investments, &c. . . .	8·341	Shares: Dividend, &c. . .	121·547
Estates	9·502	Reserve	6·235
Other Receipts . . .	10·247	Surplus Profit . . .	118·483
		Total	490·390
		Charged to Capital Account (1870/1) . .	12·232
			478·158
		Carried forward 'en fonds special'	2·148
	480·306		480·306

The surplus profit was distributed as follows:

		Thousand francs.
Shareholders	71 per cent.	84,122
Egyptian Government . .	15 ,,	17,774
Founders' shares . . .	10 ,,	11,847
Directors	2 ,,	2,370
Staff	2 ,,	2,370
Total		118,483

The surplus profits distributed to shareholders started with 1·88 frs. per share in 1875 and reached 63·657 frs. in 1883, or 12·73 per cent. in addition to the 5 per cent. of statutory dividend. Taken over the whole fourteen years from 1870, the shareholders' portion of 'surplus' profits averaged 6,008,000 frs. annually or 15 frs. per share, say 3 per cent., making 8 per cent. in all, but up till 1880 they drew but little over 5 per cent. from an undertaking which at its inception was undoubtedly risky. The directors also in 1883 could have drawn about 30,000 frs., say £1,200 for each of the twenty-four, but 1882 was the first year in which a director could have drawn more than £1,000 a year, and up till 1881 their drawings were meagre.

In 1871–6 about 6,010,000 frs. were spent in completing the canal and in improvements, and in the next seven years, 1877–83, about

---

[1] Includes besides bond interest a few other small items. A further loan of 27 million francs at 3 per cent. was raised in 1880, bringing up the share and bond capital to 373 million francs.

8,320,000 frs. were spent in improvements—rather more than the million francs annually for which Sir John Stokes had stipulated. In addition 7,011,000 frs. were spent on the Fresh-water Canal, writing off plant, &c., and, in 1883, plant, &c., for new works was purchased to the value of 2,366,000 frs.

The traffic through the canal was only 437,000 net tons in 1870, it exceeded a million tons net in 1872 (1,161,000 tons), and successive additions of a million were reached in 1875 (2,010,000 tons), in 1880 (3,057,000 tons), in 1881 (4,137,000 tons), and in 1882 (5,075,000 tons), while in 1883 the aggregate was 5,776,000 tons. British tonnage was 66·4 per cent. (289,000 tons) in 1870, but was 71·8 per cent. in 1871, and grew regularly till it reached 82·9 per cent. (3,430,000 tons) in 1881; there was an increase to 4,126,000 tons in 1882, but the percentage fell to 81·3; in 1883 the tonnage was 4,406,000 tons and the percentage 76·3. Particularly rapid was the growth in shipping from Australia—46,000 tons in 1878, 489,000 tons in 1883.

1884–1913

Up to 1884 the management of the canal had been entirely in the hands of the French Company and changes in dues had been nego-tiated with it by the British Government, as the largest shareholder, after a basis had been imposed by an International Commission and the Sublime Porte. The changes in the dues on ships with cargo (a rebate of 2·50 frs. being allowed on vessels in ballast) were as under:

15 Nov. 1869 . . .	10 fr. per net ton
5 July 1872 . . .	10 fr. per gross ton
20 Apr. 1874 . . .	13 fr. per net ton
1 Jan. 1877 . . .	12·50 fr ,,
1 Jan. 1879 . . .	12 fr. ,,
1 Jan. 1881 . . .	11·50 fr. per net ton
1 Jan. 1882 . . .	11 fr. ,, ,,
1 Jan. 1883 . . .	10·50 fr. ,, ,,
1 Jan. 1884 . . .	10 fr. ,, ,,

The rates of dividends (including the statutory 5% and share of surplus profits) and dues during the next thirty years, free of tax in all cases, was as under:

	DIVIDENDS		DUES
Year.	*Per Share francs.*	*Per cent.*	*Francs per net ton.*
1883	88·657	17·731	10·50
1884	87·252	17·450	10·00
1885	85·405	17·081	9·50
1886	75·335	15·067	,,
1887	78·325	15·665	,,

	DIVIDENDS		DUES
Year.	Per Share francs.	Per cent.	Francs per net ton.
1888[1]	84·478	16·896	9·50
1889	85·894	17·179	,,
1890	86·751	17·350	,,
1891	87·150	17·430	,,
1892	92·366	18·473	,,
1893	90·373	18·075	,,
1894	90·000	18·000	,,
1895	92·500	18·500	,,
1896	92·500	18·500	,,
1897	90·000	18·000	,,
1898	100·000	20·000	,,
1899	108·000	21·600	,,
1900	108·000	21·600	,,
1901	125·000	25·000	,,
1902	125·000	25·000	,,
1903	126·000	25·000	8·50

In 1900 it was clear that the dividends payable by the Company would reach the figure of 25 per cent., thus bringing into force the provisions of 'The London Programme' of 1883 whereby all further surplus profits were to be devoted to lowering dues, until these reached the minimum figure of five francs. The President of the Suez Canal Company thereupon approached the London Committee, the other party to 'The London Programme' in the settlement of which, according to the official view, Her Majesty's Government took no part. The London Committee were asked and agreed to waive the stipulation mentioned above, as being unduly onerous, and in its place to agree that 'every fresh reduction of tariff should be preceded by an increase of dividend'. A mistake was made, as in 1883, in not following the precedent created in 1876 by Sir John Stokes when he stipulated for a minimum annual expenditure on improvements, the necessity for which was apparently the reason which induced the London Committee to accept with such complacence this unilateral abrogation of an important condition in the agreement of 1883. Their decision was apparently taken on the ground that it afforded 'an incentive to the Company, which would not have existed under the original arrangement, to make such improvements as will tend to increase the tonnage passing through the Canal'. The figures given on page 115, however, show that the average sums spent annually on improvements from 1904 to 1913 were less than between 1884 and 1893: they also

[1] See Appendix.

show that reductions in dues did not, in fact, follow the same course as dividends. The improvements did not tend to increase the tonnage passing through the canal; they were necessary if the canal was to continue to serve the purpose for which it had been constructed.

In the years following, the London Chamber of Shipping, who appear to have been unaware of the action of the London Committee, were frequently pressed to take action in matters relating to the Suez Canal Company. The Report of the Chamber for 1905 states, 'Your Council dealt in their last three Annual Reports with the varying phases of the lengthy controversy in which they have been engaged with the Suez Canal Company upon (1) the charging of Suez Canal tonnage Dues on partially enclosed spaces; (2) the unsatisfactory nature of the composition of the 'London Committee' of the Suez Canal Company; and (3) the increased dividends paid to the shareholders of the Suez Canal Company in contravention of the 'London Agreement' which was entered into in the year 1883 between M. Charles de Lesseps and British Shipowners'. The Chamber had already pointed out to the Board of Trade, in a letter dated 15th March 1904, that circumstances had materially altered since 1883. They said: 'In the year 1883 the proportion of Suez Canal Dues to the freight earned was very much less than it is at the present time. A vessel taking coal to ports east of the Suez Canal may now have to pay about one-half of her outward earnings and one-fourth of her homeward earnings in Canal dues alone'. An interview was secured with Lord Lansdowne, the Foreign Secretary, on 9th February 1905, but it was not till nearly ten months later and only after much pressing that a definite reply was given to the representations of the shipowners. The material parts of the Foreign Office letter of 30th November 1905 were as follows:

'With regard to the appropriation of Canal profits to the reduction of dues, I am to state that the London Agreement or London Programme of 30th November 1883, in the settlement of which Her Majesty's Government took no part, consists of a series of proposed concessions on the part of Monsieur de Lesseps, and the preamble shows that the twelve points which form the substance of the arrangement were merely to "constitute the views desirable for the future administration of the Suez Canal".

'Whatever the character of this understanding may have been, the London Committee were consulted in 1900 by the President of the Suez Canal Company, both committee and president being the representatives of the original parties to the understanding, and they were unanimous in considering that such an onerous condition as that contained in Article 8 of that arrangement—viz., that all net profits above 25 per cent. should be applied to the reduction of dues till the latter were reduced to 5 frs. a ton—could not reasonably be maintained.

'The solution accepted by the British directors was that every fresh reduction of tariff should be preceded by an increase of dividend. Lord Lansdowne is not prepared to hold that this solution was disadvantageous to British interests, for it affords an incentive to the Company, which would not have existed under the original arrangement, to make such improvements as will tend to increase the tonnage passing through the Canal.'

The Chamber was thus forced to admit that the 'London Programme' was at best a 'gentlemen's agreement', and that the legal position is that the Canal Company are entitled to charge 10 francs a ton, though it is to be noted that the Concession specifies 'francs' only without saying whether they are gold, silver, or paper, and that the words 'not exceeding' suggest the possibility of reductions. M. de Lesseps, in fact, always declared that his policy was to reduce rates with increasing traffic. The Chamber has had, therefore, to proceed very diplomatically in negotiating with the Company whenever it considered a reduction of dues to be necessary, for any 'agitation' in the United Kingdom (as in 1873, 1883, 1904, and 1931) has always aroused much suspicion and resentment among the French shareholders.

The Chamber had from 1883 been critical of the representative character of the London Committee, and in the letter quoted above 'Lord Lansdowne agrees that the London Committee is not as closely in touch as might be desirable with the various branches of the shipping interests'.

How far this is true to-day is a matter on which I have no material to express an opinion.

From 1903 to the outbreak of the World War dividends and dues moved as follows:

| Year. | DIVIDENDS | | DUES |
	Per Share francs.	Per Cent.	Francs per ton.
1904	141	28·2	8·50
1905	141	28·2	8·50
1906	141	28·2	7·75
1907	141	28·2	7·75
1908	141	28·2	7·75
1909	150	30·0	7·75
1910	158	31·6	7·75
1911	165	33·0	7·25
1912	165	33·0	6·75
1913	165	33·0	6·25

While dividends were being increased and dues decreased, though not by any means simultaneously or in the same ratio, the canal itself was being constantly improved, as shown by the following figures:

		Aggregate thousand francs.	Yearly Average thousand francs.
	1884–93	94,655	9,465
Cost of improvements to Canal	1894–1903	32,697	3,270
	1904–13	82,515	8,252

In 1887 two loans of 73,026 and 238,964 bonds were issued at various rates for constructional purposes and produced 127 million francs. The 'ditch' which in 1870 was from 7 to 8 metres deep, 22 metres wide at the bottom, and 54 to 100 metres broad between banks, was 9 metres deep and 37 metres wide at 8 metres depth in 1905, and in 1923 was 11 to 13 metres deep, 45 to 100 metres wide at bottom, and 100 to 160 metres between banks. Electric lighting of ships had also been introduced in 1886 to allow traffic to pass through the canal by night through part of its length and in 1887 for the whole canal. Between 1909 and 1914 the canal was deepened from 28 to 36 feet throughout, and widened in proportion. There was also heavy outlay on new docks at Port Said. These developments were a necessary consequence of the growth of shipping and the increasing size of vessels. They increased the earning power of the canal but, if not undertaken, it would have soon been abandoned by shipping.

The following statement summarizes the financial accounts of the Company for the three decades before the outbreak of the World War.

Including the 5 per cent. interest and drawings of shares shown in the first table the shareholders received in the thirty years 1,527,617,000 francs for their original investment of 200 million francs—say £60,560,000, or over £2,000,000 a year. The division of the directors' shares of the surplus profits is not shown in the accounts, but altogether the 32 directors (for to that number had the Board been increased in 1883) drew £1,310,000 in the thirty years under review, and if the principle of equal distribution had been adopted they might each have drawn about £920 a year in the first decade, about £1,260 a year in the second decade, and about £1,930 a year in the period from 1894 to 1913.

The increase of traffic through the canal did not proceed without interruption. It grew to 6,336,000 net tons in 1885 and then, in the world depression of 1886, fell away to 5,768,000 tons, a smaller figure than in any of the three preceding years. Recovery was prompt and another steady rise followed, culminating in a total of 8,699,000 tons in 1891, a figure which was not to be surpassed till 1898. According to an article by A. Sauerbeck on 'Prices of Commodities in 1903'[1] the

---

[1] *Journal of the Royal Statistical Society*, 1904, Part I, p. 92.

Suez Canal Accounts 1884–1913

Particulars.	1884–93.	1894–1903.	1904–13.
Receipts:	In thousand francs		
Dues: Shipping	645,345	853,093	1,177,610
Passengers	18,090	22,954	25,183
Other	5,809	4,697	8,656
Investments, Exchange, &c. . .	13,129	16,054	22,439
Estates	9,249	2,872	2,722
Other receipts	4,821	8,337	8,541
Total	696,443	908,007	1,245,151
Brought forward	..	..	287
Taken from Reserve	1,236	1,598	14,300
	697,679	909,605	1,259,738
Payments:			
Administration	15,898	16,125	21,320
Transit	27,535	30,525	35,695
Maintenance	21,101	30,839	53,989
Lands, water, &c.	12,655	13,106	12,704
Total	77,189	90,595	123,708
Bond interest, &c.[1]	131,984	160,610	154,177
Shares, 5 per cent. Dividend . .	118,006	118,166	118,805
Reserves (statutory, special, depreciation, &c.)	..	37,296	84,532
Surplus profit	370,500	502,651	778,456
Carried forward	..	287	60
Total	697,679	909,605	1,259,738

The division of the Surplus Profits was as follows:

Surplus Profits, 1884–1913

Classes.		1884–93.	1894–1903.	1904–13.	1884–1913 aggregate.
	%	In thousand francs			
Shareholders . .	71	263,053	356,883	552,704	1,172,640
'Egyptian Govern-ment' (i.e. Credit Foncier)	15	55,574	75,396	116,769	247,739
Founders' shares .	10	37,049	50,267	77,843	165,159
Directors . .	2	7,412	10,053	15,570	33,035
Staff . . .	2	7,412	10,052	15,570	33,034
Total . .	100	370,500	502,651	778,456	1,651,607

[1] Including pension (120,000 fr.) to de Lesseps' family; Egyptian Supervision (30,000 fr.)

low points in the volume of British trade (imports plus exports) were in 1885 and 1893 and the high points in 1884, 1889, and 1903. The low points for wholesale prices were in 1887 and 1896, and the high points in 1883, 1889/1891, and 1900; after 1896 the effects of the Rand gold output became observable. There were, of course, special causes producing variations in Suez Canal traffic, apart from the changes produced by alterations in world prosperity. The year 1891 saw the start in the trade in fresh fruit from Australia and also the introduction of oil tankers to the canal route; an innovation to which other shipowners, fearing the risk to their ships, were opposed, but the British Government refused to intervene. In the same year began the 'colonization' of Africa and the building of railways in Japan and Siam. The year 1893 was marked by the coal strike in England, by the Australian financial crisis, and by bad foreign trade in the United Kingdom and France, especially in wheat, rice, and wool which were to a large extent carried via the canal. In 1895 it was reported (*Manchester Guardian*, 17th June) that 'the Czar's Government have determined to devote nearly £20 millions during the next three or four years for the purchase of any large parcels of Suez Canal shares coming into the market. No information is available as to what, if any, action was taken in this direction. The Australian situation improved in the following year and the opening of more Chinese ports improved trade with that country, but 1896 and 1897 saw famine and plague in India and in the latter year drought in Australia. With decreasing crop exports from India British exports to that country also fell off; e.g. in 1895 about 1,297,000 tons of coal were exported to India, but in 1897 only 598,000 tons. Cargoes being scarce and shipping plentiful, freight rates fell heavily; e.g. the homeward freight rate from Bombay fell by 74 per cent. between 1891 and 1897. The dependence of canal traffic on the weather in India is shown by the increase in the exports of wheat from India from 29,000 tons in 1897 to 484,000 tons in 1898, with a corresponding increase in the exports of coal to India from 598,000 tons to 666,000 tons. The year 1898 with a canal traffic of 9,238,000 tons marked the beginning of a prolonged development which continued with only minor fluctuations till 20,275,000 tons were reached in 1912. The exploitation of China, the South African War, the Russo-Japanese War and its sequelae of repatriation of troops (1903–6), the growth in the trade in manganese from India and soya-beans from Manchuria, were all 'bull' factors for canal traffic, just as droughts in India in 1900 and 1908 were depressing influences. The reaction from the trade boom which reached its height in 1913 began to show itself in various directions before the end of the year, but it was anticipated in the Suez Canal traffic which as a whole was 1·2 per cent. less than in 1912.

The following table shows the net tonnage of ships using the canal and trading inwards or outwards with countries east of Suez, beginning with 1890.

The Indian trade was 56·41 per cent. of the whole in 1891, and though by 1912 it had increased by 98·88 per cent. it was only 48·13 per cent. of the whole in the latter year. This relative decline was due to the great increase in the traffic with China, Japan, and Cochin-China. The Australian trade maintained its relative position and improved in volume by a slightly larger percentage than the whole traffic. British shipping formed 75·1 per cent. of the whole in 1891–5; 65·0 per cent. in 1896–1900; 62·2 per cent. in 1901–5; 62·5 per cent. in 1906–10; 62·4 per cent. in 1911–13. In 1913 the United Kingdom had 60·2 per cent. of the traffic; Germany 16·7, Netherlands 6·4, France 4·6, Russia 1·7, Japan 1·7, and Italy 1·5.

Suez Canal Traffic, 1890–1912

Year.	E. Africa.	W. India.	E. India.	Straits, Siam, Dutch E. Indies.	Cochin-China, China, Japan.	Australia.	Other Areas.	Total.
				In thousand net tons				
1890	149	1,988	1,882	879	928	716	348	6,890
1891	219	2,610	2,297	1,113	1,167	799	494	8,699
1893	172	2,239	1,833	1,028	1,234	798	355	7,659
1896	269	1,649	2,411	1,085	1,578	871	697	8,560
1897	303	1,269	2,419	1,033	1,705	845	325	7,899
1901	382	1,675	3,106	1,504	2,710	972	475	10,824
1905	482	2,623	3,722	1,671	2,943	995	698	13,134
1910	510	3,359	4,300	1,987	3,977	1,704	745	16,582
1912	747	4,812	4,947	2,435	4,202	2,037	1,095	20,275
				Percentages				
1891	2·52	30·00	26·41	12·79	13·42	9·18	5·68	100·00
1901	3·53	15·47	28·70	13·90	25·04	8·98	4·38	100·00
1912	3·68	23·73	24·40	12·01	20·73	10·05	5·40	100·00
1912 as % of 1891	341·11	184·37	215·37	218·78	360·07	254·94	221·66	233·07

Particulars of the weight of cargoes carried are not available for the earlier years, but in the three years 1911–13 the chief classes were as shown below:

Weight of Cargoes passing through Suez Canal, 1911–13.

Particulars.	1911.	1912.	1913.	Particulars.	1911.	1912.	1913.
Outward	In thousand tons			Inward	In thousand tons		
Coal . .	1,091	967	1,192	Wheat .	1,643	1,925	1,490
Iron and steel	1,320	2,035	2,898	Rice . .	1,628	1,702	2,061
Salt . .	455	432	449	Sugar .	798	400	53
Petroleum .	485	465	510	Copra .	654	587	537
Other . .	6,145	5,883	6,271	Oil seeds .	1,481	1,293	1,394
				Tea . .	487	398	393
				Jute . .	730	886	840
				Wool .	392	314	309
				Cotton .	305	188	294
				Manganese	561	623	869
				Benzine.	235	271	291
				Other .	6,138	7,075	5,924
Total . .	9,496	9,782	11,320	Total .	15,052	15,662	14,455

1914–31

The War naturally affected canal traffic and receipts profoundly, as the following table shows:

Year.	Net Tonnage. Th. net tons.	Passengers Thous.	Transit Dues. Th. francs.	Passenger Dues. Th. francs.	Transit Dues per net ton. Francs.	Dividend.	
						Per Share. Francs.	Per Cent.
1911–13 Average	19,545	275	128,985	2,635	6·75	165	33·0
1914	19,409	392	117,307	3,735	6·25	120	24·0
1915	15,266	211	90,281	2,005	6·25	120	24·0
1916	12,325	283	76,120	2,802	6·75 (1 Apr.) 7·25 (1 Sept.)	90	18·0
1917	8,369	142	61,076	1,415	7·75 (1 Jan.) 8·50	65 100	13·0
1918	9,252	106	79,340	1,050	8·50	192	20·0
1919	16,014	528	136,970	5,164	8·50		38·4 (paper) 28·6 (gold)[1]

Regular traffic fell to low levels and the canal was largely dependent on the passage of troops and of war supplies, though the traffic was only interrupted for one day. The year 1919 showed a very large 'passenger'

[1] Francs in 1919 averaged 74.61 per cent. of gold parity.

movement due to the repatriation of soldiers. The transit dues were restored to the level of 1903/5 or the return to the shareholders would have been much worse; even so it was 21·7 per cent. (gold) on the average of the six years 1914–19. In addition 252,655 new 5 per cent. bonds were issued in 1915–18, producing 119,514,000 francs, and in the period 1914–19 over 63·7 million francs were spent in improvements. The finance accounts of the canal in these six years, stated in gold francs, are as follows:

Suez Canal, 1914–19

Receipts.	Thous. gold francs	Payments.	Thous. gold francs
Dues: Shipping . . .	561,094	Administration . . .	17,683
Passenger . . .	16,171	Transit . . .	32,258
Other . . .	11,889	Maintenance . . .	34,769
		Lands, water, &c. . .	11,116
Total . . .	589,154	Bond: interest, &c. . .	110,605
Investments, Exchange, &c. .	59,391	Shares: dividend, &c. . .	84,278
Estates	1,053	Reserve (housing, &c.) .	27,000
Other receipts . . .	12,492	Surplus profit . . .	350,433
From Special Reserve . .	6,500	Carried forward . .	508
Brought forward . .	60		
Total . . .	668,650	Total . . .	668,650

The paper franc was at a discount on gold during this period and profits were made on the remission of funds from Egypt, amounting in 1919 to 29,278,000 francs.

Surplus Profits were divided as follows:

			Thous. francs
Shareholders	71 per cent.		248,808
Egyptian Government . . .	15 ,,		52,565
Founders' shares . . .	10 ,,		35,045
Directors	2 ,,		7,008
Staff	2 ,,		7,007
Total	100 ,,		350,433

The world went through a re-stocking boom in the second half of 1919 and the first half of 1920; over-hasty speculation was followed by a depression from which most countries did not begin to emerge till some time in 1923. Good trade followed till it was brought to an end by the American crash in the autumn of 1929, when the present universal depression set in. Traffic through the canal changed with changing trade, as the following figures of tonnage using the canal show:

Year.	*Total.*	*British.*	*Year.*	*Total.*	*British.*
	Th. net tons	Th. net tons		Th. net tons	Th. net tons
1920	17,575	10,838	1927	28,963	16,534
1921	18,119	11,397	1928	31,906	18,124
1922	20,743	13,383	1929	33,466	19,114
1923	22,730	14,264	1930	31,669	17,600
1924	25,110	14,995	1931	30,028	16,624
1925	26,762	16,016	1932	28,340	15,721
1926	26,060	14,969			

The tonnage using the canal in 1931 was very nearly one-half greater than that passing in 1912, and in 1929 it was over 65 per cent. larger, but in 1932 there was a fall of 15·3 per cent. from 1929.

In considering the accounts of this period the depreciation of the franc must be borne in mind. Receipts and expenses were recorded in gold francs and the profits on remissions of funds were then brought in for distribution as profits. This course was adopted up to the stabilization of the franc, and from 1928 the accounts are in new francs. This makes it advisable to consider 1920–7 separately. The average annual sterling-franc and dollar-franc exchange rates were as below:

Exchange.	*Par.*	*1920.*	*1921.*	*1922.*	*1923.*	*1924.*	*1925.*	*1926.*	*1927.*
Francs to £ .	25·225	52·78	51·90	54·60	75·66	85·27	102·51	152·76	123·86
Cents to franc .	19·293	6·71	7·46	8·19	6·07	5·23	4·77	3·25	3·92
Franc in per cent. of gold parity	100·00	34·80	38·66	42·45	31·46	27·11	24·72	16·81	20·32

Suez Canal Accounts, 1920–7

Receipts.	*1920–3.*	*1924–7.*	*Payments.*	*1920–3.*	*1924–7.*
	Thous. francs	Thous. francs		Thous. francs	Thous. francs
Dues: Shipping .	623,663	759,833	Administration .	30,891	47,368
Passenger .	12,305	10,752	Transit . .	50,625	52,552
Other .	7,858	6,135	Maintenance .	66,010	67,043
			Estates, water, &c.	21,199	25,280
Total .	643,826	776,720	Bonds: interest, &c.	69,814	67,542
Investments .	42,054	85,248	Shares: dividends,		
Estates . .	4,094	4,454	&c. . .	57,910	40,324
Other receipts .	7,598	7,513	Reserves (statutory,		
Conversion of			special, deprecia-		
Funds . .	554,731	1,774,470	tion, &c.) .	203,000	294,000
Brought forward	508	3,735	Surplus profit .	749,627	2,054,879
			Carried forward .	3,735	3,152
Total .	1,252,811	2,652,140	Total . .	1,252,811	2,652,140

The Surplus Profits were divided as under:

			1920–3	1924–7
			Thous. francs	Thous. francs
Shareholders	. . . .	71 per cent.	532,235	1,458,963
Egyptian Government .	. .	15 „	112,445	308,231
Founders' shares .	. . .	10 „	74,962	205,488
Directors .	. . . .	2 „	14,993	41,098
Staff	. . . . .	2 „	14,992	41,099
			749,627	2,054,879

From 1924 onwards the 500-franc shares were divided into two of 250 francs each. After converting the dividends declared (including the original 5 per cent.) on shares at the average discount on gold for the year, so as to obtain amounts in gold francs for comparison with previous year, we can compare dividends and transit dues.

Year.	Dividends.			Transit Dues.
	in Current Francs.	in Gold Francs.	Per Cent. (in gold).	Francs (gold) per net ton.
1920	243·851	84·8	16·96	8·50 8·25 (1 Oct.)
1921	245	94·7	18·94	8·00 (1 Oct.)
1922	320	135·8	27·16	8·00
1923	430	135·3	27·06	7·75 (1 Mar.)
1924	265	71·8	28·72	7·50 (1 Jan.)
1925	300	74·2	29·68	7·25 (1 Apr.)
1926	420	70·7	28·28	7·25
1927	455	92·5	37·00	7·25

After the franc was devalued so that 4·925 new francs were equal to one gold franc (or 1 new franc = 3·918 cents. or £1 = 124·213 new francs) the accounts of the Company were kept in new francs from 1928 onwards. The interest on the outstanding bonds was still paid in gold francs, so that it was given a 'majoration' of 66·2 million new francs. The 5 per cent. dividend on shares was paid in new francs till 1931 when, in consequence of a lawsuit decided in the Egyptian courts on 18 June and 10 December of that year, it had to be paid in gold; amortised shares were, therefore, also paid in gold. The accounts for the five years 1928–32 are summarized in the following table:

Suez Canal Accounts, 1928–32

Receipts.	Payments.
	In thousands of new francs

Receipts		Payments	
Dues: Shipping .	4,882,707	Administration	177,207
Passenger .	66,983	Transit	351,325
Other .	35,551	Maintenance	372,085
Total .	4,985,241	Estates, water, &c.	167,274
		Bonds: interest, &c.	415,720
Investments .	176,937	Shares: dividend, &c.	129,520
Exchange profits .	26,761	Reserves (statutory, special, depreciation, &c.)	431,000
Estates . .	29,600	Surplus profit	3,285,592
Other receipts .	51,114	Carried forward	4,531
From Reserve .	61,449		
Brought forward .	3,152		
Total . .	5,334,254	Total . .	5,334,254

Surplus Profits were divided as follows:

Thousand new francs

Shareholders	. . . .	71 per cent.	2,332,771
Egyptian Government	. . .	15 ,,	492,839
Founders' Shares .	. . .	10 ,,	328,558
Directors	. . . . .	2 ,,	65,712
Staff .	. . . . .	2 ,,	65,712
	. . . . .	100 ,,	3,285,592

The remuneration received by the directors was about £529,000 in the five years or nearly £3,300 a year for each director.

The first two years were highly profitable and the transit dues were reduced in 1928 by 25 centimes to 7 francs (gold) per ton and in 1929 to 6·90 francs. A further reduction to 6·65 francs was made as from 1st September 1930, and the dues on vessels in ballast were fixed for the future at half the cargo rate instead of the rebate of 2·50 francs. As the world depression deepened and the complaints of shipowners grew, a further reduction to 6 francs was made as from 15th November 1931, but as 'a temporary measure only', and at present the regulations state that it 'will remain in force until December 31st 1933'. The relation between dividends and dues is shown below:

Year.	Dividends.			Transit Dues.
	Paper francs.	Gold francs.	Per cent.	Gold francs per net ton.
1928	510	103·55	41·42	7·25 7·00 (1 Apr.)
1929	530	107·61	43·04	6·90 (1 Jan.)
1930	545·67	110·80	44·32	6·65 (1 Sept.)
1931	466·64	94·75	37·90	6·00 (15 Nov.)
1932	389·01	78·99	31·60	6·00

Up to the end of 1919 nearly 743·3 million gold francs had been spent on the original cost (291·3 million frs.) and in improvements to the canal. In 1920–7 a further sum of 140·9 million francs was expended and in 1928–32, 294·5 million new francs (equivalent to 59·8 million gold francs). The total cost of 944 million gold francs has been met as follows:

Year.	Redeemable by Drawings.	Outstanding 31.12.32 Number.	Total mill. gold francs.
	Shares, 800,000 at 250 fr., 5% in 99 years	667,204	200·0
	Bonds, 400,000 at 85 fr., 5% (for arrears of interest) 1882/1922 . . .	none	34·0
1867/8	Bonds, 333,333 at 300 fr., 5% at 500 fr. in 1868/1918	none	100·0
1871	Bonds, 120,000 at 100 fr., 3% at 125 fr. in 1873/1902	none	12·0
1880	Bonds, 73,026⎫ ⎧3%, 1880/1930	7,907	27·0
1887	„ 238,964⎬ at ⎪3%	189,143	100·0
	„ 75,000⎪different⎨	56,001	30·5
1915–18	„ 252,655⎭ rates ⎩5%	156,296	119·5
			623·0
1864/9	Indemnities, sales, &c.		121·4
To 1870	Other receipts from canal services		29·8
1870–1932	„ „ „		169·8
			944·0

The following is a summary of the Balance Sheet on 31st December 1932:—

Balance Sheet, 31 December 1932

Assets.		Liabilities.	
	mill. frs.		mill. frs.
Head Office, Paris . .	7·0	Statutory Reserve	200·0
Buildings, Egypt . .	424·3	Insurance Fund, &c. . . .	9·7
Plant and machinery in use:		Improvements Fund . . .	36·4
On Works . . 338·9		Depreciation, &c., of plant .	546·6
On Water-supply . 89·1		Depreciation of buildings . .	292·4
Other . . 20·1		Special Building Fund . .	14·5
	448·1	Total Reserve and other funds . .	1,099·6
Material in store . .	49·9	Interest, &c., due . . .	30·2
Material in process . .	20·5	Staff share of profits: Capital Fund .	69·4
Buildings being erected .	19·0	Sundry creditors and bills payable .	95·3
Cash, &c. . . .	63·5		
Investments . . .	659·8	Total	1,294·5
Bills receivable and sundry creditors . . .	112·2	Net profits from 1932 Account . .	505·3
		Carry forward	4·5
Total . . .	1,804·3	Total	1,804·3

The following summary of net profits 1870–1932 is interesting:

	Million gold francs.	*Million £ sterling.*
Shareholders	2,467·1	97·8
Egyptian Government . . .	521·2	20·6
Founders' shares . . . - .	347·5	13·8
Directors	69·5	2·8
Staff	69·5	2·8
	3,474·8	137·8

Sterling exchange is taken at the old par (25·225 francs = £1).

In addition the shareholders have received 5 per cent. on shares not amortised. The receipts of the shareholders should not, however, be attributed entirely as a reward for the investment of their original 200 million francs. Considered as an undertaking the canal is a vastly improved construction compared with its condition when opened, and about 653 million francs (gold)—say £26 million—have been spent in extensions and improvements. Funds were raised by loans which were paid off out of the profits as they accrued; this is equivalent to the familiar factory practice of putting profits back into the business for extensions, and if no fresh issue of shares is made the dividend falling to the small nominal capital from additional capital applications may become very large and raise the market value of the shares to a great height. The share of the Egyptian Government was intended as compensation for the restriction of sovereign rights consequent on the concession and for the sums which they had to pay for the recovery of some of those rights and for the cancellation of corvée labour. It is not the fault of the Company that the Khedive parted with this valuable property in 1880 in order to satisfy his creditors. The founders' shares were awarded to M. de Lesseps, partly as his personal reward— which no one would grudge—and partly to persons of influence who had helped him;[1] the character of the payment depends on the nature of the services rendered. The 2 per cent. falling to the staff for pensions, &c., and the directors' share of the same amount are in a different category. There are valid objections to making either the pensions and other provident funds, or the salaries of directors of an international public utility or a monopoly, dependent upon profits.

---

[1] It has been stated that when the founders' shares were distributed by de Lesseps many people to whom they were offered refused them as valueless.

Dues and Goods

The quantity of goods carried at different periods is shown below:

Year.	Inward.	Outward.	Total.
	In thousand tons		
1904	9,960	8,240	18,200
1905	9,980	7,840	17,820
1911	15,050	9,500	24,550
1912	15,660	9,780	25,440
1913	14,450	11,320	25,770
1927	18,440	11,080	29,520
1928	20,660	11,960	32,620
1929	21,620	12,900	34,520
1930	19,080	9,430	28,510
1931	17,950	7,380	25,330[1]

The principal classes of goods carried in 1929–31 were:

Inward.	1929.	1930.	1931.	Outward.	1929.	1930.	1931.
	Million tons				Million tons		
Mineral oils . .	4·90	4·06	3·31	Metals and machinery .	3·59	2·61	1·90
Vegetable oils, oil-seeds, nuts . . .	3·71	3·87	4·12	Fertilisers .	0·89	0·68	0·70
Cereals . . .	2·61	2·15	2·84	Cement . .	0·77	0·55	0·34
Textiles . . .	2·45	2·12	1·82	Coal . .	0·77	0·45	0·30
Minerals . . .	2·30	2·09	1·32	Railway material	0·64	0·43	0·23
Other . . .	5·65	4·79	4·54	Other . .	6·24	4·71	3·91
Total . .	21·62	19·08	17·95	Total .	12·90	9·43	7·38

The burden of transit dues on particular classes of goods varies according to circumstances. The dues are levied on the whole usable space of a cargo vessel whether it is all occupied or not, and a ship may be 'down to her marks' with space unused; if a ship goes outwards in ballast and comes back with cargo the ballast dues have obviously to be borne by the inward cargo. In the case of a passenger-cargo liner it is a question whether the transit dues on passenger-space as well as the passenger-tax should be charged against passenger-fares or whether all transit dues should be charged against freights and only the passenger-tax against fares. No accurate account of the burden of dues on cargo can, therefore, be rendered. The following short statement summarizes the aggregate figures for each of the four years 1929, 1930, 1931, and 1932:

[1] 1932: 23,632,000 tons.

Year.	Vessels.	Net Tonnage.	Cargo.	Canal Dues.	'Surplus Profits.'	Dues per net ton.	Dues per cargo ton.	Surplus Profits per net ton.	Surplus Profits per cargo ton.
	No.	Mill. tons	Mill. tons	Mill. frs.	Mill. frs.	frs.	frs.	frs.	frs.
1929	6,274	33·47	34·52	1,100	737	32·88	31·88	22·04	21·36
1930	5,761	31·67	28·51	1,023	718	32·30	35·88	22·68	25·20
1931	5,366	30·03	25·33	918	612	30·58	36·26	20·39	24·17
1932	5,032	28·34	23·63	784	505	27·65	33·16	17·83	21·36

Taking the average exchange of each year we get the following approximate sterling equivalents:

	Dues per Net ton.	Dues per Cargo ton.	Surplus Profits per Net ton.	Surplus Profits per Cargo ton.
	s. d.	*s. d.*	*s. d.*	*s. d.*
1929	5 3·6	5 1·7	3 3·7	3 5·3
1930	5 2·6	5 9·5	3 7·9	4 0·8
1931	5 3·5	6 3·3	3 6·3	4 2·2
1932	6 2·4	7 4·8	4 0·0	4 9·5

Since the United Kingdom went off the gold standard the burden of dues paid in gold is naturally much heavier. The tax of 6 francs gold or 29·55 paper francs per net ton was at 89·195 francs to the £ (the average exchange in 1932) equivalent to 6s. 7·5d. per net ton, Suez Canal measurement, was about a fifth heavier than the tax of 6·90 francs in 1929, equivalent on the average of that year to 5s. 5·8d. per net ton. The Canal Company had remarked in its Report for 1931, issued in June 1932, 'la dépréciation de la livre sterling venait infliger à la majorité des armateurs clients du Canal une aggravation peut-être temporaire, mais assurément importante, de la charge que constitutent les droits de transit'. For this reason and on account of the depression in shipping the reduction from 6·65 frs. to 6·00 frs. was made as from 15th November 1931, but, as appears from what is said above, the reduction was not equivalent to the depreciation of sterling.

The calculations as to rates per ton of cargo made in the table in the preceding paragraph were based on the assumption that *all* the transit dues were attributable to cargo, whereas, as has already been said, that may not be the case. Coal, however, is a typical full cargo commodity, and if we take a collier of 2,900 net tons and approximately 3,700 tons, Suez Canal measurement, the transit dues on such a steamer in 1929 would have been 25,530 francs gold or £1,012 at par, which on a cargo of 7,120 tons would be equal to 2s. 10d. per ton. At 6 francs a ton in 1932 the dues would have been 22,200 francs, or £1,226 at the average exchange of that year; this is equivalent to about 3s. 5·3d. per ton of cargo for a transit of 100 miles. In 1929 about 112,000 tons of coal were shipped from the United Kingdom to Ceylon and in 1932 about 37,000 tons, the f.o.b. value being in each case about 19s. 3d. per ton; canal dues alone added to that value about a seventh in 1929 and over a sixth in 1932.

In 1931 the 30,028,000 net tons (Suez Canal measurement) passing through the Suez Canal were in gross measurement 41,743,000 tons, or 100 Suez Canal tons to 139 gross tons; taking 100 gross tons as equivalent to about 60·7 tons of British registered tonnage, 100 net tons are raised to 118·5 by Suez Canal measurement.[1] The rate of 6 frs. per Suez Canal ton now current is thus equivalent to 7·11 frs. per British net ton, or, at the average exchange for 1932, about 7s. 10d. per net ton British registry. Taking this as the average rate for occupied space (neglecting unoccupied cargo space and passenger space) the rates per cargo ton on certain British imports and exports is shown below, the average stowage space for each class of goods being taken.

Commodity.	Stowage per ton weight.	Transit Dues per ton weight.		Value per ton, 1932.			
	cubic feet	s.	d.	£	s.	d.	
Australian wheat	50–53	4	5	6	6	2	c.i.f.
„ wool .	240	18	9½	83	10	9	„
„ butter	52–55	4	2¼	95	14	1	„
„ frozen beef .	95–98	7	6¾	29	12	7	„
Oil-seeds .	58–75	5	2⅔	7	4	0	„
Jute .	60–64	4	10¼	18	4	2	„
Copra .	80–120	7	10	14	14	9	„
Rails .	12–18	1	2	9	0	6	f.o.b.
Cotton piece goods	80–84	6	5	227	19	0	„
Woollen piece goods .	80–84	6	5	627	14	10	„
Textile machinery	100–120	8	7½	87	7	8	„

Outward cargoes through the canal are from one-half to two-thirds the average annual cargo carried inward, so that unoccupied space materially increases the above rates in British exports. Moreover, some types of steamer are heavily hit by the Suez Canal measurement, which may be a third more than British net tonnage instead of the 18·5 per cent. used above.

[1] 'Roughly speaking, the maritime world imposes charges on 61 per cent. of a ship's gross tonnage; the Suez Canal management on 72 per cent.' B. Olney Hough, *The American Exporter*, 1914, p. 20: 'The American rules produce a net tonnage averaging 66 per cent. of the gross tonnage' (idem. p. 23).

The Report of the Liverpool Steam Ship Owners' Association for 1930 remarked (p. 14) that 'a considerable amount of tonnage' had been diverted 'to the Panama Canal', and even after the reduction of dues in 1931 the Report for 1932 asserted (p. 19) that 'it is notorious that the present cost is keeping shipping away from the [Suez] Canal'. Comparing 1931 with 1929 the number of ships passing through the Suez Canal fell off by 14·5 per cent., the net tonnage by 10·3 per cent., and the cargo carried by 26·6 per cent. As dues are charged on space they only fell off by 16·5 per cent., but freight is charged on cargo, and as world trade has declined heavily it has not been possible to pass on the cost of running lightly laden ships to the owners of such cargo as was carried. The grumbles of 1930 were natural, but the directors of the Canal Company lent a deaf ear and, as they said in their Report for 1931, 'nous nous refusions absolument à céder à la pression de réclamations formulées à l'égard de la Compagnie sous une forme agressive'. This somewhat haughty attitude had to be modified as trade got worse, and the retreat was covered by the assertion that 'l'agitation soulevée contre la Compagnie avait complètement pris fin et les excellentes relations qui avaient régné pendant tant d'années entre votre entreprise et ses clients étaient rétablies'. Unfortunately, the shipowners were not able to retain for themselves the benefit of the concession, so great was the superfluity of shipping and so limited the co-operation between owners.

It will be recalled that in 1883 a possible reduction of transit dues to 5 francs per ton was contemplated. In 1929 when the dues were 6·90 francs gold the average per net ton was 6·676 gold francs; on this basis a rate of 5 francs would have reduced the earnings by about 303 million francs and the shareholders' total dividend to about 26 per cent. (in gold) instead of about 43 per cent.; similarly it is likely that the dividend in 1931 on a 5-franc basis would have been about 26 per cent. instead of 31·6. On the one hand, it is possible that a reduction to 5 francs would not have benefited the shipowners, for they would have been forced to pass it on to the shippers, thus, in any case, by lowering costs, stimulating the interchange of goods; on the other hand, it is at least debatable whether the 1904 ideal of a dividend in excess of 25 per cent. (which was realized for ten years) should still be regarded as attainable in gold in a world where all values have been completely transmuted. The Liverpool Steam Ship Owners' Association estimated that the canal dues 'amount to upwards of 14 per cent. of the gross freights' in 1931, and the average freight rate in 1932 was about 5 per cent. below the average for 1931, so that the burden has increased. The Association, supported by the Chamber of Shipping, sought to have the basic rate reduced to the 5 francs gold contemplated in 1883, but Lord Inchcape, as Chairman of the Canal Company, replied (*The Times*, 13 May 1931): 'Since 1883 the increase in dividends has given the shareholders £59,000,000, while the reduction in dues has given the shipowners £60,000,000. Since 1920 the shareholders have received an increase in dividends of £13,700,000 and the shipowners have gained £11,700,000 by reduction of dues; but since 1913 the shareholders have received £2,400,000 less in dividends than if the 1913 dividend had been maintained.' But the dividend in 1911–13 was 33 per cent., and the real question remains unanswered. Is a monopolist company entitled to distribute huge dividends at the expense of those who make use of its services and of those whom its clients serve?

TABLE I

SUEZ CANAL RECEIPTS

Year.	Transit and Navigation.				Invest-ments, &c.	Estates.	Other Receipts.[1]	Total.
	Ships.	Passengers.	Pilotage, &c.	Total.				
				In million francs				
1870	4·35	0·26	1·11	5·72	0·22	0·29	3·04[2]	9·27
1871	7·60	0·46	1·19	9·25	0·08	1·07	2·88	13·28
1872	14·34	0·68	1·57	16·59	0·46	1·06	0·21	18·32
1873	20·83	0·73	1·64	23·20	0·45	0·98	0·20	24·83
1874	22·65	0·74	1·72	25·11	0·48	0·50	0·64	26·73
1875	26·43	0·84	1·85	29·12	0·63	0·85	0·25	30·85
1876	27·63	0·72	1·80	30·15	0·29	0·54	0·19	31·17
1877	30·18	0·73	2·04	32·95	0·25	0·54	0·24	33·98
1878	28·34	0·99	1·96	31·29	0·44	0·52	0·25	32·50
1879	27·13	0·85	1·90	29·88	0·35	0·44	0·28	30·95
1880	36·49	1·01	2·49	39·99	0·56	0·55	0·72	41·82
1881	47·19	0·91	3·64	51·74	1·91	0·55	0·48	54·68
1882	55·43	1·31	4·34	61·08	1·31	0·54	0·48	63·41
1883	60·55	1·19	4·40	66·14	0·91	1·09	0·38	68·52
1884	58·63	1·52	2·49	62·64	0·94	1·43	0·40	65·41
1885	60·06	2·06	0·36	62·48	0·98	1·18	0·41	65·05
1886	54·77	1·71	0·32	56·80	1·00	0·69	0·53	59·02
1887	55·99	1·83	0·30	58·12	0·92	0·84	0·63	60·51
1888	63·04	1·84	0·36	65·24	1·15	0·83	0·48	67·70
1889	64·41	1·81	0·37	66·59	1·40	1·29	0·48	69·76
1890	65·43	1·61	0·39	67·43	1·67	0·89	0·47	70·46

[1] Including receipts for previous years.
[2] Recettes d'ordre 2,674,000 frs.

SUEZ CANAL RECEIPTS (*cont.*)

Year.	Transit and Navigation.				Investments, &c.	Estates.	Other Receipts.	Brought Forward.	From Reserve.	Total.
	Ships.	Passengers.	Other Dues.	Total.						
					In million francs					
1891	81·54	1·95	0·46	83·95	1·82	0·63	0·47	..	..	86·87
1892	72·61	1·90	0·38	74·89	1·69	0·78	0·45	..	..	77·81
1893	68·86	1·87	0·38	71·11	1·55	0·69	0·49	..	2·74	76·58
1894	72·12	1·66	0·35	74·13	1·38	0·53	0·91	..	..	76·95
1895	75·93	2·17	0·32	78·42	1·15	0·29	0·84	..	..	80·70
1896	76·49	3·08	0·39	79·96	1·19	0·32	0·75	..	..	82·22
1897	70·92	1·91	0·38	73·21	1·29	0·33	0·77	..	1·60	77·20
1898	82·66	2·20	0·47	85·33	1·40	0·25	0·93	..	..	87·91
1899	88·70	2·21	0·45	91·36	1·92	0·16	0·88	..	..	94·32
1900	87·28	2·83	0·60	90·71	1·68	0·13	0·93	0·99	..	94·44
1901	97·04	2·70	0·60	100·34	1·61	0·16	1·01	0·35	..	103·47
1902	101·03	2·23	0·44	103·70	2·01	0·42	0·72	0·01	..	106·86
1903	100·94	1·96	0·69	103·59	2·42	0·26	0·61	1·24	..	108·12
1904	113·18	2·11	0·68	115·97	2·33	0·27	0·61	0·28	..	119·46
1905	110·62	2·53	0·72	113·87	2·46	0·33	0·65	0·15	..	117·46
1906	103·70	3·54	0·86	108·10	2·70	0·45	0·74	0·02	3·80	115·81
1907	112·80	2·44	0·84	116·08	2·76	0·49	0·79	0·06	..	120·18
1908	105·40	2·19	0·85	108·44	1·86	0·30	0·89	0·05	7·00	118·54
1909	117·76	2·13	0·80	120·69	1·61	0·24	0·94	0·18	..	123·66
1910	127·20	2·34	0·86	130·40	2·07	0·25	0·98	0·40	..	134·10
1911	131·04	2·75	0·97	134·76	2·23	0·16	0·89	0·22	..	138·26
1912	132·93	2·50	1·00	136·43	2·34	0·13	1·02	0·34	..	140·26
1913	122·99	2·65	1·04	126·68	2·09	0·10	1·06	0·47	3·50	133·90
1914	117·31	3·73	1·10	122·14	1·70	0·07	1·21	0·06	..	125·18
1915	90·28	2·01	1·67	93·96	2·66	0·08	1·53	18·70	..	116·93
1916	76·12	2·80	1·56	80·48	6·80	0·07	1·70	11·45	..	100·50
1917	61·08	1·41	1·59	64·08	5·66	0·11	2·18	10·34	..	82·36

Year.	Transit and Navigation.				Investments.	Exchange Profits.	Estates.	Other Receipts.	Brought Forward.	From Reserve.	Total.
	Ships.	Passengers.	Other Dues.	Total.							
					In million francs						
1918	79·34	1·05	3·01	83·40	5·92	0·40	0·13	3·12	3·98	6·50	103·45
1919	136·97	5·16	2·96	145·09	7·38	28·88	0·58	2·78	0·53	..	185·24
1920	144·59	4·75	2·58	151·92	10·88	101·77	1·00	1·89	0·51	..	267·97
1921	144·49	2·73	2·07	149·29	9·05	98·61	1·01	2·17	0·32	..	260·45
1922	162·61	2·55	1·69	166·85	9·55	126·17	1·06	1·83	0·95	..	306·41
1923	171·96	2·28	1·53	175·77	12·59	228·17	1·02	1·70	2·11	..	421·36
1924	182·57	2·45	1·47	186·49	4·80	314·60	0·96	1·74	3·73	..	512·32
1925	189·43	2·49	1·54	193·46	27·41	384·80	1·14	1·87	2·50	..	611·18
1926	183·87	2·64	1·58	188·09	24·22	531·08	1·21	1·95	2·07	..	748·62
1927	203·97	3·17	1·55	208·69	28·82	543·99	1·14	1·95	0·92	..	785·51
1928	1,057·52	14·25	7·62	1,079·39	44·18	26·76	10·74	10·74	3·15	..	1,170·26
1929	1,100·34	14·84	9·29	1,124·47	49·05	..	5·66	10·77	4·11	..	1,194·06
1930	1,022·96	13·84	7·32	1,044·12	37·97	..	5·84	10·62	5·26	..	1,103·81
1931	918·38	12·24	6·42	937·04	26·08	..	6·14	10·61	1·44	50·00	1,031·31
1932	783·50	11·82	4·89	800·21	19·66	..	5·92	8·37	3·90	11·45	849·51

NOTE. From 1928 amounts are in new francs, 4·925 of which are equal to one gold franc.

TABLE II

SUEZ CANAL PAYMENTS

Year.	Administration.	Transit.	Maintenance.	Estates, Water, &c.	Interest and Drawings. Bonds.	Shares and Consol. Coupons.	Reserve.	Total.
			In million francs					
1870	1·07	1·22	2·76	3·27	10·54	..	..	18·86
1871	0·96	1·72	1·80	0·88	10·56	..	..	15·92
1872	0·90	1·61	1·57	0·75	11·42	..	..	16·25
1873	0·92	1·53	2·31	0·86	11·73	5·00[1]	..	22·35
1874	0·94	1·51	3·04	0·80	12·38	10·00[1]	..	28·67
1875	0·97	1·58	2·83	0·98	11·58	12·25[2]	0·06	30·25
1876	1·06	1·56	2·30	0·71	11·64	11·79	0·11	29·17
1877	1·14	1·62	2·28	0·76	11·66	11·78	0·24	29·48
1878	1·17	1·60	1·87	0·64	11·62	11·78	0·19	28·87
1879	1·07	1·54	1·78	0·48	11·41	11·78	0·14	28·20
1880	1·14	1·56	2·08	0·69	11·59	11·78	0·65	29·49
1881	1·14	1·67	1·97	0·54	11·60	11·78	1·30	30·00
1882	1·28	2·43	2·14	0·79	11·63	11·80	1·67	31·74
1883	1·49	2·34	2·24	1·17	11·73	11·80	1·89	32·66
1884	1·44	2·28	1·90	1·00	11·92	11·80	..	30·34
1885	1·41	2·43	2·06	1·23	12·09	11·80	..	31·02
1886	1·45	2·27	2·10	0·80	12·24	11·80	..	30·66
1887	1·42	2·41	1·54	1·15	12·20	11·80	..	30·52
1888	1·54	2·61	1·99	1·29	12·20	11·80	..	31·43
1889	1·73	2·82	2·34	1·62	12·24	11·80	..	32·55
1890	1·58	2·89	2·42	1·45	12·19	11·80	..	32·33
1891	1·66	3·24	2·50	1·78	15·30	11·80	1·50	37·78
1892	1·82	3·27	2·09	1·25	15·85	11·80	..	36·08
1893	1·85	3·30	2·16	1·09	15·76	11·80	..	35·96
1894	1·53	3·12	2·07	1·32	15·99	11·80	0·75	36·58
1895	1·47	3·03	3·48	1·52	16·14	11·80	1·29	38·73
1896	1·46	3·00	3·80	1·48	16·17	11·80	2·23	39·94
1897	1·46	2·92	2·58	1·26	16·27	11·80	..	36·29
1898	1·64	2·84	2·34	1·44	16·21	11·80	5·02	41·29

Year.	Administration.	Transit.	Maintenance.	Estates, Water, &c.	Interest and Drawings. Bonds.	Shares.	Reserves. Statutory, Special, Depreciation, &c.	Carried Forward.	Total.
			In million francs						
1899	1·79	3·18	2·47	1·20	16·22	11·80	5·13	0·99	42·78
1900	1·63	3·21	3·03	1·15	16·62	11·80	5·08	0·35	42·87
1901	1·62	3·16	3·35	1·22	16·39	11·80	4·59	0·01	42·14
1902	1·72	3·02	3·75	1·20	15·31	11·88	7·24	1·24	45·36
1903	1·81	3·04	3·96	1·31	15·30	11·88	5·97	0·28	43·55
1904	1·86	3·15	3·93	0·92	15·30	11·88	11·34	0·15	48·53
1905	1·86	3·07	3·72	0·91	15·29	11·88	9·54	0·02	46·29
1906	2·04	3·26	4·69	0·98	15·28	11·88	6·24	0·06	44·43
1907	2·04	3·45	5·41	1·09	15·27	11·88	9·60	0·05	48·79
1908	2·21	3·50	6·70	1·20	15·26	11·88	6·16	0·18	47·09

[1] July 1870, Coupon.
[2] Including £466,000 Sinking Fund, 1870–4.

SUEZ CANAL PAYMENTS (*cont.*)

Year.	Administration.	Transit.	Maintenance.	Estates, Water, &c.	Interest and Drawings. Bonds.	Shares.	Reserves. Statutory, Special, Depreciation, &c.	Carried Forward.	Total.
				In million francs					
1909	2·09	3·51	5·03	1·38	15·49	11·88	6·40	0·40	46·18
1910	2·27	3·61	4·86	1·55	15·58	11·88	11·70	0·22	51·67
1911	2·30	4·01	5·73	1·55	15·58	11·88	9·79	0·34	51·18
1912	2·29	4·10	6·30	1·59	15·57	11·88	10·77	0·47	52·97
1913	2·36	4·03	7·60	1·55	15·56	11·88	3·00	0·06	46·04
1914	2·61	4·10	5·63	1·45	16·15	11·88	3·00	18·70	63·52
1915	2·32	4·54	4·37	1·39	16·41	11·88	3·00	11·45	55·36
1916	2·38	4·63	5·15	1·62	19·79	11·88	1·00	10·34	56·79
1917	2·59	4·78	4·82	1·74	23·21	11·88	..	3·98	53·00
1918	3·10	5·97	4·39	2·01	19·15	16·38	2·00	0·53	53·53
1919	4·69	8·24	10·40	2·90	15·90	20·37	18·00	0·51	81·01
1920	6·29	11·40	16·65	4·13	18·14	19·38	48·00	0·32	124·31
1921	7·71	13·05	17·31	5·89	17·91	18·37	30·00	0·95	111·19
1922	8·35	12·93	17·68	5·69	16·93	10·08	40·00	2·11	113·77
1923	8·54	13·25	14·37	5·49	16·84	10·08	85·00	3·73	157·30
1924	11·29	13·24	13·07	5·79	16·78	10·08	85·00	2·50	157·75
1925	10·01	13·15	18·09	6·09	16·92	10·08	70·00	2·07	146·41
1926	13·22	13·16	20·04	6·39	16·92	10·08	69·00	0·92	149·73
1927	12·86	13·01	15·84	7·01	16·92	10·08	70·00	3·15	148·87
1928	31·20	66·63	77·52	35·37	83·16	10·08	150·00	4·11	458·07
1929	34·77	76·38	80·67	36·33	83·09	10·08	130·00	5·26	456·58
1930	38·12	73·65	83·05	36·00	83·16	10·08	60·00	1·44	385·50
1931	38·73	73·37	66·32	33·88	83·15	49·64	70·00	3·90	418·99
1932	34·38	61·30	64·52	25·70	83·16	49·64	21·00	4·53	344·23

NOTE. From 1928 amounts are in new francs, 4·925 of which equal one gold franc.

TABLE III

SUEZ CANAL—DIVISION OF SURPLUS PROFITS

Year.	Total.	Shareholders. 71%	Egyptian Government. 15%	Founders' Shares. 10%	Directors. 2%	Staff. 2%
		In million francs				
1870	−9·59 ⎫	Deficit carried to 'premier établissement'.				
1871	−2·64 ⎭					
1872	2·07	Profit carried forward to next year.				
1873	4·55	,,	,,	,,		
1874	2·61	,,	,,	,,		
1875	2·15	,,	,,	,,	'en fonds special'.	
1875	1·06	0·75	0·16	0·11	0·02	0·02
1876	2·00	1·42	0·30	0·20	0·04	0·04
1877	4·50	3·20	0·67	0·45	0·09	0·09
1878	3·63	2·58	0·55	0·36	0·07	0·07
1879	2·75	1·95	0·41	0·27	0·06	0·06
1880	12·33	8·75	1·85	1·23	0·25	0·25
1881	24·68	17·52	3·70	2·47	0·50	0·49
1882	31·67	22·49	4·75	3·17	0·63	0·63
1883	35·86	25·46	5·38	3·58	0·72	0·72
1884	35·07	24·90	5·26	3·51	0·70	0·70
1885	34·03	24·16	5·10	3·41	0·68	0·68

TABLE III (*cont.*)

Year.	Total.	Shareholders. 71%	Egyptian Government. 15%	Founders' Shares. 10%	Directors. 2%	Staff. 2%
			In million francs			
1886	28·36	20·13	4·25	2·84	0·57	0·57
1887	29·99	21·29	4·50	3·00	0·60	0·60
1888	36·27	25·75	5·44	3·63	0·72	0·73
1889	37·21	26·42	5·58	3·72	0·74	0·75
1890	38·13	27·07	5·72	3·81	0·77	0·76
1891	49·09	34·86	7·36	4·91	0·98	0·98
1892	41·73	29·63	6·26	4·17	0·84	0·83
1893	40·62	28·84	6·09	4·06	0·81	0·82
1894	40·37	28·66	6·06	4·03	0·81	0·81
1895	41·97	29·80	6·30	4·20	0·84	0·83
1896	42·28	30·02	6·34	4·23	0·84	0·85
1897	40·91	29·05	6·14	4·09	0·82	0·81
1898	46·62	33·10	6·99	4·67	0·93	0·93
1899	51·54	36·60	7·73	5·15	1·03	1·03
1900	51·57	36·61	7·74	5·16	1·03	1·03
1901	61·33	43·54	9·20	6·13	1·23	1·23
1902	61·50	43·66	9·23	6·15	1·23	1·23
1903	64·57	45·84	9·69	6·46	1·29	1·29
1904	70·93	50·36	10·64	7·09	1·42	1·42
1905	71·17	50·53	10·67	7·12	1·42	1·43
1906	71·38	50·68	10·71	7·14	1·43	1·42
1907	71·39	50·68	10·71	7·14	1·43	1·43
1908	71·45	50·73	10·72	7·14	1·43	1·43
1909	77·48	55·01	11·62	7·75	1·55	1·55
1910	82·43	58·53	12·36	8·24	1·65	1·65
1911	87·08	61·83	13·06	8·71	1·74	1·74
1912	87·29	61·98	13·09	8·73	1·75	1·74
1913	87·86	62·38	13·18	8·79	1·75	1·76
1914	61·66	43·78	9·25	6·17	1·23	1·23
1915	61·57	43·71	9·24	6·16	1·23	1·23
1916	43·71	31·03	6·56	4·37	0·88	0·87
1917	29·36	20·84	4·40	2·94	0·59	0·59
1918	49·92	35·44	7·49	4·99	1·00	1·00
1919	104·23	74·00	15·64	10·43	2·08	2·08
1920	143·66	102·00	21·55	14·37	2·87	2·87
1921	149·26	105·98	22·39	14·93	2·98	2·98
1922	192·64	136·78	28·90	19·26	3·85	3·85
1923	264·06	187·48	39·61	26·41	5·28	5·28
1924	354·57	251·75	53·19	35·45	7·09	7·09
1925	464·77	329·99	69·71	46·47	9·30	9·30
1926	598·89	425·21	89·83	59·89	11·98	11·98
1927	636·64	452·02	95·50	63·66	12·73	12·73
1928	712·19	505·66	106·83	71·22	14·24	14·24
1929	737·48	523·61	110·62	73·75	14·75	14·75
1930	718·31	510·00	107·75	71·83	14·36	14·37
1931	612·32	434·75	91·85	61·23	12·25	12·24
1932	505·28	358·75	75·79	50·53	10·10	10·11

NOTE. Distribution was made in gold francs to 1919 and then in current francs up to the stabilization of the franc in May 1928; thereafter in new francs 4·925 of which equal one gold franc.

TABLE IV

SUEZ CANAL TRAFFIC—BY NATIONALITIES

The British Government directors began in 1884 to report to the Foreign Office (Commercial, No. 25/1884) the nationalities and 'net tonnage' of ships passing through the Suez Canal. Prior to that year gross tonnage was recorded, except that from 1881 an 'official' tonnage was given in the statistical reports published by the Egyptian Ministry of the Interior which did not correspond with the net tonnage; e.g., for 1881 the gross tonnage was 5,794,000 tons in the Canal accounts and 5,823,000 tons in the Egyptian bluebook, while the 'net tonnage' was 4,137,000 tons, and the 'official' tonnage 3,216,000 tons, so that the 'official' would appear to be British net tonnage and the 4,137,000 tons 'Suez Canal measurement'. Particulars of the movement of ships of the leading nationalities are given in the following table. During the War the Austro-Hungarian flag disappeared, and since 1915 Denmark has been substituted in the Table.

In thousand tons

Year	Total	United Kingdom	France	Netherlands	Germany	Italy	Austria-Hungary	Spain	Norway	Russia	Japan	United States
1870	436	289	85	..	..	6	19	1	..	1	..	..
1871	761	546	89	7	2	27	39	1	..	1	..	..
1872	1,439	1,060	163	26	12	48	39	3	1	5	..	4
1873	2,085	1,500	222	73	36	59	53	8	4	13	..	1
1874	2,424	1,797	223	106	40	63	91	31	9	14	1	2
1875	2,941	2,181	226	131	46	80	92	50	13	12	1	..
1876	3,072	2,344	237	147	41	82	76	44	21	25	1	5
1877	3,419	2,698	234	156	57	86	73	55	21	24	..	1
1878	3,291	2,630	251	151	31	65	64	51	21	..	..	3
1879	3,237	2,506	262	159	22	94	71	56	8	..	9	3
1880	4,376	3,461	275	173	54	105	116	86	9	9	2	2
1881	5,823	4,832	290	188	61	116	127	102	11	47	1	1
1882	5,075	4,126	286	188	127	108	88	57	14	49	1	..
1883	5,776	4,406	557	229	157	132	99	107	26	23	..	..
1884	5,872	4,467	568	264	169	114	103	96	24	28	4	1
1885	6,336	4,864	574	252	199	159	120	96	24	30	13	5
1886	5,768	4,437	476	230	210	125	137	59	38	47	4	3
1887	5,903	4,517	384	221	220	252	141	62	35	36	5	6
1888	6,641	5,223	387	218	238	267	123	65	36	34	3	1
1889	6,783	5,353	362	262	289	187	117	72	49	28	6	1
1890	6,890	5,331	366	249	491	144	118	72	66	34	4	2
1891	8,699	6,838	407	269	596	180	112	70	57	35	4	1
1892	7,712	5,827	416	320	554	128	125	69	84	39	8	..
1893	7,659	5,753	461	327	556	120	167	69	108	44	4	1
1894	8,039	5,997	467	357	626	119	188	71	89	54	1	3
1895	8,448	6,063	673	366	694	146	166	82	68	77	12	3
1896	8,560	5,818	532	380	806	392	158	96	109	87	2	2
1897	7,899	5,139	520	382	859	129	184	182	74	134	30	..
1898	9,239	6,298	572	382	970	137	213	138	87	144	114	4
1899	9,786	6,586	599	419	1,071	133	266	149	81	153	183	2
1900	9,738	5,605	752	507	1,071	133	266	114	124	172	225	68
1901	10,823	6,253	757	509	1,763	176	409[1]	110	68	307	246	54
1902	11,248	6,773	769	520	1,707	167	418	113	76	364	237	45
1903	11,907	7,404	781	549	1,773	149	407	87	71	349	221	24

[1] At about this time the Austro-Hungarian Government repaid to ships flying the national flag all Canal Dues paid by them (see Hansard, 11.6.07).

TABLE IV (cont.)

Year.	Total.	United Kingdom.	France.	Netherlands.	Germany.	Italy.	Austria-Hungary.	Spain.	Norway.	Russia.	Japan.	United States.
					In thousand tons							
1904	13,402	8,834	778	583	1,970	205	455	88	146	154	21	24
1905	13,134	8,357	884	578	2,113	190	458	75	116	177	..	13
1906	13,446	8,300	856	561	2,156	181	483	81	80	330	147	68
1907	14,728	9,496	807	632	2,254	202	440	75	54	239	259	13
1908	13,633	8,302	815	744	2,311	190	388	78	62	252	286	..
1909	15,408	9,592	802	801	2,382	208	520	76	77	222	358	..
1910	16,582	10,424	833	855	2,564	218	643	71	46	288	351	9
1911	18,325	11,716	820	971	2,791	202	622	72	60	311	362	2
1912	20,275	12,848	799	1,240	2,825	368	814	73	91	363	320	3
1913	20,034	12,052	928	1,287	3,352	291	846	76	93	341	343	7
1914	19,409	12,910	800	1,389	2,119	369	632	72	97	200	354	3
							Denmark					
1915	15,266	11,656	666	1,334	..	363	166	73	136	60	566	3
1916	12,325	9,788	774	643	..	439	145	66	167	27	70	35
1917	8,369	6,164	579	126	..	778	35	21	66	1	155	28
1918	9,252	7,356	380	3	..	477	..	26	83	..	502	8
1919	16,014¹	11,355	475	755	..	317	315	98	257	55	1,450	168
1920	17,575¹	10,838	775	1,426	15	606	230	72	172	46	1,601	724
1921	18,119	11,397	968	2,032	171	934	232	31	259	12	1,042	672
1922	20,743	13,383	997	2,161	735	858	280	46	309	41	928	668
1923	22,730	14,264	1,294	2,178	1,214	1,043	300	37	331	74	986	614
1924	25,110	14,995	1,497	2,488	1,647	1,483	345	52	367	62	872	795
1925	26,762	16,016	1,628	2,699	1,791	1,416	360	68	372	35	1,067	812
1926	26,060	14,969	1,736	2,859	2,154	1,348	331	49	452	44	946	710
1927	28,962	16,534	1,807	3,025	2,764	1,514	292	30	662	59	914	682
1928	31,906	18,124	1,927	3,330	3,300	1,650	354	18	687	68	940	729
1929	33,466	19,114	2,166	3,544	3,455	1,525	404	18	702	104	952	705
1930	31,669	17,600	2,002	3,313	3,389	1,503	432	9	966	130	939	670
1931	30,028	16,624	2,084	2,848	3,315	1,424	366	..	746	175	1,153	625
1932	28,340	15,721	2,037	2,364	2,506	1,609	438	..	861	274	1,440	526

1 Including 317,000 tons in 1919 and 526,000 tons in 1920 described as 'Inter-Allied'.

BIBLIOGRAPHY

Julien (Raymond): *Le Trafic du Canal de Suez*. Conjoncture Économique et Prévisions. Preface by M. George Edgar-Bonnet, Directeur adjoint de la Compagnie du Canal Maritime de Suez.

This book, published in October 1933, appeared too late to be utilized, or analysed, in this chapter.

Foreign Office: Annual Returns of Shipping and Tonnage.

TABLE V
TRAFFIC THROUGH SUEZ CANAL
WITH COUNTRIES EAST AND SOUTH

The Reports of the Suez Canal Company give for 1890 and subsequent years the particulars set out in the following table:

Year.	Total.	Red Sea and Gulf of Aden.	East Africa (to Cape) and Islands.	Persian Gulf.	India.		French Indo-China and Siam.	Straits, Dutch East Indies.	Australia, New Zealand, New Caledonia.	China, Japan, Siberia, Philippines.	Other Regions and Ports for Orders.
					West Coast.	East Coast, Burma, Ceylon.					
					In thousand net tons						
1890	6,890	..	149	..	1,988	1,882	879		716	928	348
1891	8,699	..	219	..	2,610	2,297	1,113		799	1,167	494
1892	7,712	..	232	..	2,083	2,152	966		795	1,105	379
1893	7,659	..	172	..	2,239	1,833	1,028		798	1,234	355
1894	8,039	..	193	..	2,106	2,242	970		798	1,347	383
1895	8,448	..	357	..	2,015	2,417	1,003		840	1,400	416
1896	8,560	..	269	..	1,649	2,411	1,085		871	1,578	697
1897	7,899	..	303	..	1,269	2,419	1,033		845	1,705	325
1898	9,238	..	341	..	2,034	2,652	1,048		820	1,851	492
1899	9,896	..	378	..	1,846	2,892	1,265		922	2,175	418
1900	9,738	..	404	..	1,128	2,763	1,372		864	2,756	451
1901	10,824	..	382	..	1,675	3,106	1,504		972	2,710	475
1902	11,248	..	397	..	1,962	3,478	1,539		981	2,486	405
1903	11,907	..	477	..	2,405	3,481	1,435		926	2,665	518
1904	13,402	..	450	..	3,033	4,006	1,722		924	2,665	602
1905	13,134	..	482	..	2,623	3,722	1,671		995	2,943	698
1906	13,445	..	484	..	2,557	3,817	1,537		1,155	3,299	596
1907	14,728	..	454	..	3,329	3,823	1,708		1,318	3,375	716
1908	13,633	..	436	..	2,193	3,769	1,945		1,234	3,489	567
1909	15,407	..	454	..	3,114	4,214	1,655		1,544	3,874	552
1910	16,582	..	510	..	3,359	4,300	1,987		1,704	3,977	745
1911	18,325	..	710	..	3,723	4,639	2,331		1,904	4,060	958
1912	20,275	..	747	..	4,812	4,947	2,435		2,037	4,202	1,095
1913	20,034	..	816	..	4,129	5,058	2,383		2,104	4,548	996
1914 1915 1916 1917 1918	Not published										
1919	16,014	84	1,372	646	2,604	3,289	265	2,144	2,595	2,615	400
1920	17,575	141	1,586	666	2,986	3,753	403	2,523	1,359	3,796	362
1921	18,119	526	893	1,253	2,802	3,786	625	2,398	2,097	3,699	40
1922	20,743	489	841	1,956	3,436	4,338	270	2,455	2,406	4,472	80
1923	22,730	554	1,051	2,301	3,709	4,399	500	2,587	2,477	4,979	173
1924	25,110	512	1,123	2,607	4,116	5,016	480	2,693	2,529	5,671	363
1925	26,762	456	1,303	2,960	3,610	5,460	614	2,802	3,388	5,709	460
1926	26,060	400	1,475	3,384	2,819	4,932	598	2,847	3,163	5,888	554
1927	28,963	530	1,682	3,615	3,399	5,619	694	3,094	3,473	6,383	474
1928	31,906	507	1,832	3,876	3,659	5,970	901	3,955	3,435	7,186	585
1929	33,466	680	1,928	4,190	3,321	5,925	854	4,475	3,942	7,669	482
1930	31,669	502	1,875	4,517	2,988	5,588	827	3,912	3,703	7,350	407
1931	30,028	355	1,750	4,326	2,951	5,280	864	3,214	3,601	7,243	444
1932	28,340	599	1,624	4,589	2,445	4,486	875	2,863	3,334	7,102	423

CHAPTER IX

THE SUEZ CANAL DURING THE GREAT WAR

Position on outbreak of war. Enemy merchant ships. Declaration of War by Turkey. Canal defended. Activity of spies. Sir John Maxwell takes command. Defensive system. Attacks by the Turks. Mines placed in canal. Advanced line of defence organized. Effect of abandonment of Gallipoli. Sir A. Murray succeeds Sir John Maxwell. Ocean wharves constructed at Qantara: railway developments. Lt.-Col. Elgood's comments.

THE Suez Canal had always been regarded in Germany as the 'jugular vein' of the British Empire: its somewhat anomalous, even dubious, status in international law tended to obscure the realities of strategical and political action even to the canal officials who were, on the outbreak of war in 1914, somewhat uncertain as to their proper duties and sphere. The immediate result was serious delay to many ships consequent on the inability of the owners to pay dues in Paris in the usual way,[1] and the British Government had to intervene to induce the Suez Canal Company to delegate authority to the London Office to accept payment of dues in London. It was a bad beginning, but the matter was adjusted, though not before much resentment had been aroused.

Great Britain's first care was *aperire terram gentibus,* to keep open and protect the Suez Canal, in terms of the Convention of 1888, as applied by the Anglo-French Agreement of 1904. To do this it was necessary to occupy strategic points on the Canal Zone, which may be regarded as a technical but excusable breach of the Convention of 1888.

Soon after the declaration of war a number of enemy merchant ships took refuge at Port Said and Suez in order to avoid capture: they were allowed to do so, and it was not until several masters of enemy ships were found to be using their wireless apparatus for illegitimate purposes that the Company went so far as to dismantle the apparatus. Sir J. Maxwell records that in September a German sailor swam round a British warship waving a German flag and shouting abuse without being molested, and there were other incidents even more serious and more grotesque. Neither the troops nor the ships of war at Port Said and Suez were there to forbid the right of passage, but to ensure it. The Canal Company was, in the words of the Official History of the War, 'sensitive', and was not consoled even by the fact that the British Mediterranean Fleet was under the orders of the French Commander-

---

[1] Hansard, 6th Aug. 1914.

in-Chief, whilst several British cruisers were at the southern end to assure the safety of the canal. Not until Turkey declared war were their doubts removed and their difficulties solved. It was soon decided that there was no right of asylum in the canal, and the Egyptian Government called on the enemy ships that had taken refuge to leave its waters, escorting them with Egyptian gunboats beyond the three-mile limit, where captors awaited them.

Precautions were taken to prevent damage to the canal: the Egyptian Camel Corps patrolled either bank: the Bikanir Camel Corps from India arrived next, followed by the Divisions from India which replaced the British Garrison, the armed forces in Egypt being under the control of Major-General Sir John Maxwell, whose experience of Egypt dated from Tel-el-Kebir in 1882.

In October a German, an officer of the Alexandria Police, was arrested: in his possession were maps of the Suez Canal, and large numbers of detonators as well as a secret code. He was a Turkish emissary. Egypt was full of enemy subjects—at least 600[1] apart from 200 men interned from captured ships. Many of the Suez Canal pilots were Austrians, some of whom were apparently still in the service of the Suez Canal Company in 1916.[2] It is difficult to know whether to praise the Company for retaining in its service men in whom it felt complete confidence, regardless of nationality, or to blame it for subjecting the divided loyalty of such men to so severe a test. The Company, however, declared their services to be indispensable, and guaranteed their devotion to the service of the Canal: the result justified their confidence.

Sir John Maxwell took over charge in September; most of the troops under his command arrived in October: by December the defence of the canal had been organized. It was divided into three sectors for defence: Suez to the Bitter Lakes; Deversoir, north of the Great Bitter Lake, to El Ferdan; El Ferdan to Port Said. Force head-quarters and the general reserve were at Ismailia. Small detachments guarded the Sweet-water Canal and supply depots. In January 1915 a camel transport corps was formed. Old French and British warships were permanently stationed in the canal in berths, sometimes specially dredged, prepared to act as floating batteries, and there were a few British and French aircraft. The line of defence was, at first, the canal itself—the main line of communication of the British Empire thus becoming an obstacle in front of a fire trench. It was thus liable to interruption, which might be serious, but no other scheme was, in the first instance, practicable.

---

[1] There were 70,000 Turkish nationals: of these but a few were potentially dangerous.
[2] Hansard, 6th Jan. 1916.

The Canal Company's fleet of small and large craft, its engineers and their local knowledge were placed at the disposal of the Defence Force: large areas on the east bank of the canal were flooded, thus narrowing the area to be defended.

More rain fell that winter than usual, and in January 1915 a force of some 5,000 Turks were within striking distance of the canal, relying for victory on a rising of Egyptian Nationalists, which was to synchronize with the attack on the canal and to be ushered on by the murder of leading Europeans. The presence of Australians in the capital discouraged such manifestations.

The attack, gallantly delivered on 3rd February between Lake Timsah and Great Bitter Lake, failed, though three Turkish pontoons contrived to cross the canal. A Turkish 15 cm. Howitzer battery nearly succeeded, by accurate shooting at 9,200 metres, in sinking one of His Majesty's ships—the *Hardinge*—a R.I.M. transport vessel, in the fairway, and a French battleship, the *Requin*. On a British ship, the *Clio*, the Turks did 'some remarkably pretty shooting'.[1]

The attack was not repeated. The canal traffic, which was suspended for a few nights and for the daylight hours of 3rd February, was resumed. One civilian was wounded—a pilot of the Canal Company, Mr. George Carew, who, though he had a leg shot off and an arm broken, brought the *Hardinge* safely into the Timsah. He was awarded the Legion of Honour.

The immediate menace to the canal was thus removed, but the threat to the canal, though more distant, remained, for some 30,000 Turkish troops were at Beersheba and there were indications that a fresh attack was in contemplation whilst mines were being laid in the Red Sea and Gulf of Suez by Turkish vessels operating from Akaba. Ample rains had fallen in Sinai, facilitating every movement and, in March, fresh attacks were made and repulsed. On 8th April a hostile patrol appeared near Kantara: its tracks were followed eastward for 15 miles, where a large packing-case was found among the dunes. The canal was then dragged and the mine brought up on the night of the 10th. Several ships had passed over the spot in the time intervening. On 28th April fresh attacks were made near the Ismailia ferry post, and repulsed. On 30th May fresh activity developed. A party was detected approaching the canal; they retreated, but not till they had buried a mine, destined for the canal, in the sand, three quarters of a mile from the east bank, where it was discovered. On 30th June the Holt liner *Teiresias* struck a mine in the Little Bitter Lake, despite the fact that the lake had been regularly patrolled by three armed launches, manned by naval ratings. The ship swung across the channel, blocking it

[1] *Official History*, i. 45.

completely, but the Canal Company was able to reopen it for traffic that night.

The Turks now abandoned, for the time, further efforts in this field. Their principal efforts were being made in the Dardanelles, and thither most of the regular troops who had opposed us in the Sinai peninsula were transferred. The abandonment of Gallipoli was already under consideration and the British Government now had to decide, in communication with the French, how best to secure for the future the safety of the canal. Action in the Gulf of Alexandretta, to cut the railway to Palestine, was considered, and abandoned. A scheme of defence on a line 12,000 yards east of the canal over a distance of 87 miles was worked out, it was considered to require five mounted and eight infantry divisions, with 19 batteries of siege and heavy artillery, armoured cars and additional aircraft, with war material, wire, telephonic and cable communication, water arrangements and light railways. This plan was, eventually, rejected, but it serves to show both the difficulty of, and the importance attached to, the defence of the canal.

The abandonment of Gallipoli in December 1915 made the Suez Canal once more an important potential theatre of war, and it was to Egypt that the troops withdrawn from Gallipoli were sent. Lord Kitchener was deeply impressed by the danger in store for the country when the hands of the Turks were freed. He knew Egypt, and like General Maxwell was not inclined to count upon the goodwill of the people if once a powerful Turkish force appeared within striking distance of the canal; it was estimated that by April, 1916, the Turks could mass 130,000 men against us in this theatre.

The commands in the Mediterranean were reorganized, and responsibility for the defence of Suez Canal was vested in Lt.-General Sir Archibald Murray. Arriving on 9th January, 'He found' in the words of the *Official History* (i. 95)

'the Canal a scene of great activity. Fleets of *dahabiehs* had been brought from the Nile to the Canal and were carrying stone and railway material to the termini of the roads and railways on the east bank, and pipes for the pipe-lines which were to run out into the desert at right angles to the line of the Canal. Light railways in the Delta had been picked up and transferred to the Canal Zone. Hundreds of *dahabiehs* sailed each day from Port Said with hurdles, unloaded these at various points, then went on to Suez to fetch road-metal. The pipes came in the first place from India, about 130 miles of piping being obtained from this source. Thereafter it had to be purchased in the United States, and its arrival was awaited with anxiety. A single submarine might at this stage throw all plans out of gear and delay progress for many weeks.

'It was fortunate that the foundations of the new scheme of defence had been laid by Sir J. Maxwell. It demanded a great effort from all departments of the Government, intimate knowledge of men, of resources, of procedure, and the tact which only experience can fully develop. A new commander and staff would have found it a matter of extreme difficulty to set in motion this complicated machinery; they certainly could not have achieved so much in the time with all the good will in the world.'

The force under Sir A. Murray's command was now regarded as an Imperial Strategic Reserve. No more suitable spot could have been chosen from a geographical point of view, and few ports were better fitted for the purpose of receiving and dispatching military units than Port Said. The work of embarkation and disembarkation, of refitting and of refuelling both naval and military units involved the closest co-operation with the officials of the Company, who never failed us. It was done without any considerable delay to the vast commercial traffic which continued to pass through the Canal in almost undiminished volume, and the dividends of the shareholders remained unaffected.

Ocean wharves were constructed, with the consent of the Company, at Kantara, which has been connected by rail with the Egyptian railway system and was also the terminus of the military railway system on the east bank. From Kantara 600,000 gallons of fresh water were pumped daily through the pipe-lines which ran eastwards into the desert, where an elaborate system of more distant defence was constructed, designed to prevent the enemy from bringing the canal under gun-fire.

From March 1916 to October 1917 the ration strength of the British force in Egypt ran from 150,000 to 200,000 and probably at least as large a number of Egyptians were being paid from Army Funds.

In June 1917 Sir A. Murray was replaced by General Sir E. Allenby, and the British advance was continued to El Arish. Sinai was clear of the enemy and all danger to the Suez Canal was removed.

Lt.-Col. P. G. Elgood, who was on duty at Port Said during 1915 and 1916, writes as follows of the services rendered during this period by the Canal Company to the British Expeditionary Forces:

'During the years of the military occupation of the Suez Canal, rarely a day passed that British commanders were not in communication with the Company. They had, thus, ample occasion to form their own judgement upon its methods of business, and a more single-minded associate in a common cause they hardly could hope to meet. Its wealth of plant and efficiency of personnel filled naval and military officers with constant wonder and admiration: and fortunate it was for the defenders of the Canal that the Company had so great resources at command. It was a poor return for the open-handed manner in which these resources were placed later at the disposal of the British military authorities, that frequently the latter would borrow plant and omit to acknowledge receipt, despite a promise that a formal letter would be sent. Instances occurred again and again in the early days of the military occupation of the Canal, when senior officers hurriedly would descend upon Port Said, borrow craft from the Company, and forget later to perform their own part of the contract. Such omissions were the more reprehensible since the Canal Company made no charge but actual out of pocket expenses for the use of plant. So frequent were these cases that in the spring of 1916 the Company declined to allow any further loan of craft or stores from Port Said, unless the military authority of that area signed the demand.

Throughout the War the attitude of the Canal Company towards the military was distinguished by great generosity. For the use of quays, warehouses, and so on, not a penny of rent ever was asked. It is true that from August 1914 to December 1916 the troops were engaged directly in protecting the property of the lender, and, since no suggestion was made that the latter should contribute towards the heavy expenditure incurred on the defence, the Company might be well expected to place its resources at the British Commander's disposal without charge. But from 1917 onwards a new situation arose. The Expeditionary Force was well into Palestine, and the Suez Canal relieved from danger of further attack. If the Company had pressed from that date for payment from the military, it is difficult to perceive how such a claim could be resisted. But no such demand ever was preferred. Many months after the Armistice, indeed, the Army was continuing to occupy extensive storage areas, to the injury of the Company's revenue; and doubtless would be there to this day had not the Company finally, and in self-defence, fixed a definite date when the troops either must evacuate the ground or pay for the use of it.'

The writer of these words does, perhaps, less than justice to the military officers whose conduct he criticizes; but his testimony to the honourable part played by the Canal Company's officials is well deserved, and was confirmed by Sir John Maxwell in his dispatch of the 16th February 1915 in the following words:

'I take this opportunity of bringing to the notice of the Secretary of State for War the great services rendered by the Comte de Serionne and the officials of the Suez Canal Company; they have one and all been most helpful, and have unreservedly placed their own personal service and the entire resources of the Company at my disposal. The success of our defence was greatly assisted by their cordial co-operation.'

BIBLIOGRAPHY

Official History of the War.
Malcolm, Sir Ian. 'The Suez Canal', *National Review*, May 1921; 2nd edition, May 1923; 3rd edition, June 1924.

MAPS

Map of the Suez Canal. Scale 1 : 250,000. G.S.G.S. No. 3753. War Office, 1925.
Canal Maritime de Suez. Plan Général. Scale 1 : 50,000. Compagnie Universelle du Canal Maritime de Suez. [Paris], 1920. 4 sheets.
Monumenta Cartographica. Africae et Aegypti. Par Youssouf Kamal. Tome deuxième, fascicule iv. Atlas Antiquus et Index, 1933.

CHAPTER X

THE PANAMA CANAL: A RIVAL ROUTE

The Panama and Suez Canals compared. Tolls. Transits. Tonnage. Receipts. Expenses. Deficits. Nationality of Shipping. Effect on Trade of U.S.A. Relative distances via Suez and Panama.

THE Suez Canal was opened to traffic in 1869; the Panama Canal in 1914. Unlike the Suez Canal, the Panama Canal is owned and controlled by the Government of the United States, who constructed it at the cost of the State and who maintain and operate it in virtue of a series of international treaties. The Suez Canal is about a hundred, the Panama Canal fifty, miles long. The Suez Canal runs at sea-level—the Mediterranean tide being negligible, and that of the Red Sea only some 5 feet. The Panama Canal rises by three locks at each end to a height of 85 feet above sea-level. The Suez Canal cost, in all, £30 millions to build, the Panama Canal £75 millions, and the cost of maintenance and operation is in about the same proportion. The ends of both canals are joined by a railway. The Suez Canal is unfortified, is open to the commerce of all nations in peace or in war, provided they can reach it, on payment of the authorized dues. The Panama Canal is a fortified zone under the military occupation of the forces of the United States Government—an *imperium in imperio* or enclave within the body of the Republic of Panama. The Panama Canal zone is governed by an official appointed by the President of the United States, and is subject to American law. The governor's salary is £2,500 a year or so ($10,000)—less than that of any of the thirty-two directors of the Suez Canal. The Suez Canal zone is only administered by the Canal Company so far as necessary for the purposes of its business, and is an integral part of Egypt.

Tolls.—The Hay-Pauncefote Treaty of 1901, between Great Britain and the United States, provided that the canal should be free and open to the vessels of commerce and of war of all nations, on terms of entire equality without discrimination as to conditions or charges on traffic. The same applies to the Suez Canal.

Panama Canal tolls are one dollar per net ton and sixty cents per net ton for vessels in ballast, net tonnage being fixed by special Panama Canal Rules of Measurement.[1] Suez Canal tolls are now six and three gold francs, respectively, per net ton, fixed by Suez Canal Rules.

---

[1] 'Taking freight vessels as they run, the net tonnage as determined by British rules is about 61 per cent. of the gross. The American rules produce a net tonnage averaging 66 per cent. of the gross, while the Suez Canal rules make the average net tonnage of all

Dealing with the period before Great Britain was forced off the gold standard, and converting dollars and francs into sterling at the average rates for 1929, 1930, and the first half of 1931, we get the following comparison between the Suez Canal and the Panama Canal dues:

		Per net ton of Shipping.	*Per ton of Cargo.*
Suez Canal . .	1929	5·302 *Shillings.*	5·140 *Shillings.*
	1930	5·215 ,,	5·793 ,,
	1931	5·289 ,,	6·271 ,,
Panama Canal . .	1929–30	3·716 ,,	3·712 ,,
	1930–1	3·649 ,,	4·045 ,,
	1931–2	4·176 ,,	4·982 ,,

Approximately the Suez Canal dues were higher in 1931 than the Panama Canal's by more than 25 per cent. per net ton of shipping passing, and by about 30 per cent. per ton of cargo carried; the exact figures are not shown in the accounts.

'The Suez Canal dues', says the Liverpool Steam Ship Owners' Association in their Report for 1930 (p. 14), 'compare very unfavourably with those of the Panama Canal; the net tonnage as calculated by the Suez Canal Company is considerably greater than the British registered net tonnage, whereas on the Panama Canal basis of calculation it is less. . . . The effect of this difference in tolls has been to divert a considerable amount of tonnage to the Panama Canal. Further, trade with the East from the Atlantic coast of America proceeds through the Panama Canal and has the advantage of the lower charges, whilst such trade from Japan, India, and the Pacific coast of America has no such expenditure at all to bear. The result is that British trade to the East is saddled with a heavy burden from which its competitors are in whole or in part free.'

The following table gives a few of the leading particulars relating to traffic through the Panama Canal; the years quoted are of twelve months to 30th June:

Particulars.	*Unit.*	*1929–30.*	*1930–1.*	*1931–2.*
Transits, paying toll .	Number	6,185	5,529	4,506
Transits, free (U.S. Govt. vessels) . . .	Number	600	568	473
Net tonnage . .	Th. net tons	29,981	27,792	23,625
Cargo carried . .	Th. tons	30,030	25,083	19,808
Receipts from tolls . .	Th. dollars	27,077	24,645	20,707
Tolls per net ton . .	Dollars	0·903	0·887	0·876
Tolls per ton of cargo .	Dollars	0·902	0·983	1·045

For the Suez Canal the corresponding figures, as far as I have been able to obtain them, for twelve months ending 31st December are: vessels using that canal 72 per cent. of the gross.' (Professor Emery Johnson, *Report to Congress on Panama Canal Traffic*, 1914.)

Particulars.	Units.	1929.	1930.	1931.	1932.
Transits, paying toll	Number	6,274	5,761	5,366	
Transits, free	..	Nil	Nil	Nil	Nil
New tonnage	Thousand tons	33·47	31·67	30·03	28·34
Receipts from tolls.	Millions of francs paper	1,100	1,023	918	784
Tolls per net ton	Frs. paper	32·88	32·30	30·58	27·65
Tolls per ton of cargo	Frs. paper	31·88	35·88	36·26	33·16

The drop in dues per ton of shipping reflects the increase in ballast traffic; the increases in dues, per ton of cargo, show that in the last two years vessels were more lightly laden than before.

The financial results of the Panama Canal may be summarized as follows:

Particulars.	1929–30.	1930–1.	1931–2.	Aggregate 1914–32.
	In million dollars.			
Tolls	27·1	24·6	20·7	292·6
Licences, fees, &c. . . .	0·3	0·4	0·3	4·5
Total canal receipts . . .	27·4	25·0	21·0	297·1
Net canal expenses . . .	9·3	10·4	9·8	143·0
Net revenue	18·1	14·6	11·2	154·1
Fixed capital charge . . .	15·2	15·2	15·1	174·2
Deficit on all transactions (canal, railway, business, &c.) . .	*	0·8	4·2	13·3[1]

* Profit 2·7 million dollars.

The particulars of Panama Canal expenses in 1931–2 were as follows:

Particulars.	Expenses.	Earnings.	Net Expenses.
	In thousand dollars.		
Executive department . .	672·4	238·5	433·9
Accounting department .	572·0	373·4	198·6
Washington office . .	284·7	40·4	244·3
Civil Government . .	1,383·2	90·6	1,292·6
Health department . .	1,648·3	873·7	774·6
Technical divisions . .	231·8	131·6	100·2
Public buildings . .	375·9	169·9	206·0
Marine division . . .	1,456·0	843·5	612·5
Locks operation, &c. . .	1,531·1	12·4	1,518·7
Dredging division . .	2,502·5	97·1	2,405·4
Municipal expenses . .	224·9	..	224·9
Miscellaneous . . .	1,827·6[2]	..	1,827·6
Total . . .	12,710·4	2,871·1	9,839·3

[1] After allowing for business profits aggregating 9·3 million dollars.
[2] Depreciation of fixed property $1,006,000; Annuity to Panama Republic $250,000; Proportion of general stores expenses $300,000.

Thus in the 18 years that have elapsed since 15th August 1914, when the canal was opened, till 30th June 1932 the total revenue has been 297·1 million dollars, of which 292·6 million dollars were derived from tolls. Net canal expenses were 143 million dollars, leaving a net revenue of 154·1 million dollars. About 174·2 million have been paid in interest at 3 per cent. on capital, and after allowing for ·business profits, &c., the computed loss is about 13·3 million dollars or about £2,730,000 at par. In the first 18 years of the Suez Canal receipts were 730·3 million gold francs, of which 692·3 million francs were from transit and navigation dues; expenses were 97·7 million francs (after deducting deficits for 1870 and 1871—12·2 million francs—carried to capital account), leaving a net revenue of 632·6 million francs. After paying about 209·6 million francs in interest at 3 per cent. on bonds, 168·7 million francs in a 5 per cent. dividend on shares, and placing 8·4 million francs to reserves, there remained 245·9 million francs (about £9,750,000 at par), which was divided between the shareholders, the Egyptian Government, the founders, the directors, and the staff.

Over the whole period the net canal expenses of the Panama Canal were over 48 per cent. of the canal revenue, while for the Suez Canal gross expenses (excluding bond interest) were under 13½ per cent., but leaving out the loans of 1887, about 39 million francs were raised in bonds for improving the Suez Canal. For the last ten account years Panama Canal net expenses were under 37 per cent. of receipts, while Suez Canal gross expenses (excluding bond interest) were about 16·8 per cent. of receipts. But out of a total of $9,839,000 for net canal expenses in 1931–2, about $4,055,000 were in respect of civil government, health, and other services not strictly belonging to the running of the canal. If these sums be deducted, canal expenses were about 27 per cent. of canal and business receipts for 1931–2, as compared with 20·2 per cent. for the Suez Canal in 1931 and 22·3 per cent. in 1932. Still in 1931–2 there was a total deficit of $4,162,000 in the Panama Canal accounts.

In 1928–9, out of 9,882,000 tons of cargo passing from east to west through the Panama Canal, 2,350,000 tons were iron and steel, whereas in 1929 there passed eastwards through Suez 3,590,000 tons of metals and machinery and 640,000 tons of railway material out of a total of 12,900,000 tons. Iron and steel goods, such as rails, are close-stowing and dues would be of little importance, but in the case of machinery, especially of the finer kinds, 100 to 120 cubic feet or more per ton weight would be needed, and dues become important as an element in shipping cost even if they are low in proportion to the value of the goods. With heavy low-value goods like cement (37s. 3d.

per ton f.o.b. ex-United Kingdom in 1932) and salt (49s. 9d. per ton f.o.b.) dues might be the deciding factor. Over a fifth (4,900,000 tons out of 21,620,000 tons) of the cargo coming westwards through the Suez Canal in 1929 consisted of mineral oils, and it fell to 3,310,000 tons out of 17,950,000 tons in 1931. In 1928–9 about 807,000 tons of mineral oil passed from east to west and 5,198,000 tons from west to east through the Panama Canal out of totals of 9,883,000 tons and 20,780,000 tons respectively; in 1931–2 westward-bound oil was 518,000 tons out of 5,635,000 tons, and eastward-bound oil 3,117,000 tons out of 14,173,000 tons. Oil carriage is more important to the Panama Canal than to the Suez Canal, and in 1928–9, tankers paid 18·9 per cent. of the Panama Canal tolls and in 1931–2, 15·4 per cent.; of course much of this traffic is between the east and west coasts of the United States.

Owing to the different periods for which the accounts are kept, close comparison cannot be made between the working of the two canals, but the figures below are significant.

	Suez Canal.				Panama Canal.			
	Calendar Years.				Years to 30th June.			
	1929.	1930.	1931.	1932.	1930.	1931.	1932.	1933.
Shipping using canal (thousand net tons)	33,466	31,669	30,028	28,340	29,981	27,792	23,625	
Cargo carried (thousand tons) . .	34,520	28,510	25,330	23,630	30,030	25,083	19,808	
Cargo per hundred net tons . . .	103·14	90·02	84·35	83·36	100·17	90·25	83·84	
Dues per net ton (canal measurement) .	Francs. 32·88	Francs. 32·30	Francs. 30·58	Francs. 27·65	Cents. 91·76	Cents. 88·68	Cents. 87·65	
Dues per ton of cargo .	31·88	35·88	36·26	33·16	90·16	98·26	104·54	
	At average exchange of period.							
Dues per net ton (canal measurement) .	s. d. 5 3·6	s. d. 5 2·6	s. d. 5 3·5	s. d. 6 2·4	s. d. 3 9·3	s. d. 3 7·8	s. d. 4 6·8	
Dues per ton of cargo.	5 1·7	5 9·5	6 3·3	7 5·2	3 6·0	4 0·8	5 4·4	

Panama Canal dues are 120 cents per net ton, Panama Canal measurement, for vessels with cargo, and 72 cents per ton for vessels in ballast, subject to the condition that these dues must not be more than 125 cents per net ton United States measurement nor less than 75 cents per ton. As Panama Canal measurement is about 35 per cent. greater than United States measurement, the latter is chosen at the higher rate. United States measurement is very nearly the same as British measurement; it may be about three-quarters of one per cent. less on the average, differing according to the type of ship. Panama Canal dues may thus be taken at 126 cents per British net ton or 7s. 2¼d. per British ton, compared with 7s. 10d. per British net ton for Suez Canal dues, francs and dollars being converted to sterling at the average rates of 1932. At par and per British net ton the Suez Canal dues of 6 francs would be equivalent to 5*s*. 9·6*d*., while the Panama Canal dues of 126 cents would equal 5*s*. 2·1*d*. The Suez Canal dues of 6·90 francs in 1929 were equivalent to 6*s*. 5·8*d*. per British net ton, the Panama dues being then still between 5*s*. 2*d*. and 5*s*. 3*d*. These calculations relate to the maximum Panama Canal rate. The actual average charge in 1931–2 was 87·65 cents per canal net ton, equal to 119 cents per British net ton, or 6*s*. 1·5*d*. at the average exchange of the 12 months. Suez Canal dues in 1931 were 30·58 francs per Suez Canal ton, or 36·24 francs per British net ton, or 6*s*. 3·2*d*. The corresponding rates per ton of cargo are shown in the table p. 148. The drop in the value of the dollar relatively to sterling is likely to have the effect, unless counterbalanced by a corresponding reduction in Suez Canal dues, of encouraging shipping via Panama in preference to via Suez. During the week ended 6th August, 1933, for example, the average exchange value of the £ was $4·497 or 84·76 fr., and on these values the maximum charge per British net registered ton would be about 8*s*. 3*d*. by the Suez Canal and about 5*s*. 7*d*. by the Panama Canal.

There are, of course, other factors than tolls. The cost of fuel, the cargo available at intermediate ports, and weather are of great importance. The distance from Liverpool to Sydney via Suez is less by 150 miles than via Panama; to New Zealand is longer by 1,000 miles. Hongkong is nearer New York by Panama than by Suez, Singapore is nearer via Suez. Yokohama is only 700 miles nearer to Liverpool by Suez than Panama. Shanghai is almost exactly as far from New York via Panama as from Liverpool via Suez. Thus the eastern seaboard of North America is on an equality with western Europe as regards its intercourse with the mainland of Eastern Asia, whilst in the case of Japan it has a slight advantage. Oil fuel is at present cheaper at Panama than at Suez. The all-important factor is still the amount of available cargo, but the next most important is the incidence of canal dues. In the total expenses of modern ships, running expenses have a much smaller, and harbour and canal dues a larger, proportion than formerly. Hence the importance that attaches to a comparison between Suez and Panama Canal rates.

The Panama Canal has, as was anticipated, had a very beneficial effect upon the trade of the United States. Before the war, the United States purchased 48 per cent. of its imports in Europe and 16 per cent. in Asia. In 1924 it purchased 29 per cent. in Europe and 31 per cent. in Asia.[1] China, Japan, and Australia have bought more in North America and less in Europe since the canal was opened.

[1] League of Nations Memo., 1927.

Japan sent 23 per cent. of its exports to Europe in 1914, and only 6 per cent. in 1924, a point which is not without significance at the present moment.

On the other hand, the Suez Canal route normally offers better prospects of continuous freight earning and keeping ships at sea with full cargoes.

The maximum traffic passing through the canal was shown in 1929–30 when the total was 29,981,000 tons Panama Canal measurement; in 1931–2 the aggregate fell to 23,625,000 tons, the lowest figure since 1924–5. The tonnage of the principal flags in the two years was as follows:

	1929–30. In thousand tons	1931–32. Canal measurement.
United States	14,534	10,791
United Kingdom . . .	8,007	5,906
Norway	1,660	1,530
Germany	1,433	1,281
Japan	803	980
Netherlands	671	553
France	628	455
Sweden	572	539
Italy	429	479
Denmark	382	561

Tanker steamships have been the mainstay of both canals. In 1924 oil tankers were nearly 40 per cent. of the Panama traffic; in 1928 only 20 per cent. Tankers are at present some 15 per cent. of the total Suez Canal traffic, but with the completion of the Iraq pipe-line this will probably be reduced; it is already falling, as tankers are going round the Cape to avoid dues.

The following table, taken from Hallberg's very useful study of the subject, shows the relative advantages of the two routes in point of mileage.

	Saving via Suez over Panama (in marine miles).	Saving via Panama over Suez (in marine miles).
London to Fremantle . . .	5,210	..
New York to Fremantle . . .	593	..
London to Melbourne . . .	1,803	..
New York to Melbourne . . .	..	2,294
London to Sidney . . .	28	..
New York to Sidney . . .	..	2,460
London to Wellington . . .	..	1,077
New York to Wellington . . .	..	4,597
London to Calcutta . . .	9,310	..
New York to Calcutta . . .	4,790	..
London to Singapore . . .	7,339	..
New York to Singapore . . .	2,819	..

	Saving via Suez over Panama (in marine miles).	Saving via Panama over Suez (in marine miles).
London to Manila	4,700	..
New York to Manila	180	..
London to Hongkong	4,729	..
New York to Hongkong	219	..
London to Shanghai	4,989	..
New York to Shanghai	..	1,081
London to Yokohama	1,748	..
New York to Yokohama	..	2,772
London to Coronel	..	837
New York to Coronel	..	3,118
London to Valparaiso	..	1,417
New York to Valparaiso	..	3,732
London to San Francisco	..	5,538
New York to San Francisco	..	7,853

The dividing line in the East between the two routes would seem to be somewhere from Hongkong to Manila. For European trade with Eastern Asia, including Australia but not New Zealand, the Panama Canal offers no competition with Suez. The only points where the Panama Canal can compete with Suez are north-eastern Asia, eastern Australia, New Zealand, and the west coasts of North and South America.

It is clear that the Panama Canal is a powerful instrument in the hands of the President of the United States: he cannot, it is true, give financial preferences to American ships, but the lower the dues, the easier for American shipping to compete with that of Europe. Much of the trade of Asia has, as a consequence of the Panama Canal, been diverted to the United States from Europe; of that we have no right to complain. This tendency has been accentuated by the increasing disparity between Suez and Panama Canal rates, which unless corrected will have serious results for Europe.

CHAPTER XI

COMMENTS, CRITICISMS, AND REPLIES, 1931–3

Post-War Decline in Shipping. Protests of Liverpool Shipowners. Reply of Suez Canal Company. Protest of British Shipping and Commercial interests. Reply of Lord Inchcape. Rejoinder of Liverpool Steamship Owners' Association. Questions and Answers in Parliament. The question re-opened in March 1933. Views expressed to Royal Central Asian Society. Reply of the Marquis de Vogüé. Further addresses. Articles in 'Nineteenth Century and After'.

THE progressive decline in the prosperity of shipping which started in 1920 inevitably led shipowners and others to scrutinize closely all overhead charges. International and national agreements regulating seamen's wages, port and light dues were all in turn examined with a view to securing some relief: attempts were made to eliminate competitive services, to fix freights at a remunerative level, however low, and to replace the older ships by new vessels of economical design. Ships do not indeed create traffic, they only carry it, on margins of profit so slender that relatively small fixed charges, such as canal and port dues, may be decisive factors in competitive trade. Price is the one and only common language of the world of commerce. Four-fifths of the world's international commerce by value and probably a larger proportion by weight is sea-borne. Transportation services are the servants of trade, and are subject to the influence of the general economic situation: competition between different services is subject not only, or in these days even principally, to factors controllable by those who direct them, but to the influence of shipping subsidies, preferential harbour lighting and port dues and flag discriminations of various countries.

It was for these reasons that the Versailles Treaty (Art. 23 (*e*)) pledged the signatories 'to make provision to secure and maintain freedom of communications and of transit and equitable treatment for the commerce of all Members of the League', and it was in these circumstances inevitable that the dues levied by the Suez Canal Company should come under examination. It was not, however, until 1931 that criticism became vocal in various quarters. On 23rd March the question was raised at a meeting of Liverpool shipowners by Mr. F. J. Marquis and Major Leonard Cripps, a director of the Holt Line.

'The British Government', said Mr. Marquis,[1] 'owned 44 per cent. of the shares in the Suez Canal Company. Those shares had earned £36,000,000 in

[1] *The Times*, 24 March 1931.

dividends, but it was not for the purpose of making dividends that they were bought. They were bought to protect British interests. We in Lancashire think the time has arrived to ask the British Government whether they have forgotten the purpose for which they acquired this financial interest in the canal. We know that this Government, and Mr. Graham in particular, have very strong views on the subject of the exploitation of monopoly values. Is the British Government quite certain that, as the principal shareholder in the Suez Canal, it is exercising the control that lies within its power in dealing with this monopoly, the Suez Canal? . . .

'The Company passed in 1929 a dividend at the rate of 267 per cent., after making very adequate provision for the costs of maintaining the canal. It is administered in Paris, and the people of that capital take a dominant part in the control of the finances of the company. The French nation is not a ship-owning nation. It is not primarily interested in the export of goods to the Far East. It has during the last decade exhibited considerable powers of financial conservation. We find ourselves in this country meeting the cost of much of that conservation, and the general sentiment of business men here is that we have carried financial consideration of the position in France to a quixotic extent. The time has come to urge the British Government to assert its rights, recognize its obligations, and secure that representations should be made to Paris to make it clear that the Suez Canal rates at present charged constitute a serious exploitation of a monopoly, at once bad for trade and repellent to the modern social conscience.'

'The dividend of 1929', added Major Leonard Cripps, 'even on the basis of the current exchange, stood at over 50 per cent., yet the dues were still 6·65 gold francs per ton. It was only by the intervention of the British Government, as the largest shareholder in the company, that shipping owners could expect to get fair play and recognition of the obligations of the London agreement. To go on as at present was to damage British trade and to bring into disrepute the manner in which the British Government discharged its international obligations as the chief shareholder in a world highway.'

Councillor R. J. Hall emphasized the greater seriousness of the burden of the Suez Canal dues for the trade and commerce of the North of England, with its weaving industries and low-priced commodities, as compared with the higher-priced commodities and lighter weights sent from the Southern ports. A shilling a ton or 3s. a ton placed on iron and steel, or coal or galvanized sheets, meant a complete block on trade and the loss of markets to the Northern industries.

The Suez Canal Company replied a few days later in an official statement from which the following is an extract:

'For the great bulk of goods passing through the Canal the dues represent but a fraction—1 or 2 per cent.—of their value. Therefore the effect of the dues on the total commerce passing through the Canal is negligible, and may indeed be dismissed as practically nil so far as the Europe-bound traffic from countries beyond Suez is concerned.

'In reality, then, even if it be admitted that a reduction would favour certain branches of traffic forming only a minor proportion of the whole, its only general effect would, in the present economic conditions, be to impose a sacrifice on the company's shareholders which, without benefiting commerce as a whole, would not be offset by any appreciable increase in traffic. . . .

'It is certainly true that, as compared with 1928, commerce in 1929 between Great Britain and the principal markets of the Far East showed a diminution, and that the fall in British exports to the Far East was particularly marked. For the rest of Europe, on the other hand, this commerce increased, from which it is evident that the diminution referred to above is in no way attributable to the canal dues, but rather to the difference between the British costs of production and those of the other countries.

'The events of 1930 confirm this conclusion. While British exports to the Far East showed a greater reduction than those from America, the American trade, in its turn, diminished to an appreciably greater extent than those of Germany. There are thus other and more important causes of all these commercial movements and their variations than the Suez Canal dues, and they must be sought either in the exporting countries or those to whom their goods are consigned.

'It has also been alleged that a part of the Suez Canal traffic has been diverted to the Panama Canal. But an analysis of commercial movements shows clearly that traffic for which the two canals may compete is of little importance compared with the total traffic of the Suez Canal. Moreover, it is instructive to note that although the Panama Canal dues are a little lower than those of the Suez Canal the traffic figures for both show a remarkable similarity in their variations.'

Some comment on this exchange of views is necessary. The Suez Canal Company's views as to the 'negligible effect' of a levy of 1 or 2 per cent. on the value of goods passing through the canal (the actual figures vary from an average of 3 per cent. to as much as 30 per cent. in certain cases) is wholly untenable. So keen is competition in world markets that, as Councillor F. J. Hall remarked, great contracts are lost or won, and industries maintained, or the reverse, on a margin of no more than a shilling a ton.

The statement that Panama Canal dues were 'a little lower' than those of the Suez Canal was seldom true: they have never been less than 20 per cent. lower and are now about 33 per cent. lower than those of the Company.[1] The relative steadiness of German exports in 1930 was due to internal stresses, of Italian commerce to the fact among others that all canal dues on Italian vessels were paid by the Italian Government. To argue that the Suez Canal dues are a negligible factor is not consistent with known facts, for it was common knowledge even in 1931 that molasses tankers from Java and the Philippines and oil tankers from the Persian Gulf were reaching Europe via the Cape, and that

---

[1] The present Suez Canal dues of 6 francs per Suez Canal ton, at the average exchange value of the £ for the week ending 6th August (84·76 francs or 4·497 dollars), works out at 8s. 3d. per British net registered ton. The dues levied in the Panama Canal are about 5s. 7d.; when allowance is made for certain fixed charges levied in the Suez Canal and not at Panama, the Panama Canal dues on any given ship are two-thirds, or even a little less, of those levied at Port Said.

cargoes of grain from Melbourne were reaching Trieste and Alexandria via Gibraltar.

A month later, on 22nd April, a deputation, stated to represent the whole of the shipping and commercial interests of the United Kingdom, was received by the late Lord Inchcape, chairman of the London Committee of the Suez Canal Company. The Government directors were not present. The deputation urged that the Company should take immediate steps to reduce the dues, and that an understanding as to the future should be reached. Lord Inchcape undertook that his British colleagues and he would lay the views of the deputation before the Board at their next meeting in Paris in May, and expressed the hope that, in the meantime, the Associations concerned would suspend criticism of a company which had rendered, and was rendering, public services of the greatest value to trade and commerce. The deputation expressed their appreciation of the undertaking which Lord Inchcape had given, and agreed to await the result of the May meeting.

On 13th May he published a copy of a letter which he had sent on 11th May, with the entire concurrence of his French and British colleagues, to the Secretary of the Liverpool Steamship Owners' Association. After a lengthy disquisition on the past history of the canal and of the numerous improvements effected (without which the canal would have ceased to earn any dividends at all) he stated that no further immediate reduction of dues was possible in view of the actual and prospective falling off both in tonnage and receipts.

'Interested in shipping as the majority of the British directors are, they must at the same time as directors of the company have regard to all the interests involved. The last reduction in September was obtained at the instance of the British directors, whose representations were met in a spirit of acquiescence on the part of their French colleagues. The question of further diminutions was, by agreement of both sides, left to be raised as circumstances justified. The dues are never a closed question and negotiations are always open. Machinery is in existence for laying before the Board, as occasion requires, suggestions as to the scale of charges in relation to the earnings of the company. Working on these lines, I am assured that some further reduction will be agreed to by the Board to take effect as soon as the appropriate circumstances arise. An agitation by the shipowners, however, to get an immediate reduction in dues, carrying with it a reduction in the dividend, will have the effect of alienating the French shareholders, who are aware that the concession from the Egyptian Government comes to an end in 1968. The shareholders must therefore provide practically the whole of their own amortization.

'It was pointed out to us that the transit dues represent a very insignificant amount on the value of the commodities passing through the canal, only about 1 to 2 per cent., and on the south to north traffic not so much as this. The dues to-day, it was pointed out, are two-thirds of the maximum provided by the Act of Concession. Since 1883 the increase in dividends has given the shareholders £59,000,000, while the reduction in dues has given the shipowners £60,000,000. Since 1920 the shareholders have received an increase in dividends of £13,700,000, and the shipowners have gained £11,700,000 by reduction in dues; but since 1913 the shareholders have received £2,400,000 less in dividends than if the 1913 dividend had been maintained. The dividend for 1930 will have to be slightly reduced from that paid in 1929, and the proposed dividend, even at the reduced rate, can only be paid by decreasing amortization for depreciation of plant, &c.

'Considering the reductions in dues in the last ten years, some soreness was expressed by our French colleagues that the present agitation should have been started. What I have ventured to put before the Liverpool Steamship Owners' Association in this letter may not altogether satisfy them; but in the interests both of the shipping and of the trade of Great Britain I do most sincerely hope that the agitation against the directors of the Suez Canal Company and its shareholders may be discontinued, as the effect otherwise will be unfortunate and the end in view may be retarded.'

The Association replied on 16th May that they were bitterly disappointed with his letter, which was no answer to their request for a reduction in the dues.

'They contemplate with growing concern a monopolistic company, which can with modesty describe its results as "brilliant", paying dividends year after year out of earnings of which every penny has been contributed by the shipping industry during a period of unparalleled trade depression. The Association feel that it is not unreasonable to request that some small sacrifice of that prosperity should be made by the company to mitigate the hardships now being suffered by every one of its clients.

'The Association have not criticized the efficiency of the Canal service, nor have they suggested that the Canal staff are anything but courteous and obliging at all times, but that your Lordship should have been requested to draw attention to these matters would appear, in the opinion of the Association, to show a complete lack of appreciation, on the part of the Board, of the vital importance of the point at issue.

'Your Lordship is concerned with the fact that, as the concession expires in 1968, the investors in the company must provide practically the whole of their own amortization with this end in view. But what in fact does this amount to? If the case of the British Government's holding be considered, the true position of the original shareholders is clear beyond dispute. In 1875 Mr. Disraeli purchased on behalf of the British Government 44 per cent. of the shares in the company. The purchase price of these shares was £4,000,000, but since the date on which they were purchased the British Government have received in dividends and interest the sum of £38,000,000. If no more than 1 per cent. of the purchase price had been put aside annually the whole sum would have been amortized twenty years ago.

'Can it be said, therefore, that those fortunate investors who purchased the original shares of the company have reasonable grounds for complaint if a reduction in the dues be made? On the other hand, have those who purchased the shares in the open market by way of investment or speculation the right to expect that the profits of the company should be maintained at their present rate merely because the concession is due to expire in 1968—a fact which they must have known when they purchased the shares and which must assuredly at all times influence the market price of the shares?

'The Association note that the small percentage which the transit dues bear to the value of the commodities passing through is again brought forward as an argument, but, apart from the fact that even the smallest relief is of great importance to trade in present circumstances, their statement that the dues amount to upwards of 14 per cent. of the gross freights remains unchallenged.

'The Association desire me to emphasize also the fact that, while the total amount which is to be distributed in dividends for the year 1930 shows a decrease when compared with that which was distributed for the year 1929, nevertheless the Ordinary shareholders are to receive for each 250 fr. share a dividend at an increased rate—namely, 577 fr. for the year 1930, as compared with 530 fr. for the year 1929.

'With regard to the comparison made in your Lordship's letter between the increase since 1883 of £59,000,000 in the dividend and the reduction since 1883 of £60,000,000 in dues, the Association would point out that the greater part of the reduction was made in accordance with the London Agreement of that year, the terms of which obliged the Canal Company to allocate part of the surplus profits after payment of a 25 per cent. dividend to reducing the dues until the transit rate reached a level of 5 fr. (gold) per ton. The Association would be more disposed to attach importance to the comparison if to-day the dues were 5 fr. (gold) and not 6·65 fr. (gold) and the rate of the dividend 25 per cent. and not 46 per cent.'

On 15th November the dues were 'temporarily' reduced from 6·65 francs gold to 6·00 francs gold; as however, Great Britain had meanwhile been forced off the gold standard the actual incidence of the dues on laden vessels was over one shilling per Suez Canal ton higher than before.

On 10th December 1931 Mr. J. R. Robinson, M.P., asked whether His Majesty's Government would take the necessary steps to subdivide its holding so as to use its maximum voting power at future meetings of the Suez Canal in favour of an investigation into the management of the company in order to bring about a reduction in the expenses of management and a reduction of the Canal Tolls.

He also asked whether His Majesty's Government would use its shareholding power to urge a reduction of costs of management including directors' fees.

Mr. Neville Chamberlain replied that His Majesty's Government had recently received an assurance from the Company that all possible economies consistent with efficiency have been carried out[1] both as regards work and personnel. The diminution of traffic and recent reduction of dues would entail considerable reduction in amount of directors' fees. No useful purpose would be served by proposing an investigation into the management of the Company.

Some months later (14th June 1932), the Financial Secretary to the Treasury, in reply to a question in Parliament, observed that the existing incidence and possible reduction of Suez Canal dues was not the concern of the British Government but of the Suez Canal Company. It is not easy to reconcile this attitude of mind with the claim of Disraeli, and of a long line of statesmen after him, that the purchase of shares by the British Government was made with a political rather than a commercial object and has in fact been justified by results on political rather than commercial grounds. Nor is it easy to gather from questions and answers in Parliament, over many years, what purpose is served by the British Government Directors on the Board of the Suez Canal. The Prime Minister on 16th June 1925 referred to two of them as 'equipped to be of assistance to the general business of the Board by their knowledge of public affairs gained by long service in the House of Commons and in various Departments of State. The third Director (Sir John Davies) was a member of the Civil Service'. He added that the 'purely shipping and commercial activities of the Company, so far as they concern the British Empire and His Majesty's Government as principal shareholder, are carefully watched by the non-official British members, all of them experts in these matters'.

It will be noted that this reply suggests that the British Government Directors, as retired Parliamentarians or Civil Servants, can assist the

[1] Notwithstanding the Company's assurance that all possible economies had already been made, further large reductions were, in fact, effected in 1932 and 1933.

Board of the Suez Canal Company, whilst the interests of the British Empire and of His Majesty's Government are safe in the hands of the non-official directors, who are not nominated by His Majesty's Government, but by particular interests—amongst which those of the British Dominions Overseas are not included. Truly, in the words of Sir Edward Grey, the 'question of the Suez Canal is very complicated and requires to be elucidated'.

In March 1933 I took it on myself to re-open the question at a public luncheon. After complaining of the meagre information on the subject furnished to Parliament and setting forth figures, on the lines of Chapter VIII of this work, I described the Suez Canal as 'a vital artery, tenanted by growths once beneficent, but now parasitic upon the life-stream of overseas commerce'. The increase of dividends paid of recent years was proportionate to the decrease in the net earnings of shipping companies. The mercantile marine of every maritime nation had increased since 1918 except that of Great Britain, which had suffered a decrease of 20 per cent. We alone of the Great Powers did not subsidize merchant vessels: no less than £30 millions was thus spent in 1931, of which two-thirds went to support lines competing directly with British enterprise.

I reminded my hearers that when in 1931 the shipowners of Liverpool appealed for a reduction of rates, the Suez Canal Company announced that 'repeated requests render the company less inclined to reduce their charges'. Such was the language of monopolists all over the world, and it was not surprising that six of the great maritime powers had protested unofficially to Mr. Henderson in 1931 against the high level of dues charged or that Sir Arthur Michael Samuel should have felt compelled to observe, in the House of Commons, that 'the methods of the Canal Company are fast becoming a cause of international friction'.

Egypt and the Suez Canal Company could look after themselves: the British Empire needed more forceful advocacy. The Imperial Shipping Committee had had the matter on its agenda at least once. It was time to raise it again and to ensure that British official representation on the Board was not principally confined to retired private secretaries, however eminent and that, in one way or another, India, the Dominions, and the Crown Colonies should have representation.

During the next few weeks I received some forty or fifty communications including many from persons who now hold, or were holding, positions of great responsibility in political, diplomatic, consular, and commercial life both in this country and abroad, urging me to develop this thesis and to bring it prominently to public notice. I thereupon delivered an address on the subject to members of the Royal Central

Asian Society (5th April), in the hope that some rejoinder or criticism might be elicited from the Company's side. In these addresses I developed the view, set forth at length in this work:

(1) that the events of 1873 (*vide* Chap. V) established the method whereby the maritime powers could, if aggrieved at the system whereby tolls were levied by the Company, appeal to the sovereign power, then Turkey, now Egypt, which had power to impose its will;

(2) that this incident produced a general agreement among the Powers that, while the canal was an artificial channel, it was essentially a narrow strait between two bodies of open sea, and as such was a matter of international concern. It also elicited from the Powers an admission that the Canal Company had the right to levy tolls, though subject to the concessions issued by the Khedive of Egypt and confirmed by the Sultan, and in keeping with the international usage as to measurements of vessels. At the same time the operation of the canal practically, even if not formally, became subject to international law, since various Powers entered into direct negotiations with the Company, giving that body a quasi-international status;

(3) that the grant of a concession does not derogate from the 'right of eminent domain' on the part of the sovereign power, i.e. from the inherent duty, and consequently the right, to modify or even to revoke the grant should the interest of the nation, or of the world, demand such a step, subject of course to due compensation;

(4) that the Government of Egypt might reasonably be urged, on grounds of general expediency, to require, and if need be to impose upon the Company, such modification of its Statutes as will bring them into accord with modern views as to the management of public utilities and the administration of private companies. There is no precedent in the domain of municipal or international law for many provisions of the Company's Statutes in their present form;

(5) that the present constitution of the Board of the Company— 21 French citizens, 10 British, and 1 Dutch subject— was inconsistent with the specific provisions of the Statutes and constituted a breach of the terms of the concession. In this connexion I quoted the observations of a French writer, Monsieur Mimaut:[1]

'The Board rather resembles', wrote Lesage in 1905, 'a diplomatic conference on which the nations whose flag floats most frequently above the calm waters of

[1] *Les Corporations Interétatistes*, 1929.

the canal are represented—Great Britain, France, Germany, and Holland.'
Lesage recounts with satisfaction the diplomatic titles of some of the French
administrators. The recital would be even more appropriate to-day; the successors
of the former attachés of embassies are Ambassadors, or former Foreign Ministers,
or former Presidents of the Council (or, he might have added, former Presidents
of the Republic).

'The British, on the other hand', he says, 'are represented mainly by men of
business, whilst the French shareholders are represented by political figures whose
connexion with the French State is in no way hidden.

'France has lost none of the moral prestige which she reaped from the tenacity
and success of de Lesseps, which English courtesy has done nothing to diminish.
The Company's Ambassador with the Egyptian Government is French. All the
superior staff of the Canal are Frenchmen. A French Bishop occupies the epis-
copal seat recently instituted in the Governments of the Canal.

'As to Egypt, one is tempted to say that Anglo-French solidarity and the prosperity of the Canal Company have been secured at her expense. Still, the sale of
the Khedive's shareholding saved her from bankruptcy, and perhaps even from
greater dangers. Her interest was not limited to the Khedive's holding. The
Egyptian Government's share of profits appears in the annual balance sheet, but
here again Egypt has had to part with her rights. . . .

'The Company has, however, brought fresh life to Egypt, and at the end of the
concession the ownership of the Canal will revert to her. . . .

'A conjunction of political and financial circumstances has brought about a state
of affairs which represents but imperfectly the international status envisaged by
de Lesseps and dreamed of by Lord Derby. But the present régime satisfies three
main conditions necessary for the well-being of a great business of universal
interest.

'It is a *business* concern, supported by the *political* influence of the Great Powers,
and if by her own fault Germany is eliminated from the Council, the latter is still
international, for three of the principal maritime powers are represented thereon,
and can watch their own interests and those of world navigation.'

These essays elicited early in June 1933 from the Marquis de
Vogüé, chairman of the Suez Canal Company, a spirited memorandum
the principal portions of which are reproduced below, with my own
comments subjoined in the form of footnotes. Cross-headings have
been inserted.

'*Mandataire*' or '*Concessionaire*'

'The Suez Canal Company is stated to be a "mandataire" of the
Egyptian Government. It may have been possible, strictly speaking,
to describe Ferdinand de Lesseps personally as a "mandataire" of the
Viceroy when he was granted "exclusive power to set up and assume
the management of a Universal Company for the cutting of the Isthmus
of Suez". But once that Company was formed—as formed it was—
in accordance with the Viceroy of Egypt's intentions (for its articles

Y

of association were approved by the deed of concession in 1856), it was in the nature of a private concessionary company.'[1]

Right of Eminent Domain

More serious is any suggestion that it is open to a Government to amend or even to repeal in an arbitrary and one-sided manner a contract entered into with a private company, even although that company may have complied in the strictest way with the terms of its Act of Concession, which is emphatically the case in the present instance. Such a course is still considered in civilized countries as sheer robbery.

No such right of amendment or repeal was ever claimed by the Viceroy, either for himself or for his successors.[2]

Modification and Modernization of Concession and Statutes

'Our critic has in mind an intervention on the part of certain Great Powers, and more particularly Great Britain, upon whom he considers a special role to devolve owing to the fact that, for sundry political and strategical reasons, Great Britain has undertaken the responsibility of protecting the great Suez waterway.

'Here, again, there is a confusion of thought. The question of the strategical protection of the canal has been settled by the Powers who decided on the neutrality of the canal. Questions of strategy have nothing to do with the technical operation of the canal or the management of the company.'[3]

[1] Article 20 of the concession of 5th January 1856 describes de Lesseps as 'mandataire' (*vide* App. II). The Statutes, duly approved by the Khedive, were annexed to this document, which is the very basis of the Company's concession.

[2] There are good reasons for holding that the terms of the Act of Concession and the provisions of the Statutes have not in fact been complied with, notably as to the composition of the Board (Statutes XXIV) which is not now representative of the principal nationalities interested in the enterprise as users of the Canal and as to the provision (Article 2, Concession of 30th November 1854) that the Chairman of the Company should be chosen, a-far as possible from among the shareholders most interested in the enterprise (App. I). The right of amendment or repeal of a concession, subject to compensation, is the inherent right of a sovereign State. It has been repeatedly exercised in recent years and is recognized by Article 19 of the Covenant of the League of Nations which empowers the Assembly from time to time to advise the reconsideration by Members of the League of Treaties that have become inapplicable, and the consideration of international conditions whose continuance might endanger the peace of the world.

As Lord Derby wrote to Sir H. Elliot on 7th July 1874: Such being the high international importance of the Canal, its administrators have not the right to consider an infraction of the provisions of instrument governing the conditions of its administration, so far as they affect international rights, to be a matter for simply judicial action.

[3] The question of strategical protection of the canal was not settled by the Powers, but by the ineluctable fact of the position occupied in Asia by Great Britain and the British Empire. The title of the Company to levy exorbitant dues cannot be treated *in vacuo* without reference to the wider interests of world commerce.

Proposed Division of British Government Shareholding

In her dealings with the Company, Great Britain can only act in the capacity of a shareholder. This the British Government has always thoroughly understood. Under Article LI of the articles of association, one and the same shareholder is only entitled to command ten votes at the general meeting. This provision common to many leading concerns is obviously due to the desire to avoid the unrestricted preponderance of what are frequently called 'the big shareholders'.

Lesseps wanted a universal company of which no State, no one body, no individual magnate could possibly become the sole chief. The British Government, by purchasing the shares belonging to the Khedive, strictly inherited the rights of that ruler, whose approval of the articles of association had sanctioned the restriction specified in Article LI. Failing such restrictions, the preponderance of some one partner was to be feared a particularly grave risk in the case of the operation of a great sea route.

By 'cornering' the shares, any one Government—not necessarily the British Government, might have acquired exclusive control of the concern, contrary to the wishes both of the Viceroy of Egypt and the founder of the Company. The limitation of the power to vote is, in the present instance, conformable to the general interest, and surely any infringement of Article LI—inadmissible in law and dangerous in fact—would not fail to give rise to sharp diplomatic reactions.

All such considerations are lost sight of by those who ingenuously suggest that the British Government should divide up their shares among 706 mandatories, forgetting that, under Articles XLIV and XLV of the articles of association, the general meeting is made up by all the shareholders owning at least 25 shares, and that no one is entitled to represent a shareholder at the meeting unless he is himself a member. Neither directly nor indirectly can the statutory maximum of ten votes be exceeded.[1]

Dividend Payments

'Though during the war, when faced with the sudden falling off in traffic, the Company raised the canal transit dues, it did so with extreme moderation, and to an extent that was far from making up for the decline in the maritime traffic. For several years thereafter it experienced a sharp loss of revenue; in spite of which, almost immediately after

[1] This statement does not challenge but rather confirms the view that the British Government could legally divest itself of its shareholding, by disposing of them in parcels of 250 shares at current market rates to some 700 holders, individuals or corporate bodies interested in the traffic through the Canal who could, if they voted in agreement with each other, exercise through their 7,000 votes a controlling voice at General Meetings.

the war, it again proceeded to cut down its tariffs long before the receipts returned to the 1913 level, and at a time when most of the navigation companies were making substantial profits.

'Not before the financial year 1925 did the gross dividend, expressed in pre-War gold francs, once more reach the value it had in 1913, and even to-day the shareholders find that their increased dividends barely make up for the reductions suffered during the war.'[1]

Rate of Net Dividends

'Our critic would appear to have based his calculations on the average net returns distributed to the shareholders for the financial periods 1928 to 1931—namely, 495 French francs—and to have compared this figure with the nominal value of the shares, 1,250 francs, in round figures. This, indeed, is the only method whereby the percentage of income he quotes can be approximately arrived at.

'It is not with the nominal capital alone of a concern that the dividend paid should be compared, but with the whole of the capital actually invested in the concern—that is to say, in the case of the Suez Canal, with the original capital, to which should be added the proportion of profits spent on construction and improvements. Now on 31st December 1932 the capital actually invested amounted to Frs. 2,560,268,600. Thus the gross dividend distributed for 1932 represents 15·6 per cent.

'Moreover, any comparison of a dividend with the original nominal capital, or even with a capital actually invested, is necessarily devoid of significance.'[2]

---

[1] Dividends during the six years 1914–19 averaged 22·9 per cent. (see page 115) as compared with 33 per cent. for the years 1911–13. Transit dues were raised from 6·25 francs in 1914 to 8·50 francs in 1918. At no time, however, during or after the war were shipowners in general making profits on this scale. It is scarcely reasonable to suggest that Suez Canal shareholders are entitled to make good at the expense of world shipping 'the reductions suffered during the war'.

[2] The Company rightly claims that it has kept the Canal in good order and that it has spent over 2,200 million francs, the total of 'les sommes distraites chaque année des bénéfices pour les travaux d'amélioration'. In the first place, such expenditure was only sound business, and, secondly, it is folly to think that any large part thereof could have been distributed as profits. Part of Sir John Stokes's settlement was an agreement to spend an annual sum on improvements, and in 1883 the complaint of shipowners of all nationalities was that the Canal was insufficient for traffic. Improvement of facilities and limitation of dividends was then forced on the Company by the threat of applying to the Sultan for a concession for a new Canal. It is true that the British Law Officers held that M. de Lesseps had been granted a monopoly, but that opinion was never put to the only sound test. The real point is that the cost of the improvements, no less than the high dividends, came out of shipowners' pockets. One might say with truth that the old Canal has long ago, and several times, disappeared, and that the Canal of to-day has been built with the money of shipowners and their clients. Among the economies which have contributed to the

Treatment of Shipowners

'From the carrying into effect of the London programme down to and including the financial year 1932—on the one hand, the total amount of increased dividends paid to the shareholders, and, on the other hand, the total amount of the sums made over to the shipowners by way of successive abatements, it will be found that the shipowners' share exceeds that of the shareholders.'

'In consequence of the abatements granted by the Suez Canal Company since 1st January 1921, the British Government is the poorer by £6,238,000, which means that the British taxpayer has had his taxes increased proportionately. Every abatement of Frs. 50 costs the British taxpayer £250,000, on the basis of the tonnage that passed through the canal in 1932, and reckoning the pound sterling at Frs. 87·50.'[1]

maintenance of a still handsome rate of dividend is, according to the Annual Report, 'la suppression presque totale de nouveaux travaux d'amélioration et le ralentissement de ceux qui sont en voie d'achèvement'. The reduction of the grant for such works to the 'chiffre exceptionellement bas de 10 millions' (of francs) is doubtful policy.

[1] 'The public mind is greatly concerned at the concentration of the control, in a few hands, of widely distributed wealth through prevailing forms of corporate organization and management. A corporation exists by authority of law, and there is no reason why such huge aggregations of capital should not be as closely supervised by government, either federal or state, as are life insurance companies and banks.' (Nicholas Murray Butler, February 1933).

Writing on this subject in the Annual Report of the Company for 1932 the Marquis de Vogüe says that the shareholders are entitled to 'une rémunération substantielle', that they have had in increasing degree up to the last few years except for the war period. He asks, 'Celle d'aujourd'hui est elle excessive?' and answers 'No!' His reasons are, first, the additional value given to the original capital by improvements, which has been considered above. Secondly, he says:

'Il faut aussi tenir compte de ce que les actionnaires d'aujourd'hui ne sont pas ceux du début. La valeur de l'entreprise s'étant accrue peu à peu, par l'effet des travaux qui y furent effectués, la valeur des titres a progressé à même pas. Ceux qui les ont reçus en héritage ont vu, à chaque succession, augmenter leur estimation et les taxes correspondantes. Ceux qui les ont achetés de leur deniers, on sait à quel prix, pouvaient compter sur la continuation de la politique qui avait amené ces plus-values. Ce serait méconnaître les droits acquis par les uns et les autres que d'incriminer maintenant leur dividendes, et ce serait tromper leur confiance que de changer cette politique.' That is at least frank, but it is an extreme capitalist point of view which will not receive general acceptance. M. de Lesseps in previous years had to protest against the greed of speculators in Canal shares, and the widest public opinion is not likely to regard as tolerable in a private Company a policy of economic die-hardism that would be attacked in a Bon Marché. In a time of world depression, companies which control raw materials or monopolize ways of transport should not, and seldom do, exploit their customers. Now in the last four years the total remuneration earned by each 250-franc share was as follows:

	francs.		*francs.*
1929	667	1931	605
1930	650	1932	510

June 1931 and 1932 dividends were paid with the help of 50 million and 11½ million

Purchases of Plant by Canal Company

'Nothing could be calculated to mislead British opinion more completely than the statement that our plant, our service fleet, &c., are almost entirely built in France.

'For the last ten years our purchases of machinery or raw materials made in France amount to Frs. 200,000,000, those made in Great Britain to Frs. 160,000,000.'[1]

Management of the Canal Company

'The Company has been taxed with extravagant management. As a matter of fact, in the course of the last two financial years it has effected an all-round saving of Frs. 67,000,000—that is, 25 per cent. —cutting down its expenses on personnel by 27 per cent. and reducing the number of its agents or operatives by 22 per cent.'[2]

A few days later, on 12th June, the Proceedings of the Annual General Meeting of the Suez Canal Company were enlivened by a further apologia on the part of the President, couched in terms more suitable to a French audience, to which it was delivered, than to the British public to whom the memorandum of 9th June was addressed. He denounced 'un copieux mémoire, monument d'erreur et de malveillance' and, after haughtily declaring 'nous pouvions tenir pour négligeables ces attaques ridicules', asserted that 'leur auteur prouve, à tout le moins, qu'il ignore les choses dont il parle ou qu'il ne les comprend pas, ou qu'une mauvaise querelle peut devenir un bon tremplin électoral'.[3]

---

francs respectively, withdrawn from the Special Reserve which had been well fattened with surplus profits in earlier years. An average dividend exceeding 24 per cent. in four years of unparalleled depression may well excite envy and comment. If it be replied that these rates are paid in depreciated francs worth only one-fifth of a pre-War franc, one may answer by asking why, when the French Government devalued the franc in the national interest, the Suez Canal Company should expect to retain the advantages of the old economy. Accounts must be made up in the currencies of the world of to-day, not in those of a world that is dead and gone. One might ask, further, whether gold or silver francs predominated in France in the 'sixties.

[1] I am glad to give the fullest publicity to these figures, which have never before been published; queries in the House of Commons failed to elicit the information, and Sir Ian Malcolm, in his numerous contributions to the press, never mentioned them, nor, apparently, was the Department of Overseas Trade in possession of the facts. It is not, however, disputed that very few British-born subjects find employment with the Company.

[2] Here again I am particularly glad to be able to give publicity to the figures. They are the more satisfactory in that Sir Ian Malcolm's article in *The National Review* showed in successive editions (it appears to have been reprinted as a tract by the Suez Canal Company) a steady increase in the number of employees in post-War years, and the Chancellor of the Exchequer stated in December 1931 that the Company had already at that time done all that it possibly could to reduce expenditure.

[3] I yield to none in my respect for the discrimination, sagacity, and public spirit of the electors of North and West Hertfordshire, but I must on their behalf disclaim the suggestion

His defence of the Company began as usual by a reference to the early days when M. de Lesseps had to struggle against British opposition and by his fervour succeeded in inspiring French capitalists, large and small, to provide the capital for an enterprise which every one thought was extraordinarily risky. Does not such audacity, such faith, it was asked, deserve a rich reward? We may indeed grant all that has been alleged against British statesmen. We must wholeheartedly admire the genius of Ferdinand de Lesseps and the courage of the French investor. It still remains true that in the middle 'seventies the Company was on the verge of financial collapse and arbitrarily altered the basis on which dues were charged in a manner which brought it into conflict with the shipowners of Europe and with the Sublime Porte, the author of the concession. It was an Englishman, Colonel John Stokes, R.E., who negotiated with the British and Turkish Governments terms of a voluntary settlement which enabled the Company to improve the Canal and put its finances on a sound basis. Those terms included a temporary surtax of 3 francs per net ton, Suez Canal measurement, in addition to the 10 francs specified in the Concession as a maximum. The surtax was reduced at a very gradual rate, 10 francs not being again reached until 1884. During the ten years 1874–83 British tonnage averaged 78·3 per cent. of the total tonnage using the Canal, so that the surtax was no mere 'gesture' but a very solid contribution on the part of British shipowners, which might—now that the passions of the 'fifties and 'sixties have had time to die down—be regarded as offsetting former shortcomings.

The President of the Company further maintained that

'En ce qui concerne l'incidence de notre tarif sur les prix de marchandises, il est facile d'établir par de statistiques indiscutables, qu'elle est très faible. C'est ainsi que pour l'année 1932, où les prix ont été particulièrement bas, elle n'a que très exceptionellement dépassé 3 pour cent. Une détaxe, si importante qu'on puisse la supposer, n'aurait donc pas sur les prix un effet appréciable; combien ils sont plus lourdement frappés par les droits de douane et par la guerre de monnaies.'

One would wish to see these 'indisputable statistics'; practising statiicians rarely see them. In any case a general rate of 3 per cent., or any other figure, is valueless, for every one knows that bulky goods of small value cannot stand even a low rate whereas valuable goods of relatively small bulk can easily bear a high rate. In time of depression every charge becomes burdensome though in prosperity it is little felt.

of the Marquis de Vogüé that my views on the Suez Canal had any effect on their recent decision, or that, in making public in March 1933 my considered opinions on the subject, I had in mind the possibility of an electoral campaign consequent on the lamented death of Lord Knebworth some months later.

M. de Vogüé might have addressed the remark about customs dues to his own government; my object was rather to bring the force of public opinion to bear on a private corporation.

It was further maintained that the Canal Dues had not injured international trade, for 's'il est vrai que les envois de l'Europe vers le Japon ont baissé de moitié, ceux du Japon vers l'Europe ont triplé; le droit de transit n'y est pour rien'. On the contrary, even in ordinary times vessels outward from Europe through the Canal are always more lightly laden than those coming inwards, and in these latter years when the exports of manufacturing countries have been falling off, for well-known reasons, the excess of empty cargo space has raised the burden of rates on the weight of cargo—and on its diminishing value—to heights which may easily be unbearable. Japan's exports, on the other hand, have been helped by currency depreciation and by other factors.

'D'autre part', the defence goes on:

'Le Board of Trade établit que, de 1931 à 1932, les importations anglaises de toute provenance ont diminué de 18·4 pour cent.; en provenance des pays au delà de Suez, de 3·8 pour cent. seulement. Pendant la même période, les exportations anglaises ont fléchi, dans l'ensemble, de 6·6 pour cent.; vers les pays au delà de Suez, elles ont augmenté de 4·6 pour cent. Où est donc l'influence déprimante de notre tarif?'

The argument may be described as an example of the fallacy of the single cause. It would only be valid if all goods of whatever kind or of whatever origin were on every occasion subject to the same price movements. As a further contribution to the discussion the following figures (in net tons) from the 'Accounts relating to Trade and Navigation of the United Kingdom' for December of 1931 and 1932 regarding movement of British and Foreign shipping at British ports are submitted:

	Entered from		Cleared at	
	1929.	*1932.*	*1929.*	*1932.*
E. Africa, Persian Gulf, India	3,625	3,151	2,943	2,310
Eastern Asia, Pacific Islands	2,430	2,323	1,974	1,827
Countries beyond Suez	6,055	5,474	4,917	4,137
Australia and New Zealand	2,263	2,732	2,059	1,532
All Areas	62,701	56,060	68,680	53,390

This gives quite a different picture from that painted in values, but it is just as untrustworthy as a measure of magnitude of trade. Entrances from East Africa and Asia may be presumed to have used the canal, and between 1929 and 1932 they declined by 9·6 per cent., whereas entrances from all areas fell off by 10·6 per cent.; similarly the reductions in clearances were 15·9 per cent. and 22·4 per cent. respectively. All that one can conclude is that in other areas than Asia and East Africa there were stronger forces making for the reduction of trade, strong enough to outweigh the advantages of not having to pay canal dues.

When he had to consider trade with the Antipodes M. de Vogüé had to admit a reduction in canal traffic; in and out it was 3,942,000 net tons in 1929, 3,601,000 net tons in 1931, and 3,334,000 tons in 1932. But he boldly converted this disagreeable fact into an argument in defence of the canal:

'Qu'elle ait un monopole, il est un peu puéril de prétendre, puisqu'il y a d'autres voies sur les mers, et qu'une fraction de notre clientèle, indifférente à la longueur du temps, préfère passer par le Cap de Bonne-Espérance'.

In the Report it was stated that Australian wheat and Java sugar had gone by the Cape route 'dans une proportion beaucoup plus large que de coutume'. The explanation given was 'en période de dépression économique, en effet, le gain de temps que procure le passage par le Canal présente moins d'intérêt pour l'armateur'. Precisely; the heavier steaming expenses by the longer route are then less important to the shipowner and shipper than the canal dues, showing that the latter are relatively heavy, which is just what the critics have maintained. On the other hand, there was an increase from 3,310,000 tons in 1931 to 3,823,000 tons of mineral oil in 1932—'les pétroles du Golfe Persique—grâce au retour via Suez d'un grand nombre de navires-citernes qui, en 1931, avaient déserté cette route pour utiliser celle du Cap'. No explanation is given of this change.

On 19th May,[1] I read before the Royal Society of Arts a paper on 'The Suez and Panama Canals—a comparison',—the substance of which is reproduced in the foregoing chapter. On 1st June, *The Nineteenth Century and After* published an article under my signature entitled 'The Suez Canal—barrier or highway?' in which I briefly summarized some of the views expressed in this book. To this article no reply has yet (October 1933) appeared. I am far from suggesting that any valid arguments can or should be drawn from this circumstance. I merely record the fact.

---

[1] Published on 9th June 1933, vol. lxxxi, No. 4203.

CHAPTER XII

CONCLUSIONS

IT now remains to gather together the several threads of argument in the foregoing pages, in which I have dealt at some length with 'the seed-bed of the past'. The trees that were planted seventy or eighty years ago by diplomatists and engineers, soldiers and financiers, have borne fruit, and the result, taken as a whole, is worthy of their labours. But the time has come to make changes: in some directions pruning is required, both of branches and of roots, as in an orchard when trees are making wood and leaf at the expense of the fruit.

The canal itself is a product of the imagination, the pertinacity, and the diplomatic and financial foresight of one man—Ferdinand de Lesseps—though all these qualities were in some degree shared by the Khedives who supported and befriended him. It is the product of French technical and administrative skill, and of Egyptian and French capital. It has proved highly profitable to the shareholders, who except for a very brief period indeed have never been without the certainty of adequate dividends. It has almost the features of a monopoly, and the owners charge, in practice, as much as, and sometimes, as I have suggested, more than all the traffic will bear.

The possession by the British Government of nearly 46 per cent. of the shares, without corresponding voting power or representation on the Board, has not had the effects anticipated by Disraeli, and I have therefore proposed that the shares now held by Government should be sold, at current prices, in blocks of 250 shares, to persons or bodies corporate owning allegiance to His Majesty, who could thus, by their collective action as shareholders, acquire control of the Company. Such a course would, no doubt, as anticipated by the Marquis de Vogüé, provoke sharp diplomatic reactions, whence might arise in due course a solution consistent with the interests of world shipping and trade between Europe and Asia. The total volume of world trade continues to decrease, and the immediate outlook for shipping, insurance, banking, and harbour interests, which are predominantly British, is not favourable. To counteract the tendency of all countries to adopt, at whatever cost, a policy of national self-sufficiency, every channel of trade must be cleared of obstructions. One of the greatest of such channels is beyond all question the Suez Canal. One of the greatest of obstructions is, if the arguments set forth in this book are tenable, the present level of Suez Canal dues.

Other methods of securing a revision of the existing level of dues have indeed been propounded. Recourse might be had to Article 19 of the League of Nations Covenant, but that procedure has never yet been seriously attempted and the omens are not favourable, for were it once applied with success the flood-gates of peaceful revision would be opened, to the discomfiture of many.

It has been suggested that the question might be dealt with by the Communications and Transit Commission of the League, but neither the achievements nor the composition of that body give prospects of success in handling such a problem. It has also been suggested that the question might be placed on the agenda of the World Economic Conference when it next meets. It is however clear that, in the language of the stable, that horse will not run.

The Egyptian Government itself might raise the question by means of a circular letter to the Maritime Powers, as did Turkey in 1873, but the international status of Egypt and its peculiar relationship with Great Britain make it doubtful whether such a procedure would be helpful.

Lastly, the question may be left, so far as concerns official action by the maritime powers, to solve itself. In favour of this policy it is argued that if canal dues are too high, fewer ships will use the canal, more will go via Panama or the Cape, and the Company will be compelled to lower dues or to levy them on some simple *ad valorem* basis, depending on the nature and quantities of cargo in each ship. This remedy is in the hands of shippers and shipowners, and it is not unattractive. Longer sea journeys mean more ships at sea, and more employment for crews. Shipping is better so employed than lying in harbour, and would constitute a mobile reserve ready for use in other directions when needed. If all cargo (not passenger) ships between Great Britain and Asia found it desirable to go round the Cape the result might, on balance, be beneficial to this country, but for the existence, in certain markets, of American competition via Panama. This proposal, however, ignores the possibility that the Canal Company might seek to recoup themselves by charging heavier dues on that portion of the traffic which is compelled to use the canal at whatever cost, viz. passenger ships and those to or from Indian ports and Ceylon.

All these solutions are temporary, in that they neither take into account the retrocession of the canal to Egypt in 1968, nor provide a basis for the renewal of the Concession on lines which, by limiting profits, will safeguard the interests of international trade, whilst securing to Egypt a fixed sum, by way of quit-rent, in consideration of the administrative and other responsibilities imposed on her by the existence of the canal. This involves negotiations between Great

Britain and France. The sooner such discussions are undertaken, the greater the prospects of success, and of satisfaction for all parties. Canal traffic is falling to a point which forecasts the Golden Age, when, as Virgil wrote in the fourth Eclogue,

> No more shall men in tall ships cross the seas,
> Nor merchandise be carried in the same:
> All countries then all good things shall produce.

The legal position and system of administration of the canal has existed unaltered since 1854: it is no longer suited to the needs of the world. It is an anachronism. Unchanging political or commercial organizations are no more possible than unchanging species. What is living is subject to change; what is stationary has lost the power of adaptation and in a changing world must die, and in the process affect many other interests.

The task before us is to introduce into the control and administration of the Suez Canal the changes necessary to enable it to play in the future the important role which it has occupied in the past. In writing this book I have had before me no other object than to stimulate action on these lines.

APPENDICES

No. 1

Acte de Concession du Vice-Roi d'Égypte pour la Construction et l'Exploitation du Canal Maritime de Suez et Dépendances entre la Mer Méditerrannée et la Mer Rouge.—Caire, le 30 Novembre, 1854.[1]

NOTRE ami M. Ferdinand de Lesseps ayant appelé notre attention sur les avantages qui résulteraient pour l'Égypte de la jonction de la Mer Méditerranée et de la Mer Rouge par une voie navigable pour les grands navires, et nous ayant fait connaître la possibilité de constituer, à cet effet, une Compagnie formée de capitalistes de toutes les nations, nous avons accueilli les combinaisons qu'il nous a soumises, et lui avons donné, par ces présentes, pouvoir exclusif de constituer et de diriger une Compagnie Universelle pour le percement de l'Isthme de Suez et l'exploitation d'un Canal entre les deux mers, avec faculté d'entreprendre ou de faire entreprendre tous travaux et constructions, à la charge par la Compagnie de donner préalablement toute indemnité aux particuliers en cas d'expropriation pour cause d'utilité publique; le tout dans les limites et avec les conditions et charges déterminées dans les Articles qui suivent.

Article 1er. M. Ferdinand de Lesseps constituera une Compagnie, dont nous lui confions la direction, sous le nom de Compagnie Universelle du Canal Maritime de Suez, pour le percement de l'Isthme de Suez, l'exploitation d'un passage propre à la grande navigation, la fondation ou l'appropriation de deux entrées suffisantes, l'une sur la Méditerranée, l'autre sur la Mer Rouge, et l'établissement d'un ou de deux ports.

Art. 2. Le Directeur de la Compagnie sera toujours nommé par le Gouvernement Égyptien, et choisi, autant que possible, parmi les actionnaires les plus intéressés dans l'entreprise.

Art. 3. La durée de la Concession est de quatre-vingt-dix-neuf ans, à partir du jour de l'ouverture du Canal des deux mers.

Art. 4. Les travaux seront exécutés aux frais exclusifs de la Compagnie, à laquelle tous les terrains nécessaires n'appartenant pas à des particuliers seront concédés à titre gratuit. Les fortifications que le Gouvernement jugera à propos d'établir ne seront point à la charge de la Compagnie.

Art. 5. Le Gouvernment Égyptien recevra annuellement de la Compagnie 15 pour cent des bénéfices nets résultant du bilan de la Société, sans préjudice des intérêts et dividendes revenant aux actions qu'il se réserve de prendre pour son compte lors de leur émission et sans aucune garantie de sa part dans l'exécution des travaux ni dans les opérations de la Compagnie. Le reste des bénéfices nets sera réparti ainsi qu'il suit:

75 pour cent au profit de la Compagnie;
10 pour cent au profit des membres fondateurs.

Art. 6. Les tarifs des droits de passage du Canal de Suez, concertés entre la

[1] From Command Paper, C. 3805. 1883.

Compagnie et le Vice-Roi d'Égypte et perçus par les agents de la Compagnie, seront toujours égaux pour toutes les nations, aucun avantage particulier ne pouvant jamais être stipulé au profit exclusif d'aucune d'elles.

Art. 7.[1] Dans le cas où la Compagnie jugerait nécessaire de rattacher par une voie navigable le Nil au passage direct de l'Isthme, et dans celui où le Canal Maritime suivrait un tracé indirect desservi par l'eau du Nil, le Gouvernement Égyptien abandonnerait à la Compagnie les terrains du domaine public aujourd'hui incultes qui seraient arrosés et cultivés à ses frais ou par ses soins.

La Compagnie jouira, sans impôts, des dits terrains pendant dix ans, à partir du jour de l'ouverture du Canal; durant les quatre-vingt-neuf ans qui resteront à s'écouler jusqu'à l'expiration de la Concession, elle payera la dîme au Gouvernement Égyptien; après quoi, elle ne pourra continuer à jouir des terrains ci-dessus mentionnés qu'autant qu'elle payera au dit Gouvernement un impôt égal à celui qui sera affecté aux terrains de même nature.

Art. 8.[1] Pour éviter toute difficulté au sujet des terrains qui seront abandonnés à la Compagnie concessionnaire, un plan dressé par M. Linant Bey, notre Commissaire Ingénieur auprès de la Compagnie, indiquera les terrains concédés, tant pour la traversée, et les établissements du Canal Maritime et du Canal d'Alimentation dérivé du Nil, que pour les exploitations de culture, conformément aux stipulations de l'Article 7.

Il est, en outre, entendu que toute spéculation est, dès à présent, interdite sur les terrains du domaine public à concéder, et que les terrains appartenant antérieurement à des particuliers, et que les propriétaires voudront plus tard faire arroser par les eaux du Canal d'Alimentation exécuté aux frais de la Compagnie, payeront une redevance de . . . par feddan cultivé[2] (ou une redevance fixée amiablement entre le Gouvernement Égyptien et la Compagnie).

Art. 9. Il est enfin accordé à la Compagnie concessionnaire la faculté d'extraire des mines et carrières appartenant au domaine public, sans payer de droits, tous les matériaux nécessaires aux travaux du Canal et aux constructions qui en dépendront, de même qu'elle jouira de la libre entrée de toutes les machines et matériaux qu'elle fera venir de l'étranger pour l'exploitation de sa Concession.

Art. 10. A l'expiration de la Concession, le Gouvernement Égyptien sera substitué à la Compagnie, jouira sans réserve de tous ses droits et entrera en pleine possession du Canal des deux mers et de tous les établissements qui en dépendront. Un arrangement amiable ou par arbitrage déterminera l'indemnité à allouer à la Compagnie pour l'abandon de son matériel et des objets mobiliers.

Art. 11. Les Statuts de la Société nous seront ultérieurement soumis par le Directeur de la Compagnie et devront être revêtus de notre approbation. Les modifications qui pourraient être introduites plus tard devront préalablement recevoir notre sanction. Les dits Statuts mentionneront les noms des fondateurs, dont nous nous réservons d'approuver la liste. Cette liste comprendra les personnes dont les travaux, les études, les soins ou les capitaux auront antérieurement contribué à l'exécution de la grande entreprise du Canal de Suez.

Art. 12. Nous promettons enfin notre bon et loyal concours et celui de tous

[1] Abrogated by Art. 3 of Convention of 22nd February, 1866 (Hertslet's *State Papers*, vol. lvi, p. 279).

[2] Le feddan égyptien correspond à peu près à un demi-hectare.

les fonctionnaires de l'Égypte pour faciliter l'exécution et l'exploitation des présents pouvoirs.

Caire, le 30 Novembre, 1854.

A mon dévoué ami, de haute naissance et de rang élevé, M. Ferdinand de Lesseps.

La Concession accordée à la Compagnie Universelle du Canal de Suez devant être ratifiée par Sa Majesté Impériale le Sultan, je vous remets cette copie pour que vous la conserviez par devers vous. Quant aux travaux relatifs au creusement du Canal de Suez, ils ne seront commencés qu'après l'autorisation de la Sublime Porte.

(Cachet du Vice-Roi.)

Le 3 Ramadan, 1274.

Appendix 2

Acte de Concession du Vice-Roi d'Égypte, et Cahier des Charges, pour la Construction et l'Exploitation du Canal Maritime de Suez et Dépendances.
—Alexandrie, le 5 Janvier, 1856.

Nous, Mahomed Saïd Pacha, Vice-Roi d'Égypte,

Vu notre Acte de Concession, en date du 30 Novembre, 1854,[1] par lequel nous avons donné à notre ami, M. Ferdinand de Lesseps, pouvoir exclusif à l'effet de constituer et diriger une Compagnie Universelle pour le percement de l'Isthme de Suez, l'exploitation d'un passage propre à la grande navigation, la fondation ou l'appropriation de deux entrées suffisantes, l'une sur la Méditerranée, l'autre sur la Mer Rouge, et l'établissement d'un ou deux ports:

M. Ferdinand de Lesseps nous ayant représenté que, pour constituer la Compagnie susindiquée dans les formes et conditions généralement adoptées pour les Sociétés de cette nature, il est utile de stipuler d'avance, dans un acte plus détaillé et plus complet, d'une part, les charges, obligations, et redevances auxquelles cette Société sera soumise; d'autre part, les concessions, immunités, et avantages auxquels elle aura droit, ainsi que les facilités qui lui seront accordées pour son administration,

Avons arrêté comme suit les conditions de la Concession qui fait l'objet des présentes:

§ 1. *Charges.*

Article 1er. La Société fondée par notre ami M. Ferdinand de Lesseps, en vertu de notre Concession du 30 Novembre, 1854, devra exécuter à ses frais, risques, et périls, tous les travaux et constructions nécessaires pour l'établissement:

1. D'un Canal approprié à la grande navigation maritime, entre Suez, dans la Mer Rouge, et le Golfe de Péluse, dans la Mer Méditerranée;

2. D'un Canal d'irrigation, et approprié à la navigation fluviale du Nil, joignant le fleuve au Canal Maritime susmentionné;

3. De deux branches d'irrigation et d'alimentation dérivées du précédent Canal, et portant leurs eaux dans les deux directions de Suez et de Péluse;

[1] No. 1.

Les travaux seront conduits de manière à être terminés dans un délai de six années, sauf les empêchements et retards provenant de force majeure.

Art. 2. La Compagnie aura la faculté d'exécuter les travaux dont elle est chargée par elle-même et en régie, ou de les faire exécuter par des entrepreneurs au moyen d'adjudications ou de marchés à forfait. *Dans tous les cas, les quatre cinquièmes au moins des ouvriers employés à ces travaux seront Égyptiens.*[1]

Art. 3. Le Canal approprié à la grande navigation maritime sera creusé à la profondeur et à la largeur fixées par le programme de la Commission Scientifique Internationale.

Conformément à ce programme, il prendra son origine au port même de Suez; il empruntera le bassin dit les Lacs Amers et le Lac Timsah; il viendra déboucher dans la Méditerranée en un point du Golfe de Péluse qui sera déterminé dans les projets définitifs à dresser par les Ingénieurs de la Compagnie.

Art. 4. Le Canal d'irrigation approprié à la navigation fluviale dans les conditions du dit programme, prendra naissance à proximité de la ville du Caire, suivra la vallée ('ouadée') Toumilat (ancienne terre de Gessen), et débouchera dans le Grand Canal Maritime au Lac Timsah.

Art. 5. Les dérivations du Canal précédent s'en détacheront en amont du débouché dans le Lac Timsah; de ce point elles seront dirigées, d'un côté sur Suez, de l'autre côté sur Péluse, parallèlement au Grand Canal Maritime.

Art. 6. Le Lac Timsah sera converti en un port intérieur propre à recevoir des bâtiments du plus fort tonnage.

La Compagnie sera tenue, en outre, si cela est nécessaire: (1) de construire un port d'abri à l'entrée du Canal Maritime dans le Golfe de Péluse; (2) d'améliorer le port et la rade de Suez, de manière à ce que les navires y soient également abrités.

Art. 7. Le Canal Maritime, les ports en dépendant, ainsi que le Canal de jonction du Nil et le Canal de dérivation, seront constamment entretenus en bon état par la Compagnie et à ses frais.

Art. 8. Les propriétaires riverains qui voudront faire arroser leurs terres au moyen de prises d'eau tirées des Canaux construits par la Compagnie, pourront en obtenir d'elle la concession moyennant le payement d'une indemnité ou d'une redevance dont le chiffre sera fixé dans les conditions de l'Article 17 ci-près.

Art. 9. Nous nous réservons de déléguer, au siège administratif de la Compagnie, un Commissaire Spécial dont le traitement sera payé par elle, et qui représentera, près de son Administration, les droits et les intérêts du Gouvernement Égyptien pour l'exécution des dispositions du présent.

Si le siège administratif de la Société est établie ailleurs qu'en Égypte, la compagnie sera tenue de se faire représenter à Alexandrie par un Agent Supérieur nanti de tous les pouvoirs nécessaires pour assurer la bonne marche du service et les rapports de la Compagnie avec notre Gouvernement.

§ 2. *Concessions.*

Art. 10.[2] Pour la construction des Canaux et dépendances mentionnés dans les Articles qui précèdent, le Gouvernement Égyptien abandonne à la Compagnie,

[1] Abrogated by Art. 1 of Convention of 22nd February, 1866 (Hertslet's *State Papers*, vol. lvi, p. 276).

[2] Abrogated by Art. 3 of Convention of 22nd February, 1866 (ibid., vol. lvi, p. 279).

sans aucun impôt ni redevance, la jouissance de tous les terrains n'appartenant pas à des particuliers, qui pourront être nécessaires.

Il lui abandonne également la jouissance de tous les terrains aujourd'hui incultes n'appartenant pas à des particuliers, qui seront arrosés et mis en culture par ses soins et à ses frais, avec cette différence: (1) que les terrains compris dans cette dernière catégorie seront exempts de tout impôt pendant dix ans seulement, à dater de leur mise en rapport; (2) que passé ce terme, ils seront soumis, pendant le reste de la Concession, aux obligations et aux impôts auxquels seront assujetties, dans les mêmes circonstances, les terres des autres provinces de l'Égypte; (3) que la Compagnie pourra ensuite, par elle-même ou par ses ayants-droit, conserver la jouissance de ces terrains et des prises d'eau nécessaires à leur fertilisation, à charge de payer au Gouvernement Égyptien les impôts établis sur les terres dans les mêmes conditions.

Art. 11.[1] Pour déterminer l'étendu et les limites des terrains concédés à la Compagnie, dans les conditions du § 1 et du § 2 de l'Article 10 qui précède, il est référé aux plans ci-annexés; étant expliqué qu'aux dits plans les terrains concédés pour la construction des Canaux et dépendances, sans impôt ni redevance, conformément au § 1, son teintés en noir, et que les terrains concédés pour être mis en culture en payant certains droits, conformément au § 2, sont teintés en bleu.

Sera considéré comme nul tout act fait postérieurement à notre acte du 30 Novembre, 1854, qui aurait pour conséquence de créer à des particuliers, contre la Compagnie, ou des droits à indemnité qui n'existaient pas alors sur les terrains, ou des droits à indemnité plus considérables que ceux auxquels ils auraient pu prétendre à cette époque.

Art. 12.[1] Le Gouvernement Égyptien livrera, s'il y a lieu, à la Compagnie, les terrains de propriété particulière dont la possession sera nécessaire à l'exécution des travaux et à l'exploitation de la Concession, à charge par elle de payer aux ayants-droit de justes indemnités.

Les indemnités d'occupation temporaire ou d'expropriation définitive seront, autant que possible, réglées amiablement; en cas de désaccord, elles seront fixées par un Tribunal Arbitral procédant sommairement et composé: (1) d'un arbitre choisi par la Compagnie; (2) d'un arbitre choisi par les intéressés; (3) d'un tiers arbitre désigné par nous.

Les décisions du Tribunal Arbitral seront exécutoires immédiatement et sans appel.

Art. 13.[2] Le Gouvernement Égyptien accorde à la Compagnie concessionnaire, pour toute la durée de la Concession, la faculté d'extraire des mines et carrières appartenant au domaine public, sans payer aucun droit, impôt ni indemnité, tous les matériaux nécessaires aux travaux de construction et d'entretien des ouvrages et établissements dépendant de l'entreprise.

Il exonère, en outre, la Compagnie de tous droits de Douane, d'entrée et autres, pour l'introduction en Égypte de toutes machines et matières quelconques qu'elle fera venir de l'étranger pour les besoins de ses divers services en cours de construction ou d'exploitation.

---

[1] Abrogated by Art. 3 of Convention of 22nd February, 1866 (Hertslet's *State Papers* vol. lvi, p. 279).

[2] Abrogated by Art. 1 of Convention of 23rd April, 1869.

Art. 14. Nous déclarons solennellement, pour nous et nos successeurs, sous la réserve de la ratification de Sa Majesté Impériale le Sultan, le Grand Canal Maritime de Suez à Péluse et les ports en dépendant, ouverts à toujours, comme passages neutres, à tout navire de commerce traversant d'une mer à l'autre, sans aucune distinction, exclusion, ni préférence de personnes ou de nationalités, moyennant le payement des droits et l'exécution des règlements établis par la Compagnie Universelle concessionnaire pour l'usage du dit Canal et dépendances.

Art. 15. En conséquence du principe posé dans l'Article précédent, la Compagnie Universelle concessionnaire ne pourra, dans aucun cas, accorder à aucun navire, Compagnie, ou particulier, aucuns avantages ou faveurs qui ne soient accordés à tous autres navires, Compagnies ou particuliers, dans les mêmes conditions.

Art. 16. La durée de la Société est fixée à quatre-vingt-dix-neuf années, à compter de l'achèvement des travaux et de l'ouverture du Canal Maritime à la grande navigation.

A l'expiration de cette période, le Governement Égyptien rentrera en possession du Canal Maritime construit par la Compagnie, à charge par lui, dans ce cas, de reprendre tout le matériel et les approvisionnements affectés au service maritime de l'entreprise et d'en payer à la Compagnie la valeur telle qu'elle sera fixée, soit amiablement, soit à dire d'experts.

Néanmoins, si la Compagnie conservait la Concession par périodes successives de quatre-vingt-dix-neuf années, le prélèvement stipulé au profit du Gouvernement Égyptien par l'Article 18 ci-après serait porté pour la seconde période à 20 pour cent, pour la troisième période à 25 pour cent et ainsi de suite, à raison de 5 pour cent d'augmentation pour chaque période, sans que toutefois ce prélèvement puisse jamais dépasser 35 pour cent des produits nets de l'entreprise.

Art. 17. Pour indemniser la Compagnie des dépenses de construction, d'entretien, et d'exploitation qui sont mises à sa charge par les présentes, nous l'autorisons, dès à présent, et pendant toute la durée de sa jouissance, telle qu'elle est déterminée par les paragraphes 1 et 3 de l'Article précédent, à établir et percevoir, pour le passage dans les Canaux et les ports en dépendant, des droits de navigation, de pilotage, de remorquage, de halage, ou de stationnement, suivant des tarifs qu'elle pourra modifier à toute époque, sous la condition expresse:

1. De percevoir ces droits, sans aucune exception ni faveur, sur tous les navires, dans des conditions identiques;

2. De publier les tarifs, trois mois avant la mise en vigueur, dans les capitales et les principaux ports de commerce des pays intéressés;

3. De ne pas excéder, pour le droit spécial de navigation, le chiffre maximum de 10 fr. par tonneau de capacité des navires et par tête de passager.

La Compagnie pourra également, pour toutes les prises d'eau accordées à la demande de particuliers, en vertu de l'Article 8 ci-dessus, percevoir, d'après des tarifs qu'elle fixera, un droit proportionnel à la quantité d'eau absorbée et à l'étendue des terrains arrosés.

Art. 18. Toutefois, en raison des concessions de terrains et autres avantages accordés à la Compagnie par les Articles qui précèdent, nous réservons, au profit du Gouvernement Égyptien, un prélèvement de 15 pour cent sur les bénéfices nets de chaque année, arrêtés et répartis par l'Assemblée Générale des Actionnaires.

Art. 19. La liste de membres fondateurs qui ont concouru par leurs travaux, leurs études, et leurs capitaux, à la réalisation de l'entreprise avant la fondation de la Société, sera arrêtée par nous.

Après le prélèvement stipulé au profit du Gouvernement Égyptien par l'Article 18 ci-dessus, il sera attribué, dans les produits nets annuels de l'entreprise, une part de 10 pour cent aux membres fondateurs ou à leurs héritiers ou ayants-cause.

Art. 20. Indépendamment du temps nécessaire à l'exécution des travaux, notre ami et mandataire M. Ferdinand de Lesseps presidera et dirigera la Société comme premier fondateur, pendant dix ans à partir du jour où s'ouvrira la période de jouissance de la Concession de quatre-vingt-dix-neuf années, aux termes de l'Article 16 ci-dessus.

Art. 21. Sont approuvés les Status ci-annexés de la Société créée sous la dénomination de Compagnie Universelle du Canal Maritime de Suez, la présente approbation valant autorisation de constitution, dans la forme des Sociétés anonymes, à dater du jour où le capital social sera entièrement souscrit.

Art. 22. Comme témoignage de l'intérêt que nous attachons au succès de l'entreprise nous promettons à la Compagnie le loyal concours du Gouvernement Égyptien, et nous invitons expressément par les présentes les fonctionnaires et agents de tous les services de nos Administrations à lui donner en toute circonstance aide et protection.

Nos Ingénieurs, Linant Bey et Mougel Bey, que nous mettons à la disposition de la Compagnie pour la direction et la conduite des travaux ordonnés par elle, auront la surveillance supérieure des ouvriers et seront chargés de l'exécution des Règlements qui concerneront la mise en œuvre des travaux.

Art. 23. Sont rapportées toutes dispositions de notre Ordonnance du 30 Novembre, 1854, et autres qui se trouveraient en opposition avec les clauses et conditions du présent Cahier des Charges, lequel fera seul loi pour la Concession à laquelle il s'applique.

Fait à Alexandrie, le 5 Janvier, 1856.

A mon dévoué ami de haute naissance et de rang élevé, M. Ferdinand de Lesseps.

La Concession accordée à la Compagnie Universelle du Canal de Suez devant être ratifiée par Sa Majesté Impériale le Sultan, je vous remets cette copie authentique, afin que vous puissiez constituer la dite Compagnie financière.

Quant aux travaux relatifs au percement de l'isthme, elle pourra les exécuter elle-même dès que l'autorisation de la Sublime Porte m'aura été accordée.

Alexandrie, le 26 Rebi-ul-Akher, 1272 (5 Janvier, 1856).

(Cachet de Son Altesse le Vice-Roi.)

Appendix 3

Statuts de la Compagnie Universelle du Canal Maritime de Suez.— Alexandrie, le 5 Janvier, 1856.

TITRE I.—*Formation et Objet de la Société.—Dénomination.—Siège.—Durée.*

Article 1er. Il est formé, entre les souscripteurs et propriétaires des actions créées ci-après, une Société anonyme sous la dénomination de Compagnie Universelle du Canal Maritime de Suez.

Art. 2. Cette Société a pour objet:

1. La construction d'un Canal Maritime de grande navigation entre la Mer Rouge et la Méditerranée, de Suez au Golfe de Péluse.

2. La construction d'un Canal de navigation fluviale et d'irrigation joignant le Nil au Canal Maritime, du Caire au Lac Timsah;

3. La construction de deux Canaux de dérivation, se détachant du précédent en amont de son débouché dans le Lac Timsah, et amenant ses eaux dans les deux directions de Suez et de Péluse;

4. L'exploitation des dits Canaux et des entreprises diverses qui s'y attachent.

5. Et l'exploitation des terrains concédés.

Le tout aux clauses et conditions de la Concession telle qu'elle résulte des Ordonnances de Son Altesse le Vice-Roi d'Égypte, en date du 30 Novembre, 1854,[1] et du 5 Janvier, 1856:[2] la première donnant pouvoir spécial et exclusif à M. de Lesseps de constituer et diriger, comme premier fondateur Président, une Société en vue de ces entreprises; la seconde portant Concession des dits Canaux et de leurs dépendances à cette Société, avec toutes les charges et obligations, tous les droits et avantages qui y sont attachés par le Gouvernement Égyptien.

Art. 3. La Société a son siège à Alexandrie et son domicile administratif à Paris.

Art. 4. La Société commence à dater du jour de la signature de l'acte social, portant souscription de la totalité des actions. Sa durée est égale à la durée de la Concession.

Art. 5. Les comptes des dépenses faites antérieurement à la constitution de la Société, soit par Son Altesse le Vice-Roi d'Égypte, soit par M. Ferdinand de Lesseps agissant en vertu des pouvoirs dont il était investi pour arriver à la réalisation de l'enterprise, seront réglés par le Conseil d'Administration, qui en autorisera le remboursement à qui de droit.

TITRE II.—*Fonds Social.—Actions.—Versements.*

Art. 6. Le fonds social est fixé à 200,000,000 fr., représentés par 400,000 actions, à raison de 500 fr. chacune.

Art. 7. Les titres d'actions et d'obligations, dont le Conseil d'Administration détermine la forme et le modèle, sont libellés en langues Turque, Allemande, Anglaise, Française, et Italienne.

Art. 8. Le montant de chaque action est payable en espèces, dans la Caisse Sociale ou chez les représentants de la Compagnie à Alexandrie, Amsterdam, Constantinople, Londres, New York, Paris, Saint Pétersbourg, Vienne, Gênes, Barcelone, et autres villes qui seraient désignées par le Conseil d'Administration, au cours du change, soit sur Paris, soit sur Alexandrie, au choix de la Compagnie.

Art. 9. Les versements s'opèrent conformément aux appels faits par le Conseil au moyen d'annonces publiées deux mois à l'avance par l'insertion dans deux journaux, et à défaut de journaux, par l'affichage à la Bourse, dans les villes désignées à l'Article 8 ci-dessus.

Art. 10. Si le Conseil juge qu'il n'y a pas lieu d'appeler, au moment de la souscription, le versement immédiat de la partie de capital nécessaire, aux termes

---

[1] No. 1.   [2] No. 2.

de l'Article 12 ci-après, pour l'émission des titres au porteur, le premier versement peut être constaté par la délivrance de certificats nominatifs provisoires.

Ces certificats portent un numéro d'ordre; ils sont détachés d'un registre à souche et timbrés du timbre sec de la Compagnie. Ils sont signés par deux Administrateurs et un délégué du Conseil d'Administration.

Art. 11. Les certificats nominatifs peuvent être négociés, au moyen d'un transfert signé par le cédant et le cessionnaire et inscrit sur les registres établis dans les bureaux de la Compagnie ou de ceux de ses représentants désignés à cet effet par le Conseil, partout où besoin sera.

Mention est faite du transfert au dos des titres par un Administrateur ou par agent à ce commis.

La Compagnie peut exiger que la signature des parties soit dûment certifiée.

Art. 12. Les souscripteurs primitifs et leurs cessionnaires restent solidairement engagés jusqu'au payement intégral de 30 pour cent sur le montant de chaque action.

Après le versement de 30 pour cent sur le montant de chaque action, les certificats nominatifs peuvent être échangés contre des titres au porteur provisoires.

Art. 13. Chaque versement effectué est inscrit sur les titres auxquels il s'applique.

Après libération intégrale opérée, il est délivré aux porteurs des actions définitives.

Art. 14. A défaut de versement aux époques déterminées l'intérêt est dû pour chaque jour de retard à raison de 5 pour cent par an.

La Société peut, en outre, faire vendre les actions dont les versements sont en retard.

A cet effet, les numéros de ces actions sont publiés, conformément aux prescriptions de l'Article 9 ci-dessus pour les appels de fonds, avec indication des conséquences du retard apporté dans les versements.

Deux mois après cette publication, la Société, sans mise en demeure et sans autre formalité ultérieure, a le droit de faire procéder à la vente des dites actions pour le compte et aux risques et périls des retardataires.

Cette vente est faite sur duplicata, en une ou plusieurs fois, à la Bourse de Paris ou à celle de Londres, par le ministère d'un agent de change.

Les titres antérieurs des actions ainsi vendues deviennent nuls de plein droit, par le fait même de la vente; il est délivré aux acquéreurs des titres nouveaux qui portent les mêmes numéros et qui sont seuls valables.

En conséquence, tout titre qui ne porte pas la mention régulière des versements exigibles cesse d'être négociable.

Les mesures qui font l'objet du présent Article n'excluent pas l'exercice simultané par la Société, si elle le juge utile, des moyens ordinaires de droit contre les actionnaires en retard.

Art. 15. Les sommes provenant des ventes effectuées en vertu de l'Article précédent, déduction faite des frais et des intérêts, sont imputées, dans les termes de droit, sur ce qui est dû par l'actionnaire exproprié ou par ces cédants, qui restent responsables de la différence, s'il y a déficit, et qui bénéficient de l'excédent, si excédent il y a.

Art. 16. Les actions définitives sont au porteur; la cession s'en opère par la simple tradition du titre.

Les actions définitives sont extraites d'un registre à souche, numérotées et revêtues de la signature de deux Administrateurs, ou d'un Administrateur et d'un délégué du Conseil d'Administration.

Elles portent le timbre sec de la Compagnie.

Art. 17. Le Conseil d'Administration peut autoriser le dépôt et la conservation des titres au porteur dans la Caisse Sociale. Il détermine, dans ce cas, la forme des certificats nominatifs de dépôt, les conditions de leur délivrance et les garanties dont l'exécution de cette mesure doit être entourée dans l'intérêt de la Société et des actionnaires.

Art. 18. Chaque action donne droit à une part proportionnelle dans la propriété de l'actif social.

Art. 19. Toute action est indivisible. La Société ne reconnaît qu'un propriétaire pour chaque action.

Art. 20. Les droits et les obligations attachés à l'action suivent le titre dans les mains où il se trouve.

La possession d'une action emporte de plein droit adhésion aux Statuts de la Société et aux résolutions de l'Assemblée Générale des Actionnaires.

Art. 21. Les héritiers ou créanciers d'un actionnaire ne peuvent, sous quelque prétexte que ce soit, provoquer l'apposition des scellés sur les biens, valeurs, ou revenus de la Société, en demander le partage ou la licitation, ni s'immiscer en aucune manière dans son administration. Ils doivent, pour l'exercice de leurs droits, s'en rapporter aux inventaires sociaux et aux comptes annuels approuvés par l'Assemblée Générale des Actionnaires.

Art. 22. Les actionnaires ne sont engagés que jusqu'à concurrence du capital de leurs actions, au-delà duquel tout appel de fonds est interdit.

Art. 23. Le Conseil peut autoriser la libération anticipée des actions, mais seulement par mesure générale applicable à tous les actionnaires.

Titre III.—*Conseil d'Administration.*

Art. 24. La Société est administrée par un Conseil composé de trente-deux membres représentant les principales nationalités intéressées à l'entreprise.

Un Comité, choisi dans son sein, est spécialement chargé de la direction et de la gestion des affaires de la Société.

Art. 25. Les Administrateurs ne contractent en raison de leurs fonctions, aucune obligation personnelle ou solidaire. Ils ne répondent que de l'exécution de leur mandat.

Art. 26. Les Administrateurs sont nommés par l'Assemblée Générale des Actionnaires pour huit années.

Le Conseil se renouvelle, en conséquence, chaque année, par huitième. Jusqu'à ce que l'entier renouvellement du Conseil ait établi l'ordre de roulement, les membres sortants sont désignés annuellement par le sort.

Les Administrateurs sortants peuvent toujours être réélus.

Art. 27. En cas de vacances provenant de démissions ou de décès, il est pourvu provisoirement au remplacement par le Conseil d'Administration jusqu'à la prochaine Assemblée Générale des Actionnaires.

Les Administrateurs ainsi nommés ne demeurent en fonctions que pendant le temps restant à courir pour l'exercice de leurs prédécesseurs.

Art. 28. Chaque Administrateur doit être propriétaire de 100 actions, qui sont inaliénables et restent déposées dans la Caisse Sociale pendant toute la durée de ces fonctions.

Art. 29. Une part de 3 pour cent dans les bénéfices net (*sic*) annuels est attribuée aux Administrateurs en raison de leurs peines et soins.

Pendant la durée des travaux, et au besoin pendant les premières années qui suivront l'ouverture du Canal Maritime à la grande navigation, il est attribué au Conseil, pour tenir lieu de la part de 3 pour cent stipulée ci-dessus, une allocation annuelle qui sera comprise dans les frais d'administration, et dont le montant sera fixé par la première Assemblée Générale des Actionnaires.

Le Conseil d'Administration détermine l'attribution particulière qui doit être faite sur cette somme ou sur les 3 pour cent dans les bénéfices aux membres du Comité de Direction.

Art. 30. Le Conseil d'Administration nomme chaque année, parmi ses membres, un Président et trois Vice-Présidents.

Le Président et les Vice-Présidents peuvent toujours être réélus.

En cas d'absence du Président et des Vice-Présidents, le Conseil désigne, à chaque séance, celui de ses membres qui doit en remplir les fonctions.

Art. 31. Le Conseil d'Administration se réunit au moins une fois par mois. Il se réunit, en outre, sur la convocation du Président, aussi souvent que l'exigent les intérêts de la Société.

Les décisions sont prises à la majorité des voix des membres présents.

En cas de partage, la voix du Président est prépondérante.

Sept Administrateurs au moins doivent être présents pour valider les délibérations du Conseil.

Lorsque sept Administrateurs seulement sont présents, les décisions, pour être valables, doivent êtres prises à la majorité de cinq voix.

Art. 32. Le Secrétaire-Général de la Compagnie assiste aux séances du Conseil d'Administration avec voix consultative.

Art. 33. Les délibérations du Conseil d'Administration sont constatées par des procès-verbaux signés par le Président et l'un des membres présents à la séance.

Les copies ou extraits de ces procès-verbaux doivent, pour être produits valablement en justice ou ailleurs, être certifiés par le Secrétaire-Général de la Compagnie.

Un extrait des décisions rendues à chaque séance, dûment certifié, est envoyé, dans les huit jours qui suivent la réunion, à chaque Administrateur absent.

Art. 34. Le Conseil d'Administration est investi des pouvoirs les plus étendus pour l'administration des affaires de la Société.

Il arrête les propositions à soumettre à l'Assemblée Générale des Actionnaires en vertu de l'Article 16 (*sic* 36?) ci-après.

Il statue sur les propositions du Comité de Direction concernant les objets suivants, savoir:—

1. Nomination et révocation des fonctionnaires et Agents Supérieurs de la Compagnie; fixation de leurs attributions et de leur traitement;
2. Placements temporaires des fonds disponibles;
3. Études et projets, plans et devis pour l'exécution des travaux;
4. Marchés à forfait;

5. Acquisitions, ventes et échanges d'immeubles, achats de navires ou de machines nécessaires pour l'exécution des travaux et l'exploitation de l'entreprise;

6. Budgets annuels;

7. Fixation et modification des droits de toute nature à percevoir en vertu de la Concession; conditions et mode de perception des tarifs;

8. Disposition du fonds de réserve;

9. Disposition du fonds de retraite, de secours et d'encouragement pour les employés;

10. Réglementation de la Caisse des Dépôts pour les actions et obligations de la Société.

Art. 35. Le Conseil nomme ceux de ses membres qui doivent faire partie du Comité de Direction.

Il peut déléguer à un ou à plusieurs Administrateurs, aux fonctionnaires, employés de la Compagnie ou autres, tout ou partie de ses pouvoirs par un mandat spécial et pour une ou plusieurs affaires ou objets déterminés.

Art. 36. Nul ne peut voter dans le Conseil par procuration.

Lorsque le Conseil doit délibérer sur des modifications à apporter dans les tarifs ou dans les Statuts, sur des emprunts ou augmentations de capital social, sur des demandes de concessions nouvelles, des traités de fusion avec d'autres entreprises, sur la dissolution et la liquidation de la Société, les Administrateurs absents doivent, un mois à l'avance, être informés de l'objet de la délibération et invités à venir prendre part au vote, ou à adresser leur opinion par écrit au Président, qui en donne lecture en séance; après quoi les décisions sont prises à la majorité des voix des membres présents.

Titre IV.—*Comité de Direction.*

Art. 37. Le Comité de Direction, constitué en vertu des dispositions de l'Article 24 ci-dessus, est composé du Président du Conseil d'Administration et de quatre Administrateurs spécialement délégués.

Art. 38. Le Comité de Direction se réunit, à la convocation du Président, autant de fois que cela est nécessaire pour la bonne marche du service et au moins une fois par semaine.

Art. 39. Il est tenu procès-verbal des séances du Comité de Direction. Ces procès-verbaux sont signés par un des Administrateurs présents à la séance.

Les extraits de ces procès-verbaux, pour être valablement produits en justice ou ailleurs, doivent être visés par le Président et certifiés par le Secrétaire-Général de la Compagnie.

Art. 40. Le Comité de Direction est investi de tous pouvoirs pour la gestion des affaires de la Société.

Il pourvoit à l'exécution tant des obligations imposées par le Cahier des Charges et les Statuts, que des résolutions adoptées par l'Assemblée Générale et des décisions du Conseil d'Administration.

Il soumet au Conseil d'Administration les propositions relatives aux objets définis à l'Article 35 ci-dessus.

Il représente la Société et agit en son nom, par un ou plusieurs de ses membres, dans tous les cas où une disposition expresse n'exige pas l'intervention de l'Assem--

blée Générale des Actionnaires ou du Conseil d'Administration, notamment en ce qui concerne les objets ci-après:

1. Nomination et révocation des employés; fixation de leurs fonctions et de leur solde;
2. Travail des bureaux;
3. Règlements et ordres de service;
4. Ordonnancement et règlement des dépenses;
5. Transferts de rentes, d'effets publics, et de commerce;
6. Perceptions de droits, recouvrements de créances, quittances, et mainlevées avec ou sans payement, instances judiciaires et administratives, mesures conservatoires;
7. Défenses en justice, compromis, transactions, désistements;
8. Traités, marchés, adjudications, achats de mobilier, baux et locations.

Les actions judiciaires en demandant ou en défendant sont dirigées par ou contre le Président et les membres composant le Comité de Direction.

En conséquence, les notifications ou significations sont faites et reçues par le Comité de Direction au nom de la Société.

Les décisions du Comité, les actes et engagements approuvés par lui, sont signés par le Président ou par deux membres du Comité délégués à cet effet.

Art. 41. Le Comité de Direction et le Président du Conseil peuvent déléguer, par procuration authentique, à un ou plusieurs Administrateurs, fonctionnaires de la Compagnie, employés ou autres, le pouvoir de signer tous les actes et engagements mentionnés ci-dessus.

Art. 42.[1]

Un Agent Supérieur, chef des services, réside en Egypte;

Il est investi de tous les pouvoirs nécessaires pour l'exécution des travaux et la marche de l'exploitation;

Il représente la Compagnie dans tous ses rapports avec le Gouvernement Égyptien et les tiers.

Titre V.—*Assemblée Générale des Actionnaires.*

Art. 43. L'Assemblée Générale régulièrement constituée représente l'universalité des actionnaires.

Art. 44. L'Assemblée Générale se compose de tous les actionnaires propriétaires d'au moins vingt-cinq actions.

Elle est régulièrement constituée lorsque les actionnaires qui la composent sont au nombre de quarante et représentent le vingtième du fonds social.

Art. 45. Lorsque, sur une première convocation, les actionnaires présents ne remplissent pas les conditions spécifiées ci-dessus pour constituer la validité des délibérations de l'Assemblée Générale, la réunion est ajournée de plein droit, et l'ajournement ne peut être moindre de deux mois.

Une seconde convocation est faite dans la forme prescrite par l'Article 47 ci-après.

Les délibérations de l'Assemblée Générale dans cette seconde réunion ne peuvent porter que sur les objets à l'ordre du jour de la première. Ces délibérations sont valables quel que soit le nombre des actionnaires présents et des actions représentées.

[1] As modified in 1874.

Art. 46. L'Assemblée Générale se réunit, chaque année, dans la première quinzaine du mois de Mai.[1]

Elle se réunit, en outre, extraordinairement toutes les fois que le Conseil d'Administration en reconnaît l'utilité.

Art. 47. Les convocations ordinaires et extraordinaires sont faites par un avis publié un mois avant l'époque de la réunion dans les formes prescrites pour les appels de fonds, par l'Article 9 ci-dessus.

Art. 48. Les actionnaires, pour avoir le droit d'assister ou de se faire représenter à l'Assemblée Générale, doivent justifier, au domicile de la Société, au moins cinq jours avant la réunion, du dépôt fait de leurs titres dans la Caisse Sociale ou chez un représentant de la Compagnie désigné à cet effet par le Conseil d'Administration, dans les villes dénommées à l'Article 8 ci-dessus.

Les dépôts faits dans ces conditions donnent droit à la remise de cartes d'admission nominatives.

Les actionnaires porteurs de certificats de dépôt ont également la faculté de se faire représenter aux Assemblées Générales par des mandataires munis de pouvoirs réguliers, dont la forme est déterminée par le Conseil d'Administration.

Les fondés de pouvoirs doivent déposer leurs procurations au domicile de la société cinq jours au moins avant la réunion.

Nul ne peut représenter un actionnaire à l'Assemblée s'il n'est lui-même membre de cette Assemblée.

Art. 49. L'Assemblée Générale est présidée par le Président ou par l'un des Vice-Présidents du Conseil d'Administration, et à leur défaut, par un Administrateur nommé par le Conseil.

Les deux plus forts actionnaires présents au moment de l'ouverture de la séance, et qui acceptent, sont nommés Scrutateurs.

Le Président désigne le Secrétaire.

Art. 50. Les délibérations de l'Assemblée Générale sont prises à la majorité des voix des membres présents ou régulièrement représentés, conformément à l'Article 48 ci-dessus.

En cas de partage, la voix du Président est prépondérante.

Art. 51. Vingt-cinq actions donnent droit à une voix: le même actionnaire ne peut réunir plus de dix voix, soit comme actionnaire, soit comme mandataire.

Art. 52. Le scrutin secret peut être réclamé par dix membres.

Art. 53. Les délibérations de l'Assemblée Générale sont constatées par des procès-verbaux signés par le Président, par les Scrutateurs, et par le Secrétaire.

Les copies ou extraits de ces procès-verbaux, pour être valablement produits en justice ou ailleurs, doivent être certifiés par le Secrétaire-Général de la Compagnie.

---

[1] By Resolution of 1864 general meetings may take place between May 1st and August 1st.

Résolution du 6 Août, 1864.

L'Assemblée:

Conformément aux propositions développées dans sa réunion du 15 Juillet, 1863, approuve la modification de l'Article 46 des Statuts, qui fixe la réunion ordinaire de l'Assemblée Générale des Actionnaires du 1er au 15 Mai de chaque année, en ce sens que cette réunion pourra avoir lieu, sur la convocation du Conseil, du 1er Mai au 1er Août.

Adoptée à l'unanimité.

Art. 54. Une feuille de présence, destinée à constater le nombre des membres assistant à l'assemblée et celui des actions représentées par chacun d'eux, reste annexée à la Minute du procès-verbal, ainsi que les pouvoirs conférés par les actionnaires absents.

Cette feuille doit être signée par chaque actionnaire à son entrée à la séance.

Art. 55. L'ordre du jour de l'Assemblée Générale est arrêté par le Conseil d'Administration.

Aucune autre question que celles portées à l'ordre du jour ne peut être mise en délibération.

Art. 56. L'Assemblée Générale entend les Rapports du Conseil d'Administration sur la situation et les intérêts de la Société. Elle délibère sur ses propositions, en se renfermant dans les limites des Statuts et du Cahier des Charges, concernant tous les intérêts de la Compagnie. Elle nomme les Administrateurs en remplacement des membres du Conseil sortants ou à remplacer. Elle confère, lorsqu'il y a lieu, au Conseil les pouvoirs nécessaires pour la suite à donner à ses résolutions.

L'approbation de l'Assemblée Générale est nécessaire pour toute décision statuant sur les objets ci-après, savoir:—

1. Concessions nouvelles;
2. Fusion avec d'autres entreprises;
3. Modifications aux Statuts de la Société;
4. Dissolution de la Société;
5. Augmentation du capital social;
6. Emprunts;
7. Règlement des comptes de premier établissement en fin de l'exécution des travaux;
8. Règlement des comptes annuels;
9. Fixation de la retenue pour le fonds de réserve;
10. Fixation du dividende à distribuer annuellement aux actionnaires.

Art. 57. Les délibérations relatives aux objets mentionnés à l'Article 56, paragraphes 1, 2, 3, 4, 5, et 6, doivent, pour être valables, être prises par une assemblée réunissant au moins le dixième du fonds social et à la majorité des deux tiers des voix des membres présents, au nombre de cinquante au moins.

Lorsque, sur une première convocation, les actionnaires présents ne remplissent pas ces conditions, il est procédé à une deuxième convocation, conformément aux prescriptions de l'Article 47 ci-dessus.

Les délibérations de l'Assemblée Générale réunie en vertu de cette deuxième convocation sont valables quel que soit le nombre des actionnaires présents et des actions représentées.

Art. 58. Les délibérations de l'Assemblée Générale prises conformément aux Statuts obligent tous les actionnaires, même ceux qui sont absents ou dissidents.

TITRE VI.—*Comptes Annuels.—Amortissement.—Intérêts.—Fonds de Réserve.—*
Dividendes.

Art. 59. Pendant l'exécution des travaux, il est payé annuellement aux actionnaires un intérêt de 5 pour cent sur les sommes par eux versées, en exécution de l'Article 9 ci-dessus.

Il est pourvu au payement de ces intérêts par le produit des placements temporaires de fonds et autres produits accessoires, et au besoin sur le capital social.

Art. 60. Après l'achèvement des travaux, le compte des recettes et dépenses de la Compagnie pendant la durée de ces travaux est arrêté et soumis à l'Assemblée Générale des Actionnaires par le Conseil d'Administration.

Art. 61. A dater de l'ouverture du Canal Maritime à la grande navigation, un inventaire général de l'actif et du passif dè la Société au 31 Décembre précédent est dressé dans le premier trimestre de chaque année. Cet inventaire est soumis à l'Assemblée Générale des Actionnaires réunie dans le courant du mois de Mai suivant.

Art. 62. Les produits annuels de l'entreprise servent d'abord à acquitter dans l'ordre ci-après:

1. Les dépenses d'entretien et d'exploitation, les frais d'Administration, et généralement toutes les charges sociales;

2. L'intérêt et l'amortissement des emprunts qui peuvent avoir été contractés;

3. Cinq pour cent du capital social pour servir aux actions amorties et non amorties un intérêt annuel de 25 fr. par action, les intérêts différents aux actions amorties devant rentrer au fonds d'amortissement, constitué conformément à l'Article 66 ci-après;

4. Quatre centièmes pour cent du capital social également applicables à ce fonds d'amortissement;

5. La retenue destinée à constituer ou à compléter un fonds de réserve pour les dépenses imprévues, conformément aux dispositions de l'Article 69 ci-après.

L'excédent des produits annuels, après ces divers prélèvements, constitue les produits nets ou bénéfices de l'entreprise.

Art. 63.[1] Les produits nets ou bénéfices de l'entreprise sont répartis de la manière suivante:—

1. 15 pour cent au Gouvernement Égyptien;

2. 10 pour cent aux fondateurs;

3. 3 pour cent aux Administrateurs;

4. 2 pour cent pour la constitution d'un fonds destiné à pourvoir aux retraites, aux secours, aux indemnités ou gratifications accordés, suivant qu'il y a lieu, par le Conseil, aux employés;

5. 70 pour cent comme dividende à répartir entre toutes les actions amorties et non amorties indistinctement.

Art. 64. Le payement des intérêts et dividendes est fait à la Caisse Sociale, ou chez les représentants désignés par le Conseil d'Administration dans les villes dénommées à l'Article 8 ci-dessus.

Le payement des intérêts est fait en deux termes, le 1er Juillet, et le 1er Janvier de chaque année.

Le dividende est payé le 1er Juillet.

Toutefois le Conseil peut, lorsqu'il juge qu'il y a lieu, autoriser le payement d'un acompte de dividende le 1er Janvier.

Chaque payement est annoncé au moyen de publications faites conformément aux prescriptions de l'Article 9 ci-dessus pour les appels de fonds.

[1] Modified by Resolution in 1871 to give 2 per cent. to Administrators and 71 per cent. to holders of shares, whether amortized or not.

Art. 65. Les intérêts et dividendes qui ne sont pas réclamés à l'expiration de cinq années après l'époque annoncée pour le payement sont acquis à la Société.

Art. 66. L'amortissement des actions est effectué en quatre-vingt-dix-neuf ans, suivant le Tableau d'amortissement dressé en exécution des présents Statuts.

Il est pourvu à cet amortissement, ainsi qu'il a été dit à l'Article 62 ci-dessus, au moyen d'une annuité de o fr. 04 c. pour cent du capital social et de l'intérêt à 5 pour cent des actions successivement remboursées.

S'il arrivait que, dans le cours d'une ou de plusieurs années, les produits nets de l'entreprise fussent insuffisants pour assurer le remboursement du nombre d'actions à amortir, la somme nécessaire pour compléter le fonds d'amortissement serait prélevée sur la réserve, et, à défaut, sur les premiers produits nets disponibles des années suivantes, par préférence et antériorité à toute attribution de dividende.

La désignation des actions à rembourser a lieu au moyen d'un tirage au sort fait publiquement chaque année au domicile de la Société, aux époques et suivant la forme déterminées par le Conseil.

Art. 67. Les numéros des actions désignées par le sort pour être remboursées sont annoncés au moyen de publications faites conformément aux prescriptions de l'Article 9 ci-dessus.

Art. 68. Le remboursement des actions désignées par le tirage au sort pour être amorties est fait aux lieux indiqués pour le payement des intérêts et dividendes par l'Article 64 ci-dessus.

Les porteurs d'actions amorties conservent les mêmes droits que les porteurs d'actions non amorties, à l'exception de l'intérêt à 5 pour cent du capital qui leur a été remboursé.

Art. 69. La retenue opérée pour la constitution ou le complément du fonds de réserve, conformément au paragraphe 5 de l'Article 62 ci-dessus, est de 5 pour cent des produits annuels, après déduction des charges définies aux paragraphes 1, 2, 3, et 4, du même Article.

Lorsque le fonds de réserve atteint le chiffre de 5,000,000 fr., l'Assemblée Générale des Actionnaires peut, sur la proposition du Conseil, réduire ou suspendre la retenue annuelle à ce affectée ainsi qu'il vient d'être expliqué.

Cette retenue reprend cours et effet dès que le fonds de réserve descend au-dessous de 5,000,000 fr.

Art. 70. La part attribuée aux fondateurs dans les bénéfices annuels de l'entreprise par le Cahier des Charges est représentée par des titres spéciaux dont le Conseil détermine le nombre, la nature, et la forme.

Dans tous les cas, les prescriptions des Articles 17, 18, 19, et 21 ci-dessus, concernant les actions, sont également applicables aux titres des fondateurs, dont les droits suivent ceux des actionnaires sur la jouissance des terrains faisant partie de la Concession.

Titre VII.—*Modifications aux Statuts.—Liquidation.*

Art. 71. Si l'expérience fait reconnaître l'utilité d'apporter des modifications ou additions aux présents Statuts, l'Assemblée Générale y pourvoit dans la forme déterminée à l'Article 57.

Les résolutions de l'assemblée à cet égard ne sont toutefois exécutoires qu'après l'approbation du Gouvernement Égyptien.

Tous pouvoirs sont donnés d'avance au Conseil d'Administration, délibérant à la majorité des deux tiers des voix des membres présents dans une réunion spéciale à cet effet, pour consentir les changements que le Gouvernement Égyptien jugerait nécessaire d'apporter aux modifications votées par l'Assemblée Générale.

Art. 72. Dans le cas de dissolution de la Société, l'Assemblée Générale, sur la proposition du Conseil d'Administration, détermine le mode à adopter, soit pour la liquidation, soit pour la réconstitution d'une Société nouvelle.

TITRE VIII.—*Attribution de Juridiction.*—*Contestations.*

Art. 73. La Société étant constituée, avec approbation du Gouvernement Égyptien, sous la forme anonyme, par analogie aux Sociétés anonymes autorisées par le Gouvernement Français, elle est régie par les principes de ces dernières Sociétés.

Quoique ayant son siège social à Alexandrie, la Société fait élection de domicile légal et attributif de juridiction à son domicile administratif à Paris, où doivent lui être faites toutes significations.

Art. 74. Toutes les contestations qui peuvent s'élever entre les associés sur l'exécution des présents Statuts et à raison des affaires sociales sont jugées par arbitres nommés par les parties, sans qu'il puisse être nommé plus d'un arbitre pour toutes les parties représentant un même intérêt.

Les appels de ces sentences sont portées devant la Cour d'Appel de Paris.

Art. 75. Les contestations touchant l'intérêt général et collectif de la Société ne peuvent être dirigées soit contre le Conseil d'Administration, soit contre l'un de ses membres, qu'au nom de la généralité des actionnaires et en vertu d'une délibération de l'Assemblée Générale.

Tout actionnaire qui veut provoquer une contestation de cette nature doit en faire la communication au Conseil d'Administration quinze jours au moins avant la réunion de l'Assemblée Générale, en la faisant appuyer par la signature d'au moins dix actionnaires en mesure d'assister à cette Assemblée. Le Conseil est alors tenu de mettre la question à l'ordre du jour de la séance.

Si la proposition est repoussée par l'assemblée, aucun actionnaire ne peut la reproduire en justice dans son intérêt particulier. Si elle est accueillie, l'assemblée désigne un ou plusieurs commissaires pour suivre la contestation.

Les significations auxquelles donne lieu la procédure ne peuvent être adressées qu'aux dits commissaires. Dans aucun cas, elles ne doivent l'être aux actionnaires personnellement.

TITRE IX.—*Commissaire Spécial du Gouvernement Égyptien près la Compagnie.*

Art. 76. Conformément au Cahier des Charges un commissaire spécial est délégué près la Compagnie, à son domicile administratif, par le Gouvernement Égyptien.

Le Commissaire du Gouvernement Égyptien peut prendre connaissance des opérations de la Société, et faire toutes communications ou notifications nécessaires à l'accomplissement de son mandat, pour l'exécution du Cahier des Charges de la Concession.

TITRE X.—*Dispositions Transitoires.*—*Premier Conseil d'Administration.*

Art. 77. Par dérogation aux Articles 24, 26, 27, 30, 56 ci-dessus et sauf l'exception déterminée par l'Article 23 de l'Acte de Concession, le Conseil d'Administration est constitué comme suit, pour toute la durée des travaux et pendant les cinq premières années qui suivront l'ouverture du Canal Maritime à la grande navigation.

MM.————

Indépendamment des attributions déterminées par les Articles 34 et 35 des présents Statuts le Conseil d'Administration, constitué comme il est dit ci-dessus, est investi de tous pouvoirs pour assurer l'exécution de l'entreprise. A cet effet, il peut choisir le mode qui lui paraît le plus favorable tant pour l'acquisition et la revente des terrains que pour l'achat des matières, l'exécution des travaux, et la fourniture du matériel de toute nature. Il peut autoriser la mise en adjudication de tout ou partie des travaux, l'acquisition de tous biens meubles et immeubles nécessaires à l'établissement et à l'exploitation des Canaux et dépendances faisant partie de la Concession. Il peut également, et dans le même but, autoriser les travaux en régie et les marchés à forfait pour tout ou partie de l'entreprise.

Le premier Conseil d'Administration est autorisé, pendant la durée du mandat spécial qui fait l'objet du présent Article, à se compléter, en cas de vacances, de quelque manière que ces vacances se produisent.

Titre XI.—*Publications.*

Art. 78. Tous pouvoirs sont donnés au porteur d'une expédition des présentes pour les faire publier à Alexandrie et partout où besoin sera.

Nous Mohammed Saïd Pacha, Vice-Roi d'Égypte, après avoir pris connaissance du projet des Statuts de la Compagnie Universelle du Canal Maritime de Suez et dépendances, lequel nous a été présenté par M. Ferdinand de Lesseps, et dont l'original, contenant soixante-dix-huit Articles, reste déposé dans nos archives, déclarons donner aux dits Statuts notre approbation, pour qu'ils soient annexés à notre Acte de Concession et Cahier des Charges, en date de ce jour.

Alexandrie, le 26 *Rebi-ul-akhir,* 1272 (5 *Janvier,* 1856).

(Cachet de Son Altesse le Vice-Roi.)

Appendix 4

Convention entre le Vice-Roi d'Égypte et la Compagnie Universelle du Canal Maritime de Suez.—Signé au Caire, le 22 *Février,* 1866.

[Extract]

Entre Son Altesse Ismaïl Pacha, Vice-Roi d'Égypte, d'une part; et la Compagnie Universelle du Canal Maritime de Suez, représentée par M. Ferdinand de Lesseps, son Président-Fondateur, autorisé à cet effet par les Assemblées Générales des Actionnaires des 1er Mars et 6 Août, 1864, et par décision spéciale du Conseil d'Administration de la dite Compagnie, en date du 13 Septembre, 1864, d'autre part; a été exposé et stipulé ce qui suit: . . .

Art. 9. Le Canal Maritime et toutes ses dépendances restent soumis à la police Égyptienne, qui s'exercera librement comme sur tout autre point du territoire, de façon à assurer le bon ordre, la sécurité publique, et l'exécution des lois et règlements du pays.

Le Gouvernement Égyptien jouira de la servitude de passage à travers le

Canal Maritime sur les points qu'il jugera nécessaires, tant pour ses propres communications que pour la libre circulation du commerce et du public, sans que la Compagnie puisse percevoir aucun droit de péage ou autre redevance sous quelque prétexte que ce soit.

Art. 10. Le Gouvernement Égyptien occupera dans le périmètre des terrains réservés comme dépendance du Canal Maritime, toute position ou tout point stratégique qu'il jugera nécessaire à la défense du pays. Cette occupation ne devra pas faire obstacle à la navigation et respectera les servitudes attachées aux francs-bords du Canal.

Art. 11. Le Gouvernement Égyptien, sous les mêmes réserves, pourra occuper pour ses services administratifs (poste, douane, caserne, &c.), tout emplacement disponible qu'il jugera convenable, en tenant compte des nécessités de l'exploitation des services de la Compagnie; dans ce cas, le Gouvernement remboursera, quand il y aura lieu, à la Compagnie les sommes que celle-ci aura dépensées pour créer ou approprier les terrains dont il voudra disposer.

Art. 12. Dans l'intérêt du commerce, de l'industrie, ou de la prospère exploitation du Canal, tout particulier aura la faculté, moyennant l'autorisation préalable du Gouvernement et en se soumettant aux règlements administratifs ou municipaux de l'autorité locale, ainsi qu'aux lois, usages, et impôts du pays, de s'établir, soit le long du Canal Maritime, soit dans les villes élevées sur son parcours, réserve faite des francs-bords, berges et chemins de halage; ces derniers devant rester ouverts à la libre circulation, sous l'empire des règlements qui en détermineront l'usage.

Ces établissements, du reste, ne pourront avoir lieu que sur les emplacements que les ingénieurs de la Compagnie reconnaîtront n'être pas nécessaires aux services de l'exploitation, et à charge par les bénéficiaires de rembourser à la Compagnie les sommes dépensées par elle pour la création et l'appropriation des dits emplacements.

Art. 13. Il est entendu que l'établissement des services de Douane ne devra porter aucune atteinte aux franchises Douanières dont doit jouir le transit général s'effectuant à travers le Canal par les bâtiments de toutes les nations sans aucune distinction, exclusion ni préférence de personne ou de nationalité.

Art. 14. Le Gouvernement Égyptien, pour assurer la fidèle exécution des Conventions mutuelles entre lui et la Compagnie, aura le droit d'entretenir à ses frais, auprès de la Compagnie et sur le lieu des travaux, un Commissaire spécial.

Art. 15. Il est déclaré, à titre d'interprétation, qu'à l'expiration des quatre-vingt-dix-neuf ans de la Concession du Canal de Suez et à défaut de nouvelle entente entre le Gouvernement Égyptien et la Compagnie, la Concession prendra fin de plein droit.

Art. 16. La Compagnie Universelle du Canal Maritime de Suez étant Égyptienne, elle est régie par les lois et usages du pays; toutefois, en ce qui regarde sa constitution comme Société et les rapports des associés entre eux, elle est, par une Convention spéciale, réglée par les lois qui, en France, régissent les Sociétés anonymes. Il est convenu que toutes les contestations de ce chef seront jugées en France par des arbitres avec appel, comme sur-arbitre, à la Cour Impériale de Paris.

Des différends en Égypte entre la Compagnie et les particuliers, à quelque nationalité qu'ils appartiennent, seront jugés par les Tribunaux locaux suivant les formes consacrées par les lois et usages du pays et les Traités.

Les contestations qui viendraient à surgir entre le Gouvernement Égyptien et la Compagnie seront également soumises aux Tribunaux locaux et résolues suivant les lois du pays.

Les préposés, ouvriers et autres personnes appartenant à l'Administration de la Compagnie, seront jugés par les Tribunaux locaux, suivant les lois locales et les Traités, pour tous délits et contestations dans lesquels les parties ou l'une d'elles seraient indigènes.

Si toutes les parties sont étrangères, il sera procédé entre elles conformément aux règles établies.

Toute signification à la Compagnie par une partie intéressée quelconque en Égypte sera valablement faite au siège de l'Administration à Alexandrie.

Appendix 5

SUEZ CANAL: RULES OF NAVIGATION (*January* 1933)

GENERAL

ARTICLE 1

Obligation to comply with the regulations.

§ 1. Transit through the Suez Canal is open to ships of all nations, subject to their complying with the conditions hereinafter stated.

However, the Company reserves to itself the right to refuse access to the Canal to ships which it may consider dangerous to shipping generally.

On receiving a copy of these regulations, captains of ships bind themselves to abide by and conform with them in all points, to comply with any requisition made in view of their due carrying-out, and obey all signals prescribed in the special Book of Signals, of which a copy is placed at their disposal.

§ 2. Mail ships, ships carrying petroleum, or having dangerous materials on board, and ships under quarantine, must show the signals prescribed in the special Book of Signals.

§ 3. Ships carrying petroleum or dangerous materials must comply with these regulations and also with the Rules of Navigation, Appendix for ships carrying dangerous materials, a copy of which is given to captains on their arrival in one of the Canal ports.

§ 4. The navigation of ships, undecked vessels, or any other craft, measuring five hundred tons gross or under, is governed by special regulations.

ARTICLE 2

Draught of ships and seaworthiness.

At present, ships with a draught of no more than 33 English feet (metres 10·06) are authorized to transit.[1]

[1] This draught (33′ max.) of the ship is not to be confused with the depth of water in the Canal.

Ships are not permitted to transit when their draught of water exceeds the maximum, or when they are not well-found in every respect for navigation in the Canal.

ARTICLE 3

Responsibility of Captains. Pilots' Duties.

All ships measuring more than *five hundred tons gross* must take, either for entering or leaving the harbours of Port-Saïd and Port-Thewfik, or for transit through the Canal, a pilot of the Company, who will furnish all particulars as to the course to be steered.

In the case of ships measuring under five hundred tons gross the Company reserve the right of sending aboard either a pilot or a master should the requirements of the service render it advisable.

The pilots place at the disposal of captains their experience and practical knowledge of the Canal, but as they cannot be acquainted with the defects and peculiarities of individual ships and their machinery, whether in navigating, stopping, steering, &c., the responsibility of handling the ship devolves solely upon the captain.

Captains are held responsible for all damage or accidents of whatsoever kind resulting from the navigating or handling of their ships by day or by night.

Normally, the pilots' duties commence, or cease, at the exterior buoys of Port-Saïd and Port-Thewfik harbours.

ARTICLE 4

Mail Ships. Distinctive character.

Mail ships are all ships performing a regular mail service under contract with a Government, at fixed dates appointed in advance. The contract must have been duly exhibited to the Company by the owners.

ARTICLE 5

Ships in ballast. Distinctive character.

Merchant ships which are not earning freight on their voyage, and which are carrying only such fuel as is necessary for their own consumption, and only their crews with the provisions for same, are considered as being in ballast.

A ship landing her passengers or cargo before passing through the Canal and taking them on board afterwards, will in no case be considered as being in ballast.

Further, in order to be entitled to claim the benefit of the ballast rate,[1] the volume of bunker coal or fuel must not exceed 125 per cent. of the engine-room space as shown on the Suez Canal Certificate. Bunker coal or fuel should, primarily, be contained in the ship's permanent or movable bunkers. However on the Captain's application, if well founded, permission may be granted for it to be stowed on deck or in the ship's holds. In any case owners will have to take the necessary steps so that the total volume of all bunkers on board can be easily ascertained.[2]

---

[1] See Art. 7.

[2] See Art. 16 and 17 of the Regulations for the measurement of tonnage, p. 205.

ARTICLE 6

Suez Canal tonnage.

§ 1. The tonnage on which all dues and charges to be paid by ships, as specified in these regulations, are assessed, is the net tonnage resulting from the system of measurement laid down by the International Commission held at Constantinople in 1873,[1] and duly entered on the special certificates issued by the competent authorities in each country.

In assessing the dues, any alteration of net tonnage subsequent to the delivery of the above-mentioned certificates is taken into account.

§ 2. The Company's officials are empowered to ascertain whether cargo or passengers are carried in any space not included in the net tonnage entered on the ship's special certificate.

And, generally, may verify whether all spaces which ought to be included in the tonnage are entered on the certificate and are correctly determined therein.

§ 3. Every ship not provided with the special certificate showing the net tonnage prescribed by the Constantinople Commission, is measured by the Company's officials in conformity with the rules laid down by the Constantinople Commission.

The net tonnage thus arrived at is provisionally made use of for the assessing of the dues, until such time as the ship tenders a special certificate duly drawn up by the competent authorities.

ARTICLE 7

Transit dues.

§ 1. Tonnage dues are, at present, *six francs sixty-five centimes* per ton.[2]

§ 2. Ships in ballast are allowed a reduction of fifty per cent. thereon (i.e. pay *three francs thirty-two and a half centimes* per ton).[3]

§ 3. As a temporary measure, the above-mentioned dues are reduced to *six francs* for loaded ships and to *three francs* for ships in ballast. This reduction will remain in force until December 31st 1933.

ARTICLE 8

Passenger dues.

§ 1. In addition to the tonnage dues mentioned in art. 7, transit dues are charged on all passengers at the rate of *ten francs* per passenger above twelve years of age, and *five francs* per passenger between three and twelve.

Children under three years of age pay no dues.

[1] See pages 205–10:
Regulations for the measurement of tonnage.—Additional deductions allowed by the Suez Canal Company.—Rules for the measurement of deck spaces. Taxation of double-bottoms.

[2] In the present Rules all rates or tariffs are expressed in gold francs as defined by the French law of the 7th of the month of Germinal, year XI.

[3] See Art. 5.

§ 2. Sailors occasionally taken on board of ships passing through the Suez Canal are considered as passengers and are charged for as such, unless they are duly entered on the ship's articles and certified as being intended for ships belonging to the same owners.

ARTICLE 9

Berthing dues.

The rate of berthing dues at Port-Saïd, Ismaïlia and in the Company's docks at Port-Thewfik, is *two centimes* per ton, per day, whatever be the duration of the ship's stay, but the first 24 hours are not included. These dues are payable every ten days.

ARTICLE 10

Pilotage dues.

Pilotage in the Canal itself is free of charge.

The payment of dues for pilotage in or out of Port-Saïd and Port-Thewfik is charged for as follows:

1. *For ships not going through the Canal:*

By day . . . . { steamers or motor ships, 25 francs; sailing vessels, 10 francs.

By night (between sunset and { steamers or motor ships, 50 francs; sailing vessels, sunrise) { 20 francs.

2. *For ships going through the Canal:*

By day . . . . Free.

By night . . . { steamers or motor ships, 25 francs; sailing vessels, 10 francs.

The payment of these pilotage dues is compulsory on all ships above *five hundred tons gross measurement.*[1]

When the pilot is kept on board beyond the time required for pilotage proper, a charge of *forty francs* per day is due.

ARTICLE 11

Divisions of Transit.

A reduction of half the transit dues and half the passenger dues is allowed to ships and passengers using only half the length of the Canal.

No other division than one-half of the length of the Canal is admitted: between Ismaïlia and Port-Saïd being considered one-half, and between Ismaïlia and Port-Thewfik the other half, or inversely.

ARTICLE 12

Local traffic between Port-Saïd and Ismaïlia.

For ships effecting a voyage from either Port-Saïd to Ismaïlia in ballast and back from Ismaïlia to Port-Saïd with a cargo of Egyptian origin, or from Port-Saïd to

[1] See Art. 3.

Ismaïlia with a cargo for an Egyptian destination and back from Ismaïlia to Port-Saïd in ballast, the rate of tonnage dues is only two francs per ton for the entire journey.

Payment must be made in full previous to the commencement of the journey. Over and above this, the ships are subject to the same incidental charges as other ships.

The carrying of passengers only is not considered as being local traffic

ARTICLE 13

Mode of payment of dues.

§ 1. All dues and charges specified in the present rules must be paid in cash, at the Company's conditions, in Egypt, Paris, or London.

§ 2. Tonnage dues and passenger dues are payable in advance.

§ 3. In the case of payments made in Paris or London the Company will wire out to its officials in Egypt, at owner's risk and expense, due notice of the amounts paid.

Whenever amounts thus paid in advance are insufficient for the discharge in full of all charges and incidental expenses due by the ship, the balance must be paid in Egypt at the Company's Offices.

§ 4. Claims for errors in the declaration of tonnage or in the levying of the dues must be sent in within a month after the ship's passage through the Canal.

MOVEMENTS OF SHIPS

ARTICLE 14

Arrival.

§ 1. When nearing the buoys at the approach to the Port-Saïd channel, a ship wishing to enter sends up the signal for a pilot. On coming on board the pilot hands to the captain a copy of the present Rules and a pilotage form.

The captain fills up the pilotage form and gives it back to the pilot when the latter leaves the ship.

§ 2. The captain must clearly show as indicated by the pilot, when entering the channel:

(*a*) The ship's commercial number in the International Code.

(*b*) the ship's specific signal (mail-ship, coasting ship, collier, oil-ship, ship having explosives, &c.) as per the Book of Signals.

(*c*) If necessary, the signal prescribed in the Book of Signals for a ship which intends remaining more than 12 hours at Port-Saïd, or which is in need of repairs.

§ 3. The port officials direct the ship to its mooring berth either by signals hoisted at the masthead of the Company's Office, or verbally by sending a boat to meet the ship. The ship must acknowledge.

§ 4. When coming in, changing berth, or leaving, the Captain must work his hawsers by means of the ship's boats or with the help of the mooring boats of a firm approved by the Company.

Stay in the Canal ports.

§ 1. The captain is responsible for the mooring of his ship in the ports of the Canal.

§ 2. He must attend specially to the instructions in the following paragraphs:

§ 3. When the ship is moored on buoys, the hawsers must be watched and handled so as to always ensure a good mooring.

If two ships are moored to the same buoy, when one leaves, the other must rectify her mooring as necessary.

Hawsers which have been slacked down for the passage of barges or tugs must be hauled taut as soon as possible.

§ 4. Captains must conform to the advice which the port captain will give re hawsers during the stay of their ships in port, especially when, in case of impending bad weather, he shall consider it necessary that the hawsers and shackles should be inspected and, if need be, strengthened.

§ 5. When a ship is moored with her stern to the bank, the captain must keep himself continually informed of the draught of water aft, so as to avoid grounding on the submerged slope either as a result of the settling of the ship as she loads, or of her too great proximity to the bank.

§ 6. At night, the ship, either moored or manœuvring, must show the lights as prescribed by the International Regulations for preventing collisions at sea.

Moreover, ships moored at right angles with the bank must carry the forward white light at the extreme bows at a sufficient height for it to be clearly visible.

§ 7. Unless otherwised authorized, barges alongside a ship must not be more than two abreast.

§ 8. It is forbidden to try the projector, or to put in action the propellers during the process of warming up, in the absence of the pilot, or without informing him if he is on board.

§ 9. Ships must not put their engines out of working order for any cause whatsoever without informing the Company. In such cases moorings shall be strengthened to avoid danger to the ship in case of bad weather.

§ 10. The captain must always keep on board sufficient crew to ensure, beside the handling of the mooring hawsers, the manning of all available appliances for coping with a fire or a leak.

§ 11. The port captain or his delegate shall have free access on board ship to ensure the carrying out of the Regulations, to verify the ship's seaworthiness, and especially to ascertain that there is no dangerous cargo on board.

§ 12. Ships moored in the Dock at Port-Thewfik are subject to the same regulations as in the Canal over and above those set out in §§ 7 and 8 of the present article.

They cannot be authorized to effect repairs which may deprive them of the use of their motive power.

ARTICLE 16

Changing berth.

§ 1. A captain wishing to change the berth of his ship shall notify the port captain or his representative, stating the time when his ship will be ready for the move, and whether he wishes for the aid of a tug. The new berth will be allocated by the port captain.

A pilot will be sent him in due course.

The move shall take place at the time fixed by the port captain or his delegate.

§ 2. All charges entailed by a change of berth resulting from the captain's erroneous or incomplete declaration must be paid by the captain.

§ 3. The charges for changing berth are 25 francs for steamers or motor ships and 10 francs for sailing ships.

If, for want of steam, the ship has to be towed, she pays for the hire of tugs as per tariff on page 210.

§ 4. When necessary in the general interest of navigation, the port captain may order a ship to change her berth, and when so ordered the change is free of charge. The change shall be made as quickly as possible.

ARTICLE 17
Ships passing one another.

§ 1. Ships under way in the harbours or in the entrance channels shall conform to the international regulations for preventing collisions at sea.

§ 2. In the harbours the speed of ships must be reduced to the lowest limit allowing them to answer the helm. Captains must not hesitate to stop engines when passing moored ships, in order to avoid the breaking of hawsers and resulting accidents.

ARTICLE 18
Fire on board. Leak.

§ 1. In case of fire on board, or leak, when in harbour, the captain must inform the port captain at once.

At the same time he must give general warning by means of long blasts on the steam-whistle and make ready for moving his ship if requested to do so.

§ 2. Neighbouring ships must in such cases also be ready to change berths.

§ 3. The Company's officials will direct operations.

ARTICLE 19
Sailing.

§ 1. Ships which do not enter the Canal must, during their stay in Port-Saïd, report themselves at the Harbour office, and the special certificate showing the ship's capacity be produced.

§ 2. Captains of ships intending to put to sea must pay in advance the dues for pilotage and berthing, if any. They must state the hour of their departure by means of a letter or telephone message addressed to the port captain by the ship's Agent.

They will apply for a pilot by clearly exhibiting half an hour before the stated hour of departure the signal as prescribed.

§ 3. Mooring must not be changed before the pilot is on board.

The ship will get under way only if there is no signal from the Company to the contrary.

When several ships are ready to get under way, the order of their sailing either for the Canal or for sea will be fixed by the Harbour office.

§ 4. The Captain may apply for the Company's tugs to help to manœuvre his ship. Such help will be granted under the conditions of Article 20.

§ 5. When the pilot leaves ship, the Captain will hand back to him the pilotage form after having filled it in as required.

ARTICLE 20

Towage.

§ 1. Tugs may be placed at the disposal of captains to help manœuvre their ships on arrival and departure.

Such help is free of charge.

The tugs do not supply hawsers.

§ 2. Tugs may be hired for any operation where their assistance may be necessary to tow a ship, or to get her afloat, in the harbours or outer-harbours. (See tariff, page 210.)

§ 3. Whatever may be the conditions and circumstances under which the Company places a tug at a ship's disposal, the captain of the ship has exclusively the direction and control of the operations; consequently he bears the responsibility for any damage or accidents whatsoever resulting from the use of the said tug.

ARTICLE 21

Prohibitions.

§ 1. Sounding of the steam-whistle is only allowed for working the ship, or in the circumstances laid down in the present Regulations and in the International Regulations.

§ 2. Boats, other than the Canal Company's own, are not allowed to come alongside ships which are under way or manœuvring, except the following ones at their own risk:

(*a*) The Quarantine and Police boats,
(*b*) The mooring boats,
(*c*) The ship's agent's boat.

CONDITIONS OF TRANSIT

ARTICLE 22

Formalities to be fulfilled.

When a ship intending to proceed through the Canal has taken her moorings, the captain must enter his ship at the Transit-Office and pay the transit dues, as well as, when there is occasion, the dues for pilotage, towage and berthing. A receipt is delivered to him, which serves as a voucher in case of need.

The following written information must be handed in by him:

Name and nationality of the ship, authenticated by exhibiting the ship's papers respective thereto,

Name of the captain,

Names of the owners and charterers,

Port of sailing,
Port of destination,
Draught of water,
Length,
Breadth,
Number of passengers as shown by the passenger list,
Statement of crew as shown by the ship's articles,
Capacity of the ship authenticated by producing her special certificate.
The captain must also exhibit the bill of health.

ARTICLE 23

Preparations for entering the Canal.

§ 1. All ships ready to enter the Canal must have their yards braced forward, their ladders and jib-booms run in, and their boats swung in, and the derricks obstructing the view forward, lowered.

§ 2. At least 4 mooring hawsers in good condition must be in readiness at suitable points on deck in case it should be necessary to tie up in the Canal, and every arrangement must be made for their quick handling.

One or two boats, according to the size of the ship, must be in constant readiness for lowering in order to carry the hawsers to the mooring posts without any delay.

§ 3. The bow anchors must be ready to let go.

The steering gear and the engine room telegraph must be ascertained to be in good working order before entering the Canal.

§ 4. Captains must, before entering the Canal, ascertain that deck loads, if any, are stowed in such manner as not to affect the ship's stability or impede the crew.

§ 5. The captains of ships in ballast must fill all spaces intended to be used for carrying water ballast in such proportion as the officials of the Company may direct.

§ 6. Ships intending to go through the Canal by night[1] must first satisfy the officials of the Company in Port-Saïd or Port-Thewfik that they are provided with:

a. A projector (search-light) placed in the axis showing the channel 1,200 metres ahead (roughly 1,300 yards) and so constructed as to admit of rapid splitting up of the beam of rays into two separate segments of 5° each, with a dark sector in the middle also of 5°.

b. Overhead lights powerful enough to light up a circular area of about 200 metres diameter (roughly 650 feet English) around the ship.

The officials of the Company decide whether the appliances fulfil the requirements of the regulations in order to ensure safe navigation of the Canal at night.

Special insistence will be exercised on care being taken that the working of the generators does not obstruct the sight of the man at the wheel.

Night transit may be suspended in case of damage to, or imperfection in, the appliances.

§ 7. Captains shall place their wireless apparatus and equipment at the disposal of the Canal Company during transit through the Canal.

Pilots shall be allowed to receive and send free of charge to the Company all service messages which may be deemed necessary.

---

[1] See, regarding night transit, Art. 26, paragraphs 2, 3, and 4.

The wireless watch will be kept in accordance with the indications of the pilot and it may even be required that a continual watch shall be kept during the whole transit through the Canal.

ARTICLE 24

Hours of departure and movements under way.

§ 1. The Captain will apply for a pilot by clearly exhibiting, one and a half hours before the stated hour of departure, the signal as prescribed.

§ 2. Mooring must not be changed before the pilot is on board. The ship will get under way only if there is no signal from the Company to the contrary.

§ 3. When several ships are ready to get under way at the same time, the order of their sailing either for the Canal or for sea will be fixed by the Company.

The Company will prescribe the movements of ships under way in order to give full security to navigation, and to ensure, as far as possible, the speedy passage of mail ships.

Consequently no ship may demand immediate passage through the Canal, and no claim as to delay arising from the foregoing causes can be admitted.

§ 4. The Captain may apply for the Company's tugs to help to manœuvre his ship. Such help will be granted under the conditions of Article 20.

§ 5. The Captain must set a watch both by day and by night.

§ 6. All ships, tugs included, must stop whenever there is not a clear passage ahead.

They must also slow down passing sidings, sections of the banks being stone-faced or cut back, as well as all ships in sidings or under way, hoppers, dredgers, and other floating plant.

§ 7. As soon as a ship has tied up, whether in or out of a siding, she must hoist the signals prescribed in the special Book of Signals.

Ships must slack down any hawsers they may have had to run across the Canal so as to give free passage to tugs, steam or motor launches, hopper-barges and any other light draught craft that may have to pass them.

Men must be constantly at hand ready to slack down hawsers or cut them in case of need. The ship's engines must always be under steam ready to be started.

§ 8. Ships proceeding in the same direction are not allowed to overtake one another under way in the Canal.

In the case of a ship being allowed to pass another one ahead of her, this must be done comfortably with the indications given by the Company's officials.

§ 9. Captains are forbidden to anchor in the Canal, except in case of absolute necessity.

ARTICLE 25

Speed.

The maximum speed of ships passing through the Canal is normally *twelve kilometres* (6½ *nautical miles*) per hour.

Exceptionally, a speed slightly in excess of the twelve-kilometre maximum may be allowed in order to enable ships to steer better.

ARTICLE 26
Night transit.

§ 1. Navigation of sailing craft of every description by night is entirely forbidden.

§ 2. During night transit ships must keep their projector alight.[1] They must show their regulation lights and keep a man on the look-out forward.

§ 3. When a ship under transit at night is about to tie up whether in or out of a siding, she must at once extinguish her projector and turn on her overhead lights.[1] When she has completed tying-up she must extinguish her overhead lights and her navigating lights and hoist the lights prescribed in the special Book of Signals.

§ 4. Ships navigating at night in the Large Bitter Lake must extinguish their projector except in the portions immediately adjoining the outlets of the Canal into the Lake where the channel continues to run between two lines of buoys.

§ 5. Ships not provided with projectors are only allowed to transit at night under exceptional circumstances, the captain being entirely responsible for any delay, mishap or damage of any description, that may happen to his own ship, as well as for any similar accidents he may cause to other ships in the Canal or to the Company's craft, plant or installations. Ships going through the Canal under these conditions are subject to all the other rules for night transit.

ARTICLE 27
Prohibitions.

The following prohibitions are hereby notified to captains:

1. Throwing overboard in the ports of the Canal or at any point during transition from sea to sea, earth, ashes, cinders, or articles of any kind.

2. Emptying or letting flow oil, petrol, heavy oil, oil fuel, or scourings or cleansing water from tanks having contained such products. Loading, unloading, and, generally, handling of liquid fuel must be so carried out as to avoid any fuel leaking into Canal waters, failing which, the Company reserves to itself the right to stop such operations until the necessary repairs will have been effected.

3. Picking up, without the direct intervention of the Company's officials, any object that may have fallen into the Canal or its ports of access.

Whenever any object or merchandize whatsoever falls overboard, the circumstance must be immediately reported to the Canal Company.

If the Company considers that the picking up cannot be effected by the interested parties without impeding the transit, the Company proceeds to carry it out, at their expense.

4. Allowing any gun shots to be fired.
5. Burial in the banks of the Canal.
6. To take boats or floating appliances of whatever description in tow.

ARTICLE 28
Accidents.

§ 1. Whenever a collision appears probable, ships must not hesitate to run aground, should this be necessary, to avoid it.

[1] See art. 23, paragraph 6.

§ 2. Whenever a ship is accidentally stopped on her way, she must, if other ships are following her, attract their attention by sounding her steam-whistle sharply four or five times in close succession, repeating this several times at a few moments' interval until the ship following her repeats this signal, which must be taken as an order to slacken speed at once with a view to stopping, if need be.

Ships stopped accidentally at night must immediately replace their white stern light by a red light.

In case of grounding the captain must also immediately signal to that effect conformably with the indications in the Book of Signals.

§ 3. When a ship gets aground, the officials of the Company alone are empowered to prescribe and supervise all operations required to get her off, including unloading and towing if necessary, captains placing at their disposal all available means.

All attempts on the part of other ships to get off a ship aground are strictly prohibited.

§ 4. When a ship grounds or stops in the Canal in consequence of an accident other than a collision, the Company, in order to remove the obstruction in the fairway with all possible speed and to hasten the restarting of the ship, does not claim any reimbursement whatsoever of expenses incurred in getting off the ship. If once afloat, the ship continues her transit in tow, she must from this moment pay towage charges, as scheduled in the present regulations.

It is moreover well understood that ships bear all expenses incurred in repairs, or putting into condition, necessary to remedy such damage as might interfere with their restarting, whatever be the moment at which the damage may have taken place, and that they remain responsible for all damage and accidents of whatsoever kind which may be the consequence of the grounding.

§ 5. When a ship grounds or stops in the roads, or ports, from whatever cause, or in the Canal itself in consequence of collision, all charges of getting the ship off, towing, unloading, reloading, &c., are charged to the ship and must be paid, as per statement drawn up by the Company, before leaving Port-Thewfik or Port-Saïd.

TOWAGE AND CONVOYING

ARTICLE 29

Compulsory towage or convoying.

The Officials of the Company may order that certain defective ships, or ships carrying dangerous cargoes, shall be towed or convoyed in the Canal by one of the Company's tugs.

Towage charges are based on the schedule at the end of the present rules.

ARTICLE 30

Hire of tugs on a lump sum basis.

By arrangement with the Company, tugs can be hired on a lump sum basis for the towage of any type of craft or vessel which cannot transit the Canal under their own power.

ARTICLE 31

Use of private tugs.

§ 1. Shipowners are authorized to have their ships towed or convoyed by their own tugs, or tugs belonging to third parties, under their entire responsibility. Such tugs must be approved of by the Canal Company.

§ 2. Ships towed or convoyed by approved tugs pay *fifty centimes* towage dues per ton.

§ 3. Approved tugs towing or convoying ships are free of any charge.

When they go through the Canal either for the purpose of meeting ships which they are about to tow or convoy, or in order to return to their home berth after having towed or convoyed the said ships, tugs are not liable to payment of the tonnage dues, but they must take a pilot on board.

They must carry neither goods nor passengers; the fact of having on board passengers or goods renders them liable to the payment of all dues and charges to which ships in transit are subject.

§ 4. Notwithstanding the special treatment above stipulated, tugs belonging to private owners are subject to the strict observance of all other articles of the regulations relative to ships under way or berthed.

EXTRACT FROM THE REGULATIONS FOR THE MEASUREMENT OF TONNAGE

recommended by the International Tonnage Commission assembled at Constantinople in 1873

(Minutes of Proceedings, xxi, Appendix ii)

GENERAL PRINCIPLES

1. The gross tonnage or total capacity of ships comprises the exact measurement of all spaces (without any exception), below the upper deck, as well as of all permanently covered and closed-in spaces on that deck;

N.B. By permanently covered and closed-in spaces on the upper deck are to be understood all those which are separated off by decks or coverings or fixed partitions, and therefore represent an increase of capacity which might be used for the stowage of merchandise, or for the berthing and accommodation of the passengers or of the officers and crew. Thus, any one or more openings, either in the deck or coverings, or in the partitions, or a break in the deck, or the absence of a portion of the partition, will not prevent such spaces being comprised in the gross tonnage, if they can be easily closed in after admeasurement, and thus better fitted for the transport of goods and passengers.

But the spaces under awning decks without other connexion with the body of the ship than the props necessary for supporting them, which are not spaces 'separated off' and are permanently exposed to the weather and the sea, will not be comprised in the gross tonnage, although they may serve to shelter the ship's crew, the deck passengers, and even merchandise known as 'deck loads'.

2. 'Deck loads' are not comprised in the measurement;

3. Closed spaces for the use or possible use of passengers will not be deducted from the gross tonnage;

4. The determination of deductions for coal spaces may be effected either by the rules of the European Danube Commission of 1871 or by the exact measurement of fixed bunkers.

RULE II. FOR LADEN SHIPS

Art. 9.—When ships have their cargo on board, or when for any other reason their tonnage cannot be ascertained by means of Rule I, proceed in the following manner:

Measure the length on the upper deck from the outside of the outer plank at the stem to the aftside of the stern-post, deducting therefrom the distance between the aft-side of the stern-post and the rabbet of the stern-post at the point where the counter-plank crosses it.

Measure also the greatest breadth of the ship to the outside of the outer planking or wales.

Then, having first marked on the outside of the ship, on both sides thereof, the height of the upper deck at the ship's sides, girt ship at the greatest breadth in a direction perpendicular to the keel from the height so marked on the outside of the ship, on the one side, to the height so marked on the other side, by passing a chain under the keel; to half the girth thus taken add half the main breadth; square the sum, multiply the result by the length of the ship taken as aforesaid; then multiply this product by the factor 0·17 (seventeen hundredths) in the case of ships built of wood, and by the factor 0·18 (eighteen hundredths) in the case of ships built of iron. The product will give approximately the cubical contents of the ship, and the general tonnage can be ascertained by dividing by 100 or by 2·83, according as the measurements are taken in English feet or in metres.

Art. 10.—If there be a break, a poop, or other permanent covered and closed-in spaces (as defined in the general principles) on the upper deck, the tonnage of such spaces shall be ascertained by multiplying together the mean length, breadth and depth of such spaces and dividing the product by 100 or 2·83, according as the measurements are taken in English feet or metres, and the quotient so obtained shall be deemed to be the tonnage of such space, and shall be added to the other tonnage in order to determine the gross tonnage or total capacity of the ship.

DEDUCTIONS[1]

TO BE MADE FROM THE GROSS TONNAGE IN ORDER TO ASCERTAIN THE NET TONNAGE

Art. 11.—To find from the gross tonnage of vessels as above set forth the official, or net register tonnage, either for sailing vessels or for steam ships, the following mode of operation must be resorted to:

Sailing vessels.

Art. 12.—For sailing vessels deduct: the spaces exclusively and entirely occupied by the crew and the ship's officers, those taken up by the cookhouse and latrines exclusively used by the ship's officers and crew whether they be situated above or below the upper deck; the covered and closed-in spaces, if there be any situated on the upper deck, and used for working the helm, the capstan, the anchor gear, and for keeping the charts, signals, and other instruments of navigation.

Each of the spaces deducted as above may be limited according to the requirements and customs of each country, but the deductions must never exceed in the aggregate 5 per cent. of the gross tonnage.

Art. 13.—The measurement of these spaces is to be effected according to the rules set

---

[1] Extract from the final report of the International Tonnage Commission assembled at Constantinople in 1873:

§ 17. *It is recommended that a penal provision shall be enacted to the effect that if any of the permanent spaces which have been deducted shall be employed either for the use of merchandise or passengers, or in any way profitably employed for earning freight, that space shall be added to the net tonnage, and nevermore be allowed as a deduction.*

forth for the measurement of covered and closed-in spaces on the upper deck; the result, obtained by deducting the total of such allowances from the gross tonnage, represents the net or register tonnage of sailing vessels.

Steam ships.

ART. 14.—For vessels propelled by steam or any other mechanical power, deduct:

1. The same spaces as for sailing vessels (art. 12) with the limitation to 5 per cent. of the gross tonnage;

2. The spaces occupied by the engines, boilers, coal-bunkers, shaft-trunks of screw steamers, and the spaces between decks and in the covered and closed-in erections on the upper deck surrounding the funnels, and required for the introduction of air and light into the engine-rooms, and for the proper working of the engines themselves. Such deductions cannot exceed 50 per cent. of the gross tonnage.

ART. 15.—The measurement of the spaces allowed for both in sailing vessels and in steam ships (section 1 of art. 14) is to be effected according to the rules set forth in articles 12 and 13 for sailing vessels.

Spaces for which allowances are made in steam ships only (section 2 of art. 14) are measured according to the following rules:

Ships having coal-bunkers with movable partitions.

ART. 16.—In ships that do not have fixed bunkers, but transverse bunkers with movable partitions, with or without lateral bunkers, measure the space occupied by the engine-rooms, and add to it, for screw steamers 75 per cent., and for paddle steamers, 50 per cent. of such space.

By the space occupied by the engine-rooms is to be understood that occupied by the engine-room itself and by the boiler-room together with spaces strictly required for their working, with the addition of the space taken up by the shaft-trunk in screw steamers and the spaces between decks which enclose the funnels and are necessary for the admission of air and light into the engine-rooms.

These spaces are measured in the following manner:

Measure the mean depth of the space occupied by the engines and boilers from its crown to the ceiling at the limber strake, measure also three, or, if necessary, more than three breadths of the space at the middle of its depth, taking one of such measurements at each end and another at the middle of the length; take the mean of such breadths; measure also the mean length of the space between the foremost and aftermost bulkheads or limits of its length, excluding such parts, if any, as are not actually occupied by or required for the proper working of the engines and boilers.

Multiply together these three dimensions of length, breadth and depth, and the product will be the cubical contents of the space below the crown.

Then find the cubical contents of the space or spaces, if any, between the crown aforesaid and the uppermost or poop deck, as the case may be, which are framed in for the machinery or for the admission of light and air, by multiplying together the length, depth and breadth thereof.

Add such contents as well as those of the space occupied by the shaft-trunk to the cubical contents of the space below the crown; divide the sum by 100 or by 2·83, according as the measures are taken in English feet or metres, and the result shall be deemed to be the tonnage corresponding to the engine and boiler-room which serves as basis for the deductions referred to.

If in any ship in which the space aforesaid is to be measured, the engines and boilers are fitted in separate compartments, the contents of each shall be measured separately in like manner, according to the above rules, and the sum of their several results shall be deemed to be the tonnage of the engine-rooms which serves, as aforesaid, as basis for the total deductions.

Ships with fixed coal-bunkers.

ART. 17.—In ships with fixed coal-bunkers, measure the mean length of the engine- and boiler-room, including the coal-bunkers. Ascertain the area of three transverse sections of the ship (as set forth in the rules given in articles 3 and 4 for the calculation of the gross tonnage) to the deck which covers the engine.

One of these three sections must pass through the middle of the aforesaid length, and the two others through the two extremities.

Add to the sum of the two extreme sections four times the middle one, and multiply the sum thus obtained by the third of the distance between the sections. This product divided by 100, if the measurements are taken in English feet, or by 2·83 if they are taken in metres, gives the tonnage of the space in question.

If the engines, boilers, and bunkers are in separate compartments, they are separately measured, as above set forth, and the results are added together.

In screw steamers the contents of the shaft-trunk are measured by ascertaining the mean length, breadth and height, and the product of the multiplication of these three dimensions divided by 100 or 2·83 according as the measurements are taken in English feet or in metres, gives the tonnage of such space.

The tonnage of the following spaces between decks and in the covered and closed-in erections on the upper deck, is ascertained by the same method, viz.:

a. The spaces framed-in round the funnels;

b. The spaces required for the admission of light and air into the engine-rooms;

c. The spaces, if any, necessary for the proper working of the engines.

ART. 18.—Instead of the measurement of fixed bunkers, the rules for bunkers with movable partitions as set forth in article 16 may be applied.

ART. 19.—In the case of *tugs* the allowances are not limited to 50 per cent. of the gross tonnage; all the spaces occupied by machinery, boilers, and coal-bunkers may be deducted.

Nevertheless, if such vessels are not exclusively employed as tugs, the deductions in question cannot exceed 50 per cent. of the gross tonnage.

ADDITIONAL DEDUCTIONS ALLOWED BY THE SUEZ CANAL COMPANY

The Company allow the following spaces to be included in the deductions specified at Art. 12 *of the regulations for the measurement of tonnage, provided the deductions do not, in the aggregate, exceed* 5 *per cent. of the gross tonnage:*

A. The chart-room, even when also used as the captain's cabin. When, however, the captain's accommodation comprises several rooms, one of which is the chart-room, that room alone is deducted; but, in all cases, the room used as the chart-room must, if it is to be deducted, be situated on the upper deck.

B. The cabins of the ship's doctors, if actually occupied by them.

C. A mess-room, if there is one, for the exclusive use of the officers and engineers; or, if they exist, two mess-rooms: one of them for the exclusive use of the officers, the other one for the exclusive use of the engineers.

A mess-room, if there is one, for the exclusive use of the petty officers.

No deduction is allowed for the officers' mess-room in ships having passenger accommodation, which are not also provided with a passengers' mess-room.

D. All spaces fitted as bath-rooms, or lavatories, for the exclusive use of the ship's officers, engineers, and crew, with the exception of such of the said bath-rooms as is available for passengers when no bath-room for their exclusive use is provided.

E. All spaces specially provided for the storage of search-lights, the wireless telegraphy installation and the operator's berth, on condition that they are situated on the upper deck.

The above specified spaces can only be deducted if they bear a distinctly visible and permanent indication of their exclusive appropriation.

MEASUREMENT OF DECK SPACES

For ships fitted with superstructures the following rules, which concern only such spaces as are excluded from the national tonnage, are applied:

I. *Ships with one tier of superstructures only*

1. *Poop, bridge, forecastle.*

The following exemptions are allowed:

a. Such length of the poop measured from the inside of the stern timber, at half height of the said poop, as shall be equal to $\frac{1}{10}$th of the full length of the ship.

b. The portion of the bridge in way of the air spaces of the engine and boiler spaces, it being understood that such air spaces are not considered to extend beyond the forward bulkhead of the stoke-hold and the after bulkhead of the main engine-room.

c. Such length of the forecastle measured from the inside of the stem at half height of the said forecastle, as shall be equal to $\frac{1}{8}$th of the full length of the ship.

d. In each of the above three cases of superstructures, such portions as are in way of openings in the walls of the ships not provided with any means of closing and facing one another.

2. *Poop and bridge combined, or forecastle and bridge combined.*

In each of these combined spaces, the following exemptions are allowed:

a. That length only which corresponds to the openings of the engine-room and boiler spaces as specified in (1. *b*) above.

b. Such portions as are in way of openings not provided with any means of closing and facing one another in the walls of the ship.

3. *Shelter-decks.*

In the case of shelter-decks, the following exemptions are allowed:

The portions in way of openings in the side plating of the ship not provided with any means of closing and facing one another.

Such air spaces as are situated within the shelter-deck must be measured into the engine-room space and deducted together with 75 per cent. of their volume.

II. *Ships having more than one tier of superstructures.*

a. The exemptions prescribed in paragraphs 1, 2, and 3 above are applicable in their entirety to the lower tier only.

b. Tiers above the lower tier are only allowed the exemption of such portions as are in way of openings in the side plating of the ship not provided with any means of closing and facing one another.

Remark.

Should a ship, at any time, transit with passengers, merchandise of any kind, or bunker coal, or stores of any description, in any portion whatever of any exempted or deducted space, the whole of that space is added to the net tonnage and can nevermore be exempted from measurement.

TAXATION OF DOUBLE-BOTTOMS

When double-bottom spaces are utilized for the carriage of oil during the transit of the Canal their cubical capacity will be added to the tonnage.

Contrary, however, to the rules actually in force, this addition will not be of a permanent character; the cubical capacity of the said spaces will only be added to the tonnage when they are utilized.

TARIFF FOR THE HIRE OF PLANT

A tugboat	1st class	*per hour*	250 Fr.
	2nd ,,	,,	140 ,,
	3rd ,,	,,	75 ,,
	4th ,,	,,	50 ,,
A lighter	1st category	*per day*	75 ,,
	2nd ,,	,,	50 ,,
	3rd ,,	,,	25 ,,
Floating Crane of 100–150 tons	1st *hour*		150 ,,
	For each con-secutive hour after the first { at work		120 ,,
	while shifting position or waiting		40 ,,
Sheer-hulk 60 tons	1st *hour*		100 ,,
	For each con-secutive hour after the first { at work		60 ,,
	while shifting position or waiting		25 ,,
Sheer-hulks of 25, 35 and 40 tons.	1st *hour*		80 Fr.
	For each con-secutive hour after the first { at work		50 ,,
	while shifting position or waiting		20 ,,
A sheer-hulk of 12 tons. (A floating self-propelling crane.)	1st *hour*		100 ,,
	For each con-secutive hour after the first { at work		60 ,,
	while shifting position or waiting		25 ,,
Sheer-hulks of 8 and 10 tons	1st *hour*		60 ,,
	For each con-secutive hour after the first { at work		40 ,,
	while shifting position or waiting		15 ,,
Diving appliances	*Hire*	*per hour*	15 ,,
	Plus: Per hour of diving proper, reckoned from the moment the diver enters the water to the moment he leaves it		15 ,,

NOTE.—For sheer-hulks and diving appliances the hire will be increased by 50 per cent. between 6 p.m. and 6 a.m.

The same increase will be made between 6 a.m. and 6 p.m. on Sundays and holidays.

For tugboats, hire is reckoned from the time of first firing; for the other appliances, from the time they leave the depot. Hire ceases when they re-enter the depot. The charges for towage of the appliances have to be paid over and above the amount for hire.

Appendix 6
CORRESPONDENCE RELATING TO SUEZ CANAL DUES[1]
NOTE

THIS correspondence well illustrates the difficulties created by the dual position of the British Government as a large shareholder on the one hand and on the other as the authority to whom all His Majesty's subjects naturally look to secure equitable treatment for British shipping and for the products of His Majesty's Dominions and Dependencies beyond the Seas. The Governor-General suggests that His Majesty's Government should use their influence to secure a reduction of dues. The British Suez Canal Directors point out that such reduction might lead to pecuniary loss to the British Treasury. The Treasury concur in the view expressed by the British Directors. It only remains for the Board of Trade and the Colonial Office meekly to concur with the Lords Commissioners of the Treasury. The dividend payable in 1905 was 28 per cent.; it has since attained the figure of 44 per cent.; it is known that representations on the subject have been made by some Dominion and Colonial Governments and that six maritime powers protested unofficially in 1931 to the Foreign Office, but without result.

A. T. W.

No. I

Governor-General Lord Northcote to the Earl of Elgin.

My Lord,   Sydney, May 15, 1906.

I HAVE the honour to inform your Lordship that my Ministers have recently been making inquiries with a view to considering measures for the improvement of the present means of transport between Australia and Great Britain, for the purpose of the encouragement of trade and the carriage of immigrants at cheap rates.

2. In the course of inquiries the important question has arisen as to the route followed by steam-ships trading between England and Australia, the voyage via the Cape of Good Hope involving a delay of several days as compared with that via the Red Sea and the Suez Canal.

3. It has been learned that many shipowners are deterred from taking the shorter route by reason of the very heavy charges which are imposed by the Suez Canal authorities. Shipowners are compelled either to increase their rates for passage and freight by adding the Canal dues, or else to take the longer but less expensive course round South Africa. As every shortening of the voyage between Great Britain and Australia is valuable to shippers of perishable and other products, especially in certain seasons, my Ministers are anxious that no means shall be left untried to induce the ships to use the Suez Canal.

4. Seeing that the Canal dues enable shareholders to receive a dividend of 28 per cent., my Ministers are of opinion that the time has arrived for the reconsideration of the existing rates, and possibly for a substantial reduction therein, and they suggest that, on behalf of Australia, as well as of all other British possessions lying to the east of Egypt, the influence of the British Government might be employed in procuring concessions which would have an early and material effect on inter-Empire trade, as well as upon the volume of traffic which will pass through the Canal.

I have, &c.
(Signed) NORTHCOTE.

[1] From Command Paper Cd. 3345, 1907.

No. II

British Suez Canal Directors to Sir Edward Grey.—(Received 4th September.)

Sir,   Paris, August 31, 1906.

In conformity with the instructions contained in your despatch of the 13th ultimo, we have the honour to submit, for the information of the Secretary of State, the following observations.

We have perused the inclosures which are forwarded in the despatch, and have given special attention to the letter in which the Governor-General of Australia invokes the employment of the influence of the British Government to procure concessions in the way of a reduction of the existing rates of dues on vessels passing through the Suez Canal.

Lord Northcote's Ministers adduce four reasons in support of a reduction of the Tariff—

1. That shipowners are deterred from taking the shorter route on account of the very heavy charges.

2. That the dividends now paid amount to 28 per cent.

3. That the inter-Empire trade would be beneficially affected.

4. That the volume of traffic through the Canal would be increased.

Although these points have been discussed in considerable detail in previous correspondence between the Foreign Office and ourselves, we will again review the arguments briefly.

1. With regard to the first statement, the statistics of navigation by the Canal route present incontrovertible evidence that during the thirty years in which it has been in existence the number of ships which have made use of it has greatly and, with the exception of minor fluctuations, steadily increased, viz., from 2,000,000 tons net in 1876 to 13,000,000 tons in 1905.

Although it might reasonably be supposed that this six-fold increase was in the main due to the reductions which have been made in the tonnage rates, little or no relation in the way of cause and effect can be traced between them, while the increased traffic appears to be proportionate to the growth of the maritime commerce of the world in a very exact measure.

Paradoxical as it may appear, we are assured by many large shipowners that, although reductions in the Tariff are welcomed by them, these reductions have practically no effect in increasing the Canal traffic, or in diverting from the Cape to the Canal route any material amount of tonnage. Far more importance is attached by them to the widening and deepening of the Canal than to any reduction in the charges for its use.

It cannot therefore be maintained that the charges are deterrent, as alleged, but we have always supported their reduction, and we would point out that the dues, which were originally, in 1869, fixed at 10 fr. per ton, and raised to 13 fr. per ton in 1874, have by successive stages been reduced to 7 fr. 75 c. per ton, at which rate they now stand. The last reduction of 75 centimes per ton was conceded as recently as from the 1st January of this year, and followed on a reduction of 50 centimes per ton made on the 1st January 1903, amounting to a total reduction by 14 per cent. of the Tariff during the last three years.

2. While the present dividend of 28 per cent. on the 500-fr. share is an undoubted sign of the great prosperity of the enterprise, we cannot regard it as a proof that its profits are exorbitant. The arrangement which admits of this result was agreed to between the shipowners and M. Ferdinand de Lesseps in 1882, neither party at the time anticipating its realization. It must be borne in mind that from 1869 to 1870 the shareholders only received a yearly dividend of 5 per cent.; from July 1871 to July 1874 the dividend was passed and replaced by a certificate for 85 fr., which was subsequently paid. From that date to July last the average of the dividends has been 16 per cent., but from the formation of the Company to the present date it has only amounted, in round figures, to 12½ per cent.,

and, owing to the large increase in the market value of the shares, the return to the purchasers for some years past has ranged between 3 and 4 per cent.

It is manifest that the body of shareholders is interested in maintaining the growth of the dividend, and that their voting power at a general meeting would most probably be exercised in favour of further increase (with the exception, of course, of the British vote, which very inadequately represents the proportion of shares held by His Majesty's Government). We are, however, still hopeful that a method of adjusting the partition of surplus revenue, more acceptable to the clients of the Company, may be eventually arrived at.

It must not be forgotten that the Company spends every year large sums on the improvement of the Canal, and that a scheme of important works is being carried out with a view, on the one hand, to widen the Canal, which will enable the passage to be made more quickly; and, on the other, to deepen it, which would enable a large number of vessels to carry more cargo, and thus increase their freight-carrying capacity. If further sacrifices were asked and obtained from the shareholders the result would probably be a delay in carrying out the work of improvement, if not its entire cessation, a result known to be quite contrary to the wishes of the shipowners.

3. That the inter-Empire trade would be beneficially affected is, no doubt, a very valid reason for both the Home and Colonial Governments to press for further reductions; but these would obviously have a precisely opposite effect upon the foreign rivals of our maritime commerce through the Canal, and it would be futile to urge this argument upon our Continental colleagues.

4. It has often been alleged that the volume of traffic through the Canal would increase on a reduction of tariff; but this contention is not wholly borne out by the facts, for the reasons that we have already assigned. While we do not altogether deny that some slight increase of volume has followed reductions of tariff, the only conspicuous result is a diminution of receipts. This is especially apparent in the present year, when the Tariff has just been reduced by 75 centimes. The consequent loss would, at the present date, have amounted to at least 400,000*l.*, if the traffic had not been considerably increased by the return to Europe, through the Canal, of the Russian troops engaged in the Far East.

The Board of Trade, having been kept fully informed by the Foreign Office of all the somewhat complicated conditions affecting Suez Canal tariffs, will be in a position to give its views upon the points raised by Lord Northcote in his despatch. While we cordially agree in the general aspiration of the Australian Government, we have, as the representatives of the financial interests of His Majesty's Government, to protect the large revenue which now accrues to the Exchequer; and we submit that any further reductions of the Tariff would practically amount to a subsidy to ships using the Canal, at the cost, to a great extent, of pecuniary loss to His Majesty's Government.

We have, &c.
(Signed) H. AUSTIN LEE.
JOHN C. ARDAGH.
H. T. ANSTRUTHER.

No. III

Foreign Office to Board of Trade.

Sir,   Foreign Office, September 12, 1906.

WITH reference to your letter of the 6th July last, I am directed by Secretary Sir E. Grey to transmit to you, to be laid before the Board of Trade, the accompanying copy of a despatch from the British Directors of the Suez Canal Company,[1] in connection with the request of the Governor-General of Australia that His Majesty's Government should use their influence to secure a reduction in the charges imposed by the Canal authorities.

[1] No. II.

A Copy of this despatch has also been communicated to the Treasury, and Sir E. Grey would request that the reply to the Governor-General of Australia should be deferred until the Lords Commissioners have had the opportunity of expressing their views on the subject.

I am, &c.

(Signed) F. A. CAMPBELL.

No. IV

Treasury to Foreign Office.[1]—(*Received* 2 *October.*)

Sir,   Treasury Chambers, October 1, 1906.

I HAVE laid before the Lords Commissioners of His Majesty's Treasury Mr. Campbell's letter of the 12th ultimo, inclosing copy of a despatch from the British Directors of the Suez Canal Company on the subject of the Australian Government's request that the influence of His Majesty's Government may be used to secure a reduction in the charges imposed on traffic through the Canal.

In reply their Lordships direct me to acquaint you, for the information of the Secretary of State for Foreign Affairs, that they concur in the views expressed by the Directors, and that a reply to the Australian Government in that sense would meet with their approval.

While my Lords are in full sympathy with the object of the Commonwealth Ministers, they do not think that anything would be gained by the attempt to pursue that object without due regard to the interests of those who have a purely financial concern in the affairs of the Canal.

I am, &c.

(Signed) E. W. HAMILTON.

No. V

Board of Trade to Foreign Office.—(*Received* 17 *October.*)

Sir,   Board of Trade, October 16, 1906.

WITH reference to your letter of the 11th instant, transmitting a copy of a letter from the Treasury respecting the Australian Government's request that the influence of His Majesty's Government may be used to secure a reduction in the Suez Canal dues, I am directed by the Board of Trade to state, for the information of Sir E. Grey, that they propose to send a copy of the despatch from the British Directors of the Suez Canal Company which accompanied your letter of the 12th ultimo to the Colonial Office, and to communicate to that Department the substance of the Treasury letter, with an intimation that the Board, having regard to all the circumstances of the case, acquiesce in the views expressed therein.

The Board will be glad to be informed whether Sir E. Grey concurs in this proposal.

I am, &c.

(Signed) WALTER J. HOWELL

No. VI

Foreign Office to Board of Trade.

Sir,   Foreign Office, October 18, 1906.

I AM directed by Secretary Sir E. Grey to acknowledge the receipt of your letter of the 16th instant respecting a reduction of the Suez Canal dues, and to state that he concurs in the proposal of the Board of Trade as expressed therein.

I am, &c.

(Signed) E. GORST.

[1] Copy sent to Board of Trade, 11th October 1906.

No. VII

The Earl of Elgin to Governor-General Lord Northcote.

My Lord,　　　　　　　　　　　　　　　　Downing Street, October 31, 1906.

I HAVE the honour to transmit, for the information of your Ministers, the accompanying copy of a letter[1] from the British Directors of the Suez Canal Company regarding the charges imposed by the Suez Canal authorities.

I am informed that the Lords Commissioners of the Treasury and the Board of Trade concur in the views expressed by the Directors, and that although they are in full sympathy with the object of your Ministers, they do not think that anything would be gained by an attempt to pursue that object without due regard to the interests of those who have a purely financial concern in the affairs of the Suez Canal.

I am, &c.
(Signed) ELGIN.

Appendix 7

NOTE ON THE EFFECT OF THE SUEZ CANAL ON THE MIGRATION OF MARINE FAUNA[2]

THE marine fauna of the Mediterranean and the Red Seas differ widely from one another. Relatively few species are common to both seas. Since the opening of the Suez Canal, however, a considerable number of marine plants and animals have passed through from one sea to another. By 1896 creatures hitherto peculiar to the Red Sea had reached Fiume and Tunis, probably attached to the hulls of ships. The swimming crab, a staple article of food in Egypt, formerly existed only in the Red Sea: it is now found in large numbers at Alexandria and Haifa.

The canal itself is not favourable to migration; constant dredging, incessant churning of the muddy bottom, high water temperatures, and the absence of any current from one end to the other are the principal obstacles. Though there is a progressive diminution in the salt content of the Bitter Lakes, due to the inter-mingling of sea-water brought by the canal, the salinity is still very high. This is not, however, necessarily an obstacle to migration, as the fauna of the Lakes are on an average larger than the corresponding species in either sea. Red Sea species tend to predominate, owing probably to tidal currents.

[1] No II.
[2] Abstracted from the *Proceedings of the Zoological Society of London*, vol. xxii, 1926: Cambridge Expedition organized in 1924 by Professor Stanley Gardiner, F.R.S.

INDEX

EUROPEAN BUSINESS
Four Centuries of Foreign Expansion
An Arno Press Collection

Anstey, Vera, *The Economic Development of India* 1952

Baster, A. S. J. *The Imperial Banks.* 1929

Baster, A. S. J. *The International Banks.* 1935

Blount, Edward. *Memoirs of Sir Edward Blount.* 1902

Braake, Alex L. Ter. *Mining in the Netherlands East Indies.* 1944

British Electrical and Allied Manufacturers' Association. *Combines and Trusts in the Electrical Industry.* 1927

Brode, Heinrich. *British and German East Africa.* 1911

Burden, William A. M. *The Struggle for Airways in Latin America.* 1943

Calvert, Albert F. *Nigeria and Its Tin Fields.* 1910

Crouchley, Arthur Edwin. *Investment of Foreign Capital in Egyptian Companies and Public Debt.* 1936

Davies, A. Emil. *Investments Abroad.* 1927

Deterding, Henri. *An International Oilman.* 1934

Ferns, Henry S. *Britain and Argentina in the Nineteenth Century.* 1960

Fitzgerald, Patrick. *Industrial Combination in England.* 1927

Gregory, Theodore. *Ernest Oppenheimer and the Economic Development of Southern Africa.* 1962

Henry, James Dodds. *Baku.* 1906

Hussey, Roland Dennis. *The Caracas Company, 1728-1784.* 1934

Jucker-Fleetwood, Erin Elver. *Sweden's Capital Imports and Exports.* 1947

Korthals-Altes, J. *Sir Cornelius Vermuyden.* 1925

Laves, Walter Herman Carl. *German Governmental Influence on Foreign Investments, 1871-1914.* 1977

Levy, Herman. *Monopoly and Competition.* 1911

Liefmann, Robert. *Cartels, Concerns and Trusts.* 1932

Marcus, Edward and Mildred Rendl Marcus. *Investment and Development Possibilities in Tropical Africa.* 1960

Meakin, W. *The New Industrial Revolution.* 1928

Michell, Lewis. *The Life and Times of the Right Honourable Cecil John Rhodes, 1853-1902.* Two vols. in one. 1910

Miller, Benjamin L. and Joseph T. Singewald. *The Mineral Deposits of South America.* 1919

Mulhall, Michael G. *The English in South America.* 1878

Nordyke, Lewis. *Cattle Empire.* 1949

Nute, Grace Lee. *Caesers of the Wilderness.* 1943

Patterson, E. M., editor. *America's Changing Investment Market.* 1916

Pinner, Felix. *Emil Rathenau und das Elektrische Zeitalter.* 1918

Riesser, J. *The German Great Banks and Their Concentration in Connection with the Economic Development of Germany.* 1911

Rippy, J. Fred. *British Investment in Latin America, 1822-1949.* 1959

Rondot, Jean. *La Compagnie Française des Pétroles.* 1962

Roth, Cecil. *The Sassoon Dynasty.* 1941

Senior, Nassau W. *A Journal Kept in Turkey and Greece in the Autumn of 1857 and the Beginning of 1858.* 1859

Siemens, Georg. *History of the House of Siemens.* Two vols. 1957

Southworth, Constant. *The French Colonial Venture.* 1931

Spender, John A. *Weetman Pearson, First Viscount Cowdray, 1856-1927.* 1930

Thorner, Daniel. *Investment in Empire.* 1950

U. S. Department of Commerce, Bureau of Foreign and Domestic Commerce. *Investments in Latin America and the British West Indies.* 1918

U. S. Federal Trade Commission. *Report of the Federal Trade Commission on Foreign Ownership in the Petroleum Industry.* 1923

U. S. Office of the Alien Property Custodian. *Alien Property Custodian Report.* 1919

U. S. Office of the Alien Property Custodian. *Annual Reports.* Four vols. in one. 1943/45/46/47

Van Oss, S. F. *American Railroads as Investments.* 1893

van Winter, Pieter J. *American Finance and Dutch Investment, 1780-1805.* 1977

Vlekke, Bernard H. M. *Nusantara.* 1943

Wallace, Donald H. *Market Control in the Aluminum Industry.* 1937

Wellington, Dorothy Violet Wellesley. *Sir George Goldie, Founder of Nigeria.* 1934

Wheeler, John. *A Treatise of Commerce.* 1931

Wilkins, Mira, editor. *British Overseas Investments, 1907-1948.* 1977

Wilkins, Mira, editor. *European Foreign Investments, As Seen by the U. S. Department of Commerce.* 1977

Wilkins, Mira, editor. *Foreign Investments in the United States.* 1977

Wilkins, Mira, editor. *Issues and Insights on International Investment.* 1977

Williamson, John W. *In a Persian Oil Field.* 1930

Wilson, Arnold T. *The Suez Canal.* 1933

Wilson, Charles Henry. *Anglo-Dutch Commerce and Finance in the Eighteenth Century.* 1941

Wood, Gordon. *Borrowing and Business in Australia.* 1930

Wortley, B. A. *Expropriation in Public International Law.* 1959